COLLECTING THE EDGED WEAPONS OF THE THIRD REICH

VOLUME VIII

By

LTC. (RET.) Thomas M. Johnson

Published privately by the author in Columbia, South Carolina

Library of Congress Catalog
Card Number 75-15486

International Standard
Book Number (ISBN) 0-944432-05-0

First Edition

Printed in the United States of America
by The R. L. Bryan Company
Columbia, South Carolina

Cover photo—Robert Waitts Collection
Photograph by Charles H. Jenkins, III

Author's Dedication

This book is dedicated in memory of Thomas J. Gorman, Jr., a man who led an exemplary life, loved his family dearly, and still found time to build one of the most extensive edged weapon collections in this country.

and to

MGySgt. (Ret.) Elmo McAuliffe, USMC, a fellow collector and long-time close personal friend of the author's, who died suddenly during August, 1995, at his home in California. Elmo provided encouragement and support for many years with the conscientiousness he brought to every task.

Both men will be sorely missed.

Thomas M. Johnson

Nº 21

JOHNSON Reference Books

(540) 373-9150
FAX: (540) 373-0087
E-MAIL: Ww2daggers@aol.com

CONTENTS

PREFACE

Before I address the real purpose of this, the Preface to LTC (Ret.) Thomas M. Johnson's **Volume VIII** of **Collecting the Edged Weapons of the Third Reich**, I feel obligated to try to impress upon the reader the significance of having been asked to write it. While certainly I am honored to now be numbered among what I consider a rather exclusive group (those who were selected to write the Prefaces for the previous books in this series), it is far more important to myself and the entire collecting community that the series continues and that **Volume VIII** came to be written. I recall a day in early May 1981 when I received my copy of **Volume IV**, immediately opened it up and started reading. On reaching page xiv, I read with great dismay the first line of the Introduction: "This being the concluding reference to my four-volume series **Collecting the Edged Weapons of the Third Reich**. . . ." I had been collecting edged weapons for about nine years at that point and regarded LTC Johnson's references as both an essential part of my reference library and the primary impetus of my interest in the hobby. I looked through each volume countless times, comparing the few pieces in my collection to those pictured and looking wistfully at those I did not have. I still find myself doing that—I guess it is true some things never change!

Although I have since had the opportunity to spend a considerable amount of time with him, I have never heard LTC Johnson say why he made that statement or why he changed his mind and decided to continue the series. Neither is important. What is important is that there has now been a **Volume V, VI, VII** and **VIII**. In addition, the collector/researcher with a complete reference library should also be able to point to a long-awaited and much-needed cross reference for **Volumes I-V**, two fascinating references featuring German war souvenirs of all types, a second volume of **Wearing the Edged Weapons of the Third Reich**, and the beginnings of an in-depth look at Imperial German edged weapons—literally thousands of pages and fully fifteen years worth of information brought to light and made available to the collecting community after LTC Johnson wrote and, thankfully, reconsidered those words.

To look over the Table of Contents of each of those succeeding volumes, to look at the names and faces of those who had the opportunity to share their knowledge with us and might not have done so otherwise, to read and reread learning something new each time, is to begin to understand the phenomenal growth of this hobby. Each page serves to place these artifacts in their proper context as true pieces of history. With World War II now fully half a century in the past, the ranks of those who were there are shrinking dramatically. All too soon, the memories fade and the experiences and events of the war truly become history. As this happens, World War II memorabilia will assume its place alongside that of the memorabilia of the U.S. Civil War, World War I, and other conflicts. Today's collectors should consider themselves fortunate to be a part of this process. Beyond the almost certain monetary gains to be made is the knowledge collectors share about their particular items of interest, providing them with an "insider's view" of an era in history that continues to impact our world today. Edged weapons, perhaps more than any other Third Reich collectible, were present, usually in great number, at virtually every event during that turbulent period. This is witnessed by the incredible array of swords, daggers and bayonets one can observe in most period photographs of the massive early Party rallies and even informal gatherings, to the service bayonets and fighting knives seen carried and used in every theater of combat. As a result, the serious edged weapon collector will find, often by surprise, that he or she is much more knowledgeable about that period of history than their noncollecting contemporaries. Most will readily attribute a great deal of that knowledge to LTC Johnson. As a matter of fact, there is not a German edged weapon collector or dealer today, in this country or abroad, who does not owe a serious debt to Tom Johnson and his company, Johnson Reference Books, for making this interesting hobby what it is today. On a personal note, I remember Tom's seminar at the MAX II Show in St. Louis, Missouri, on the subject of how to write a reference book. He not only talked the audience through the many steps of researching, writing, and publishing a reference book, but made it clear that, "anyone burning with desire to author a separate study on German edged weapons should not be deterred by a false impression of subject-matter saturation," and adding that, . . . "every collector and researcher profits tremendously by each additional text on the subject. . . ." Was it coincidence that some two short years later I had a book on the market? I do not think so!

As with **Volumes II-VII** of this series, what readers will likely find most interesting about **Volume VIII** is the incredible variety of information found herein. They are certain to find that **Volume VIII** continues to deliver. The various types and models of Third Reich edged weapons were identified and discussed thoroughly in **Volume I**, and one wonders how many skeptics there were out there when they learned that there would be a **Volume II**. "What else is there to know? We can already tell all the daggers apart!" Fortunately, most of the skeptics long ago joined the legions of fans who now own dog-eared copies of all of LTC Johnson's previous works and eagerly await the next volume. A cursory look at the **Volume VIII** Table of Contents assures the reader that LTC Johnson and his contributors have once again produced a reference greater than the sum of its parts, as, indeed, the serious collector no doubt regards the entire series! **Volume VIII** offers a continued look at the Solingen factories and the edged weapon industry itself (most certainly a favorite topic of yours truly!); an in-depth study of the increasingly scarce edged weapons of the *RLB*; further pictorial studies to include previously unpublished rare and unusual edged weapons and accouterments, factory source documents, and edged weapons in wear; and more on Third Reich boot knives from that subject's recognized authority, Robert Heiduk.

Once again, LTC Johnson, his contributing writers, and all those concerned have provided the collecting community with a reference worthy of its predecessors while at the same time stimulating our interest and making us wonder what else there is to know and learn about this fascinating hobby. I would like to close the Preface as I began it—by stating what a privilege it is to have had a small hand in this reference—and by taking a brief opportunity, on behalf of the international collecting community, to thank LTC Johnson, his contributors, staff, and the rest of those who continue to share their knowledge and love for this hobby for their continued efforts.

March 1996

Albert "Skipper" Greenwade
Crosby, Texas
Author of *Me Fecit Solingen* and
Editor of the "MAX GAZETTE"

ACKNOWLEDGEMENTS

Occasionally I add a reference book to my personal library which is printed without an Acknowledgements Section. To this author that is sheer folly, as I submit that no reference book "worth its salt" can be researched and written in a vacuum by a single individual. Whether the assistance comes to the author in the form of advice, artwork, encouragement, experience, knowledge, research, and/or photographs, a sizeable number of persons other than the primary author make invaluable contributions to any worthwhile reference book. If my premise is correct, then these persons should certainly be duly recognized to the readers of the published work. The fact of the matter is that the contents of any usable reference book are gathered from a very wide variety of sources and individuals.

I can say without equivocation that the contributors to my ongoing series of reference books are, all-in-all, the best team available. First and foremost are the experts in this field whom I invited to pen an individual section or chapter. Major contributions to this latest volume were made by Barry Brown from England, Gailen David, Doug Gow from New Zealand, Albert "Skipper" Greenwade, Robert Heiduk, Ken Rouse from Germany, Hinrik Steinsson from Iceland, and Ben Swearingen.

In addition to the above collectors/researchers who took the time and made the effort to "take pen to paper," the following individuals also contributed in a major way. Providing much assistance to the author on the other side of the Atlantic was longtime colleague *Herr* Gunter Bastian of Solingen, Germany, who took countless hours of his time to locate all of the old edged weapon factory addresses in his hometown. Although I had personally located a number of these active and inactive buildings over the years, *Herr* Bastian knew of many more obscure companies, many of which are long out-of-business. Photographs of our many excursions throughout "the City of Swords" can be found in **Chapter 1**.

A special note of thanks to best-selling author Kenneth D. Alford of Richmond, Virginia, for taking a day out of his busy life to introduce me to the Center of Military History, the U.S. Army Agency in Washington, D.C., which is charged with the mission of safeguarding several hundred captured pieces of German artwork. Ken is the author of the best-selling book entitled, **The Spoils of World War II—The American Military's Role in Stealing Europe's Treasures**.

The author is also deeply indebted to professional photographer Jack Arnold and his firm Oneida Limited of Oneida, New York, for taking his valuable time and resources to make the author a better photographer. I mentioned to Jack during 1994 that I was well satisfied with the results of my black & white close-up photography, but not with my color work. He immediately invited me to visit his company and learn the "tricks of the trade" from true photographic professionals. Jack and his colleagues are responsible for all of the beautiful Oneida color photographs of the company's flatware, china, and crystal that we all see on a daily basis in major U.S. and even foreign magazine publications, as well as adorning the walls in numerous Oneida retail stores. Any improvements in my own photographic prowess in this volume can be directly attributed to Jack Arnold's patient tutoring.

While numerous German edged weapon collectors and/or dealers worldwide submitted quality color and black & white photographs for this volume, five who must be individually thanked for their support with literally dozens of photographs to choose from are Thomas T. Wittmann, Robert Waitts, Edmund F. Leland, Adam Portugal of Germany and Doug Gow of New Zealand. I also solicited photographs from other collectors/researchers to include in this reference. I want to personally thank each and every one who went to the trouble and expense to send material, as the response was overwhelming. I just hope that the photographers whose work is reproduced in this reference will be pleased with the presentation, as the final selection process was most difficult.

I owe a great debt of gratitude to the continuing untiring efforts of military artist Brian Molloy of Wales, England, whose impressive military art improves with each of my books. Brian has contributed his artistic talents to supplement my writings since 1978. It would be difficult for me to picture doing a worthwhile reference book without him. I would also like to welcome and thank a new military artist who also contributed his time and talent to this ongoing series of reference books, Darko Pavlovic' of Croatia. I look forward to working with Darko on future military art requirements for my publications.

Again, my sincere thanks go to *Herr* Siegfried Rosenkaimer, a <u>seventh-generation</u> Solingen edged weapon maker, for his invaluable input, guidance, and careful editing of the chapter and accompanying photograph captions on Solingen. *Herr* Rosenkaimer is a true perfectionist and insisted that I "get it right" even to the inclusion of every last German *umlaut*.

David J. Koller of Naperville, Illinois was kind enough to turn over his own personal Solingen research materials in order to make this a better reference book.

I would also be remiss by not acknowledging the meticulous German-English translations provided by Mark Ready of Albuquerque, New Mexico; Kurt Glemser of Canada; and Ms. Bonnie Jones of Fredericksburg, Virginia.

Other individuals who have played a major role in the production of this reference include my longtime personal secretary, Ms. Donna Kines, who diligently typed and proofread every word of the text; our JRB General Manager, LTC (Ret.) Michael Little, who is responsible for providing the input for countless "in-wear" photo captions; Gailen David, who was instrumental in providing assistance in updating the Current Values section for this reference; and last, but certainly not least, my wife, Tink, for her continued efforts with research and proofreading.

This book would not have been possible without the generous help of many people worldwide. I wish to express my sincere thanks to everyone who assisted, and particularly the following. The names are listed in alphabetical order as this seems the only fair way to all concerned.

Kenneth D. Alford
Jack Arnold
Kevin L. Ash
LTC (Ret.) James P. Atwood
Ronald J. Baldini
Gunter Bastian (Germany)
Howard Bayliss
Jean-Jacques Biugne (France)
David Blackmon (England)
Paul Blatner
Joe F. Bourn
Donald Boyle
Barry Brown (England)
Bernie Brule (Canada)
Joseph Buffer
Jason P. Burmeister
Derek Chapman (Canada)
James Chapman
Mike & Mark Chenault
Houston C. Coates
Gregory Colarossi
Keith Cornford (England)
Donald Covert
TSGT (Ret.) T. Wayne
    Cunningham, USAF
Thomas Curtis
Rudy A. D'Angelo
Gailen David
Ian Davidson (England)
Victor Diehl
Edward Earp, Jr.
Charles Eliopoulos
Alfred C. Ex
Volkhart Fiedler (Germany)
W. E. Fitzgerald
Johannes A. Floch (Austria)

Anthony T. Flotte, Sr. *
George R. Fuerst *
Sterling "Chip" Gambino
Barry D. Garver
Andrew Gates (England)
Peter Gauf (Germany)
J. Jay Gillespie
Benny A. Giordano
Kurt Glemser (Canada)
Thomas J. Gorman, Jr. *
Doug Gow (New Zealand)
Lynn W. Gray
Albert "Skipper" Greenwade
Joseph Gruenling
David Hall
N. Neil Hardin
Ian Hargreaves (Canada)
William Harvey
Robert Heiduk
Gordon Henger
John C. Hewitt (Ireland)
Ron G. Hickox
Doug Humer
John P. Innella
Jean-Marie Irlande (France)
Charles H. Jenkins, III
Carter Jennette
Robert Jensen
Robert P. Johns
Tink Johnson
C. R. "Jeff" Jones
Gary A. Juwell
MAJ Robert B. Kaleva, USA
Ralph Kaschai
Bernd H. Kellner (Germany)
Ian "Lemmy" Kilmister
Donna Kines

_____
* Deceased

P. L. Kingsland (Australia)
David J. Koller
Horst J. Kricheldorf (Germany)
Bavin J. Lane (England)
Fred LaRue
P. W. Lefort *
Edmund F. Leland
Bernard Levine
LTC (Ret.) Michael E. Little, USA
Randy Long
Jess Lukens
Herman A. Maeurer
CAPT (Ret.) Dennis Majerski,
   USCG
Denny Matheny
Mark D. Mattefs
Dr. John Merling
Robert Metcalf (England)
Dr. Julian Milestone
Andrew Mollo (England)
Brian Molloy (United Kingdom)
Mike Morris
Dr. Milledge Murphey
Cline Mutersbaugh
George Notarpole
Joseph Pankowski
Darko Pavlovic' (Croatia)
John P. Pearson
Tony Perry
Fred Perski (Germany)
David J. Peterson
Jonathan Pittaway (South Africa)
Adam J. Portugal (Germany)
Mark Ready
J. Rex Reddick
Bill Rice
Henning Ritter (Germany)
Randy Rodachy
David Rome
Siegfried Rosenkaimer (Germany)
SGM (Ret.) Kenneth H. Rouse
   (Germany)
Sune Sandling
W.P.B.R. Saris (Netherlands)

Herr & Frau Horst Schmidt
   (Germany)
Estel H. Schram
Robert K. Sellers (England)
Robert Sevier
William Shea
Richard Sherrod
Andreas Shoredits (South Africa)
Thomas Shutt
Hooper Skardon
Jill Halcomb Smith
Charles Snyder
Andy Southard, Jr.
Suzanne Spinnen (Germany)
Otto Spronk (Netherlands)
T. S. Stafford (England)
Dirk Stefanski (Germany)
Hinrik Steinsson (Iceland)
Mack Stephenson
Joseph Stone
John A. Swartele
Ben E. Swearingen
Charles N. Tallman
Daniel Tarkington
Alain Taugourdeau (France)
Stephen Truax, III
Willi Ulrich (Germany)
Kurt Van Laere (Belgium)
Peter Verbruggen (Belgium)
Mladen Vukusa (Croatia)
Robert Waitts
Anthony Ward (England)
A. "Bram" Wasmus (Netherlands)
Robert J. Wee
Courtney S. West
Roy White
Keith Wilson
Stewart Wilson (England)
George Winchell
Dr. W. A. Windrum (Canada)
Thomas T. Wittmann
Stephen D. Wolfe
"The Cracked Pot" Collection
"The Old Brigade" Collection

INTRODUCTION

The initial words of this introduction to **Volume VIII** of **Collecting the Edged Weapons of the Third Reich** are being penned at the U.S. Air airline terminal at Charlotte, North Carolina en route from my home in northern Virginia to my longtime printer, The R.L. Bryan Company in Columbia, South Carolina. The purpose of the trip is to put the final touches on **Volume VII** of this series and to release it for printing. What makes this worthy of mention is that, for the first time in this ongoing series of continuing reference books, a follow-on volume has been commenced before the current volume has even been printed. The reason for this is simply the vast abundance of materials which were crowded out of **Volume VII** due to space constraints. Each of the past six volumes, i.e., **Volumes I-VI**, had some materials left over after the final verbiage, photographs, and artwork had been selected, but nothing to compare to the overage factor for **Volume VII**. Sufficient quality materials were on-hand during the preparation of **Volume VII** for at least a 600-page reference. Even after "major surgery" in editing, the final book was still over fifty pages more than my signed contract with the printer. The point is that enough material was on-hand to complete two volumes and, thus, a **Volume VIII** was the only logical solution.

For the reader/collector who is yearning for more information on this fascinating and ever-growing hobby, the news is good. Rather than the usual four- to seven-year preparation period between successive volumes, **Volume VIII** was completed in record time. The contents of this volume will include an in-depth study of the following topics:

- —A first-person account of the author's ties to the German blade-producing city of Solingen.
- —The dress sidearms of the *RLB* organization.
- —An update on the status of the one-of-a-kind Hermann Göring *Reichsmarschall's* dagger.
- —More rare and unusual blades of the Reich.
- —Third Reich edged weapons in wear.
- —The Third Reich boot knife.

The news is also good on the introduction of other quality reference books on the subject of edged weapons. In the Introduction of **Volume III** I stated, "As time continues to heal the horrendous wounds of the tragic WWII era, German authors will, undoubtedly, pen their own versions of this fascinating subject—indeed, the story is <u>really</u> theirs to tell!" Since that bold prediction, the hobby has witnessed the first hardbound major reference on the subject by a German author, Ernst J. Niederhofer (pen name) entitled, **The Cold Steel Weapons of the SA, the SS, and the NSKK of the NSDAP**. This 197-page, large format reference is extremely well done and shows many quality photographs of the common as well as the rare daggers of the

SA, SS, and NSKK. Also included are many never-before-published pictures of these sidearms in wear. English-speaking collectors/researchers will be delighted to hear that portions of the German text have been translated into English. A second reference by a German author was released during 1994—a 326-page, paperback reference entitled, *Katalog Der Blankwaffen Des Deutschen Reiches 1933-1945* (Catalog of the Edged Weapons of the German Empire 1933-1945) by well-known German dealer, Andre Husken. This new reference is basically a German version of my own **Volume I** of **Collecting the Edged Weapons of the Third Reich**. As a matter of fact, the reader will recognize the vast majority of the photographs, as Herr Husken contracted with Johnson Reference Books to use my **Volume I** photographs of the actual model sidearms to augment his own previously unpublished "in wear" pictures. Like **Volume I**, the Husken reference provides the reader with current market values (in German *DMs*) for each model sidearm and its accompanying accouterments. These new foreign titles represent important references for any Third Reich dagger collector. Hopefully, these references will be the first of many to follow penned by German authors.

By the time you are reading this, my partner in the Militaria Antiques Xtravaganza (MAX) Show, Thomas T. Wittmann, will have his own dagger book on the market. Tom's book, entitled, **Exploring the Dress Daggers of the German Army**, is a major step forward into finding and analyzing the dress daggers worn by the German Army. **Exploring** . . . is intended to be the first in a series which will be devoted to detailing all Third Reich dress dagger types. Work is progressing rapidly on the second book in the series which will examine the 1st and 2nd Model *Luftwaffe* patterns.

England's Frederick J. Stephens' long-awaited reference on the Holbein series of dress daggers, e.g., the SA, NSKK, SS, and NPEA party form daggers is <u>finally</u> nearing completion and promises to be another one of Fred Stephens' best-sellers. Fred's rare research and writing abilities are widely recognized on both sides of the Atlantic Ocean. Johnson Reference Books (JRB) is presently negotiating with him to serve as the publisher of this welcomed and long-awaited reference.

Another reference work on the subject of German edged weapons which has also been years in the making (now over a decade) is the late Thomas Gorman's **German Crafted Blades: Master Identification Reference**. Although Tom, unfortunately, suffered an untimely death in late 1994, his wife, Lois, is determined to have Tom's book printed as a lasting tribute to her beloved husband. His original work has been rescheduled, reorganized, repackaged, and reduced to its present 950+ page encyclopedia format. In his introduction to **Daggers, Swords and Bayonets of the Third Reich**, author Fred Stephens states . . . "A diligent attempt to document every known pattern of bladed weapon produced during the Third Reich would necessitate hundreds, if not thousands, of pages of text and photographs." Fellow collector Tom Gorman attempted to perform this unenviable task in his **Master Identification Reference**.

Johnson Reference Books is presently negotiating with two German scholars/researchers to purchase the rights and publish the definitive work on the subject of German edged weapon portepees. The finished publication will picture in color a side and bottom view of all German military dagger, sword, and bayonet portepees, *Troddeln*, and *Faustriemen* from 1800 to 1945. This single text, when published, will provide the collector/researcher with the tool to accurately identify (to company level) any German edged weapon knot.

Another fine reference in the works is a **Volume III** of the Kurt Glemser series entitled, **A Guide to Military Dress Daggers**. Kurt, a Canadian, has gone further than anyone else in introducing the edged weapon collecting community to the numerous dress daggers and bayonets produced by countries other than Germany and the many interesting sidearms produced in Germany for export to other countries. Kurt's **Volume III** will probably not be printed until late 1996, and it will enlighten collectors worldwide with updated information on Rumanian, Czechoslovakian, Austrian, Yugoslavian and Swiss dress daggers, Italian Cadet daggers, Solingen export daggers, and the renowned Dinger family of swordsmiths. Of special note to the German edged weapon collectors, **Volume III** will feature period photographs which will prove that the Austrian Air Force daggers were worn during the Third Reich period (after the *Anschluss* in 1938) by Austrians in German *Luftwaffe* uniforms! Johnson Reference Books (JRB) is the sole international distributor for this informative reference series.

A recently released (1994) reference on the same subject of European dress daggers is **World of Dress Daggers 1900-1945, Volume I** by Robert J. Berger. This 295-page hardbound text covers nearly all of the foreign dress daggers released from 1900 to 1945 and includes the sidearms of sixteen different countries. Outstanding basic research was conducted for this book. The edged weapons of countries other than Germany are becoming increasingly popular, and this book, as well as the aforementioned Glemser books, certainly are valuable additions to the collector/researcher's library. Johnson Reference Books has also been selected by Mr. Berger to be the sole international distributor for his new reference.

Hopefully the reference books mentioned in this Introduction are the first of many to follow. This author is personally aware of additional militaria collector references being penned by well-known collectors/researchers Barry Brown of England, Gailen David, Robert Thompson, Robert Waitts, and Thomas Wittmann (a follow-on **Volume III**).

The Solingen blue and gold city crest is evident on each of the main road arteries leading into the city and welcomes visitors to the *Klingenstadt* (Blade City).

Chapter 1

THE SOLINGEN FACTORIES

"By the work one knows the workman."
— Jean de la Fontaine

Solingen. *Klingenstadt.* Blade City. Whether the name is in German or in English, the result is the same. The name itself evokes pure excitement for the connoisseur of fine edged weaponry. This industrial German city remains world renowned for cutlery and represents the absolute mecca for students and collectors of German daggers, swords, and bayonets. The famous German cutlery names of Eickhorn, Höller, Hörster, Pack, Puma, Seilheimer, WKC, etc. are as well-known to American edged weapon collectors as Ford, General Motors, McDonald's, etc.

The author certainly has an affinity for this city, having made a very comfortable living from its products for over three decades. As with the chapter on the small East German village of Steinbach (appearing in the last volume of this continuing series), I prefer to write this chapter in the first person due to a personal, long-term relationship with the city of Solingen and a sizeable number of its inhabitants working within the blade industry. My first visit occurred during the winter of 1960, and this trip has been followed by well over <u>one</u> hundred <u>and</u> fifty additional treks to its environs.

Completing four years of Army ROTC at the University of Tennessee and accepting a regular Army commission as a 2nd Lieutenant, I had the option of personally selecting my first worldwide Army assignment. With any young person's desire "to see the world," my choices were quickly narrowed to two selections—beautiful Hawaii or intriguing Germany. As the deadline for my decision grew near, I eliminated the former option due to possible "cabin fever" on being assigned to one minuscule island (Oahu) in the center of the Pacific Ocean. Thus, I selected Germany and was immediately assigned to an Armored Infantry Rifle Battalion garrisoned in the Bavarian capital of Munich.

My first introduction to the edged weaponry of the Third Reich came early in this initial tour of duty with the U.S. Army. Having a real appreciation for both the quality workmanship and the inexpensive prices of antique German clocks at the time, a kindly German clock seller, *Herr* Richard Walther, made periodic trips to my quarters in the Schwabing area of Munich to display his latest antique clock acquisitions. During one of his initial visits in 1960, I remarked to *Herr* Walther that since I was a career military officer, I should have a keen interest in military artifacts and inquired if he ever ran across any of these items in his constant searching of the Munich area to replenish his inventory of clocks. *Herr* Walther advised me that he had been a First Sergeant in the *Wehrmacht*, had numerous friends and acquaintances who had served in WWII, and promised to see what he could turn up.

On his next trip to my quarters, *Herr* Walther brought three Nazi artifacts for my inspection—a desk trophy featuring a silver closed-wing eagle and swastika mounted on a marble base complete with engraved presentation, an exquisite lead crystal ashtray with a swastika etched on the bottom, and a "German dagger." I purchased the three items and, since the dagger was complete with the "hanging straps," I allocated space on my den wall for display. During the next few weeks I had the occasion to admire the quality craftsmanship of the dagger, its scabbard, and the straps, and began to muse over the typical questions of who wore this particular sidearm during the Third Reich, for what occasions, etc. Incidently, my purchase price of the dagger and hangers was thirty-two *Deutsche Mark (DM)* which at the 1960 4-to-1 mark/dollar exchange ratio was equal to $8.00!

A few weeks later, *Herr* Walther returned to my quarters to proudly announce that he had a beautiful antique German grandfather clock with Westminster chimes to show me and another German dagger. I was naive enough to inquire about why I would need another WWII German dagger since I already had one. He smiled and returned from his automobile with a dagger that did not resemble in any way the one displayed on my den wall. *Herr* Walther explained that **both** were, in fact, WWII German daggers. (It was not until much later that I identified the first purchase as an Army Officer's and the second one as a 2nd model *Luftwaffe* dagger, also complete with hangers and portepee.) This second acquisition was made for the same 32 *DM* ($8.00) price and was mounted in my den alongside the other dagger.

The cycle repeated itself shortly thereafter with a third WWII German dagger (looking nothing like the other two) being acquired and added to the den wall (later determined to be an early SA dagger). The closest thing to an explanation from *Herr* Walther on the variant models was that different organizations under the Reich wore their own distinctive sidearms. One evening as I sat in my den and pondered the three different dagger models on the wall, I decided to make a determined effort to solve the puzzle and determine first the type daggers that I had acquired and, on a broader scale, how many different, distinct types were worn. This project proved to be a major undertaking since the available literature on the subject of WWII German daggers during this time was practically nonexistent. Although I was able to ferret out from the few available paperback pamphlets on the market the identity of the three daggers, a reference simply did not exist which explained in any detail the descriptions and values of the different model daggers, the organizations represented, the history and production aspects, etc., etc. I had a burning desire to find the answers to all of these questions, and what better place to look than the German blade city of Solingen.

This city's blades have been the absolute paragon of fine cutlery <u>since before</u> <u>the</u> <u>Middle</u> <u>Ages</u>. The first recorded mention of Solingen was in 1067 A.D., and the town was first chartered on 23 February 1374 A.D. Several natural resource advantages led to the development of what was to become the cutlery industry of Solingen. The surrounding thick forests offered virtually an unlimited supply of wood for making charcoal, and the nearby streams revealed deposits of iron ore by leaving reddish-brown sediments on their way to the Rhine River. Perhaps even more important was the geographical location, as *Koln* (Cologne), which at the time was the wealthiest trading center in all of Germany, was only some twenty short miles away. With swords and knives, the name "Solingen" became synonymous, the world over, with "excellence." In 1929, Solingen was classified as a German "large town" (over 100,000 inhabitants) through amalgamation with the neighboring small towns of Ohligs, Gräfrath, Wald, and Höhscheid. During the last census known to this author and taken in 1993, the number of inhabitants had grown to over 164,000.

I would like to digress for a moment and explain a commercial reason that also became a part of the equation dictating a journey to Solingen. Having joined my brother during the 1950s in a teenage joint venture of purchasing old, outdated Ford car parts from authorized Ford dealers in our home state of Tennessee and surrounding states, and reselling them to antique and classic car aficionados nationwide, the thought crossed my mind that, since the vast majority of these weapons were manufactured in Germany in the sole city of Solingen, perhaps the blade manufacturing firms there might still have a quantity of old parts (or better yet, completed pieces) still in stock. After all, World War II had ended only fifteen years prior to my tour of duty in Munich, and Germans, being

1930s Edged Weapon factory photo includes worker Werner Brattig of Solingen. During 1995, Herr Brattig offered to help the author with research for this chapter.

somewhat frugal, seemed predisposed to not throwing things away.

Therefore, on a <u>very</u> cold, wintry day, I drove to Solingen and began to call on the various edged weapon firms that were still in business at that time. Seeing Solingen for the first time in 1960, my first impressions were twofold: first, the city was <u>much</u> larger than I had imagined; and secondly, the cutlery firms were tucked away out of sight throughout the city and difficult to find. The typical edged weapon collector, even today, tends to expect the cutlery firms to dominate this city of swords. Not so in 1960, and certainly not so today. In fact, the Solingen cutlery industry for which the city is famous—the makers of knives, flatware, swords, razors, etc.—today represents only some twenty percent of the total value of production for the city. One can drive around the *Innenstadt* (city center) and the suburbs for sometime without locating a single firm.

However, armed with a map and asking a lot of questions, one can locate the individual firms. Every company which I visited during the winter of 1960 seemed to have the same reply, "Oh, you are an American. Do you know LTC Atwood? He bought everything we had from the old times." Although at the time I had no idea who Jim Atwood was, I would learn later that he was a fellow U.S. Army Officer serving in Berlin with the Berlin Brigade who had the identical thoughts as myself concerning the Solingen manufacturing firms, and he had made his quest to the city only a few short months before my own visit. A complete description of what Jim Atwood found (and I subsequently lost) in Solingen is explained in detail in his own words in Chapter 2 of my **Volume II** of this same series. I should add that LTC Atwood certainly had done his homework and had done an extremely thorough job, as every firm that I visited seemed to have the same, "Do you know LTC Atwood . . ." retort.

Although Jim Atwood was thorough with his Solingen factory foray, he had overlooked some items. For example, I purchased a large quantity of original sales catalogs from the large Carl Eickhorn Company (Eickhorn **Kundendienst** catalogs) and the F.W. Höller firm. *Herr* Grah, the owner of F.W. Höller at the time, also had available a large number of leftover dagger parts and even a few completed pieces.

Other early 1960s contacts on subsequent trips to Solingen included Gustav Spitzer's son and Kuno Ritter. Although elderly, *Herr* Ritter was kind enough to complete a high-quality 2nd model Navy dagger for me. Since he was quite old at the time, and there was considerable handwork required, he had no interest in honoring my request for additional examples. I remember him mentioning to me that the Navy dagger he completed was the first (and would be the last) WWII dagger that he had worked on since the late 1930s. It took *Herr* Ritter quite some time to complete this single sidearm, and he mailed it to me after I returned to the U.S. A copy of the original Ritter invoice is reproduced in this chapter. The total cost including the postage and insurance was only 100 *DM* (approximately $30.00 at the time). I kept Kuno Ritter's Navy dagger for many years but, unfortunately, sold it by mistake.

Over the past thirty-five years, I have had the opportunity to meet in person a large number of individuals working within the Solingen cutlery industry who run the gamut from blade polishers and grinders to swordsmiths and master craftsmen to company executives and factory owners. Needless to say, this long-term association has played a major role in my own knowledge and understanding of this important industry. It is difficult for me to comprehend anyone claiming to be a real expert in this field without developing some of these same associations and close Solingen ties. How any purveyor of German edged weapons can claim to really understand this hobby without spending a lot of time in Solingen is beyond me. As the old cliché goes, many of the aforementioned people in Solingen have forgotten more about

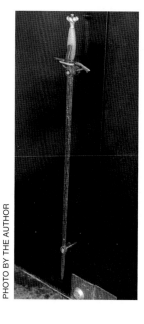

Although the *Blankwaffen* (edged weapons) industry in Solingen today is a mere fraction of former times, the city has definitely not forgotten its past, and the visitor is met with many reminders, including this sword door pull in the City Center.

◄

the manufacture of these sidearms than most "foreign" dealers and collectors will ever know. Quite simply stated, the majority of edged weapon pundits both in this country and abroad are out of touch with the edged weapon industry in Solingen. In my opinion, to fail to know and understand this city is to really fail to know and understand this hobby. I personally believe this to be true.

Unfortunately, many of the edged weapon firms in Solingen have gone out of business since my initial visit in 1960 and now cease to exist. Likewise,

Yet another example from Solingen's past. The author spotted in a residential area of Solingen a left-over Army Officer dagger pommel being used as part of a locking device on a wooden fence. ►

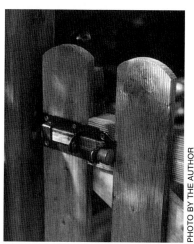

many of my early Solingen contacts have, unfortunately, expired of old age. Some of the early firms have adjusted to the changing economic demands and have managed to survive. Today, former Solingen cutlery casters supply the German automobile industry, and former ferrule makers continue in business by manufacturing umbrella frames and components for the electronics industry. The only two old firms which still maintain a large sword-producing capability are E. & F. Hörster and WKC. These two companies remain active today producing swords for other countries' military forces, as well as manufacturing dress swords for the U.S. military academies.

The pictorial section of this chapter will illustrate many of the present and former locations of a large number of the Solingen cutlery manufacturers, as well as some of the former suppliers and subcontractors to the industry. As mentioned in the Acknowledgements Section, I am indebted to my long-time Solingen colleague, *Herr* W. Gunter Bastian, for spending countless hours in locating the industry sites, to include many that have long been

A considerable part of Solingen WWI & WWII Edged Weapons were transported out of the city via the Müngstener Bridge. This amazing engineering feat was built between 1893 and 1897 and connects Solingen and the neighboring town of Remscheid. The structure passes over the Wupper River and remains Germany's highest railway bridge at *107 meters*. Kaiser Wilhelm II visited the completed Müngstener Bridge on 12 August 1899, and a monument at the base of the bridge commemorates his historic visit.

out of business. One thing that is obvious from a study of the individual black and white photographs of the various factories is that several of the edged weapon companies were not the massive corporate giants as shown in many of their letterheads. It appears that liberty was taken when doing the letterhead engraving to incorporate some of the neighboring buildings! However, these factory photographs will give the reader/researcher some indication concerning the comparative size of the various firms during the 1930s-40s. If some of the street names and/or street numbers do not match the current addresses, it is because many streets and locations throughout Germany were renamed and renumbered after the war. For example, there, obviously, are no more *Adolf Hitler Platze* in Germany (the former address of the *Gebr. Christians, Christianswerk K.G.* firm in Solingen which used the well-known "fork" trademark was *Adolf-Hitler Platz #18 & 19*).

The several-day search to locate the majority of the old edged weapon factory sites proved to be both interesting and fruitful. An original 1936 Solingen address book (pictured) and an original 1939 *Stadtplan* (city plan) proved to be most helpful in establishing the correct 1936 addresses. Many of the out-of-business edged weapon manufacturing firms have been replaced by other tenants during the years between 1945 and the present.

The former *Deutsches Klingenmuseum* in Solingen-Gräfrath, circa 1975. The building was erected as the city hall of the city of Gräfrath (today part of Solingen-Gräfrath) at the beginning of the century.

The new *Deutsches Klingenmuseum* in Solingen-Gräfrath. The museum was relocated a couple of blocks away from the original site in this large building above the centuries-old Gräfrath market square.

For example, the small factory of *C. Bertram Reinh. Sohn Fabrik*, located at *Beethovenstrasse #103* is now a Catholic church, and the large *Gottlieb Hammesfahr* buildings on *Focherstrasse* now house the huge, internationally known *Krups* household appliance and coffeemaker factory. Dagger collectors/researchers know both of these original firms by their prominent trademarks on 1933 SS dress daggers ("rooster and hen" trademark for the former and a "pyramid" for the latter). It is interesting to note that the *Gottlieb Hammesfahr* company manufactured blades (drop-forged) for many other Solingen manufacturers, as well as their own complete daggers.

In addition to researching the old factory addresses, the numerous Solingen factory photographs which accompany this chapter took several different days to shoot, due to the fact that the Solingen area seems to get more than its fair share of inclement weather. It is not uncommon for the majority of *Deutschland* to be clear as a bell, and as one approaches the beautiful *Bergisches Land* surrounding Solingen to have the weather suddenly change to fog, mist, and often rain.

Some of the old factory sites are simply empty lots. For example, the *Kamphausen & Plümacker* knife factory *(RZM 7/83)* location at *13*

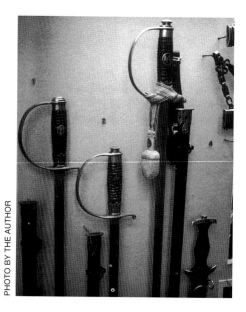

A portion of the Third Reich Edged Weapon Collection presently on display at the *Deutsches Klingenmuseum* in Solingen. Publicly displaying sidearms from the *NS* period at the *Klingen-museum* was strictly prohibited until very recently when a small collection was displayed to the public.

◄

After several years of searching for a copy, the author finally was fortunate to purchase a complete 1936 Solingen Address Book which features not only the addresses of *all* of the period edged weapon manufacturers, but also numerous interesting advertisements for Third Reich Dress Daggers and Swords. This single publication, combined with an original 1939 Solingen *Stadtplan* (city map) also in the possession of the author, were invaluable in the preparation of this chapter.

►

Mittelstrasse in Solingen-Ohligs is now an overgrown empty lot. Perhaps the proximity to the *Bahnhof* (Railroad Station) resulted in total bomb damage from World War II. Also, the site of the former *Carl Julius Krebs Fabrik* was completely cleared for the construction of a new Solingen *Autobahn* by-pass. Every attempt has been made to provide the reader/researcher with detailed, accurate former addresses in the event that a reader may want to make a personal trek to Solingen and follow in the author's footsteps.

Perhaps best known of the various trademarks applied to German Edged Weapons are the "Balanced Scales" of the Alexander Coppel (Alcoso) Factory in Solingen. The Alcoso Company manufactured a full line of Third Reich edged weapons during the 1933-45 timeframe, as well as being the predominant manufacturer and purveyor of the Third Reich miniature edged weapons (see page 222 of **Volume VII**). At the end of WWII, the Coppel plant was bombed into ruins. However, the old factory building at *Auf dem Kamp 58-62* was rebuilt and is presently rented to a firm which manufactures haircutting equipment. Note that the old Alcoso sign with the company "balanced scales" trademark remains intact.

Lastly, I tip my hat to the members of the 1930s-40s Solingen, Germany edged weapon industry from factory workers to company owners, as they have collectively created, albeit inadvertently, the intriguing and fascinating hobby of **Collecting the Edged Weapons of the Third Reich** which thousands of collectors worldwide enjoy today. Although they did not manufacture these beautiful sidearms for collectors, they did make them, and we are all the benefactors of their fine labor!

Close-up photograph of the 1933-45 Alcoso Company sign with the well-known "Balanced Scales" trademark which remained intact when this photograph was taken in 1995.

Pictured above is the former *Walter Backhaus KG* firm located at *120 Beethovenstrasse.* The old red brick factory building seen in the background is very typical of Solingen edged weapon production factories during the Third Reich period. *Walter Backhaus* operated a forge for pocket knife blades, and the company manufactured a limited number of SA daggers. The buildings are presently occupied by the printing firm *Druckerei Herbert Fuhrman.*

This Catholic Church located at *Beethovenstrasse #103* was the former *C. Bertram Reinh. Sohn Fabrik*, well-known throughout the knife world for their famous "Hen and Rooster" trademark. This small firm had always been rated at the top of the pocket-knife industry with many claiming their products to be the finest pocketknives in the world. Readers of this reference will also recall the *C. Bertram Reinh. Sohn* firm for their manufacture of 1933 SS dress daggers. When the company closed its doors several years ago, the "hen and rooster" trademark was acquired by the Robert Klaas firm in Solingen.

The modern Böker Edged Weapon Company, Solingen, Germany. The original red brick factory is visible in the background. The Böker firm is best known for their quality SS daggers manufactured during the Third Reich era. The firm suffered *major* bomb damage during World War II, and the modern building in the foreground of the picture is actually a facade over one of the original damaged red brick Böker factory buildings.

The well-known Clemen & Jung firm was located during the period of the Third Reich at *54 Florastrasse* in the Center of Solingen. Clemen & Jung was founded in 1860 as a manufacturer of tableware and household cutlery, although it also produced many dress daggers, swords, and bayonets. The firm was highly regarded for the quality of their etched and engraved blades. Collectors are very familiar with the firm's "Z in a shield" trademark. The original building like much of the downtown area of Solingen was totally bombed out late in the war, and an apartment house (pictured) was rebuilt on the old Clemen & Jung factory site. The Clemen & Jung name is still in existence, and the company manufactures handcuffs only, i.e., no sidearms production after being bombed out. The present owners are not related to the old owners.

Perhaps the best known of all of the Solingen-based cutlery firms to German Edged Weapon collectors and researchers is the *Carl Eickhorn Waffenfabrik* located at *Brühlerstrasse 55/59*. Founded in 1865 by Carl Eickhorn, the company's many trademarks were based on a squirrel device. Carl Eickhorn not only manufactured a complete line of Third Reich edged weaponry, but was also well-known for ornate Honor daggers and swords, sabers, and dress bayonets of exemplary quality. Unfortunately, the Carl Eickhorn company declared bankruptcy in 1976. The firm presently occupying the old Eickhorn buildings manufactures and sells quality *Bestecke* (tableware).

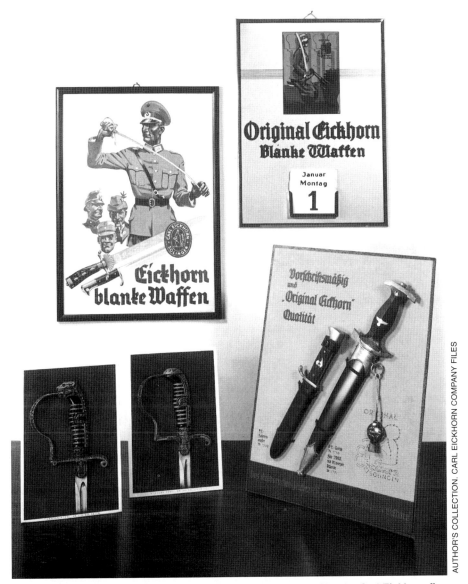

Pictured above is one of several advertising photographs used by the Carl Eickhorn firm in their *Kundendienst* catalog.

Period advertising Calendars and sales literature from the Carl Eickhorn *Waffenfabrik*. A copy of this original black-and-white photograph appears in the Eickhorn *Kundendienst* catalog.

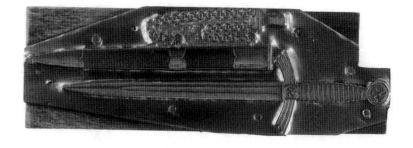

Original Carl Eickhorn Printing Clichés for the Eickhorn 1st and 2nd Model *Luftwaffe* Dress Daggers. These clichés were basically made by hand and were used in the printing of the company's sales catalogs and brochures in the 1930s. Note that the face of the 1st model *Luftwaffe* cliché is constructed of copper and the 2nd model *Luftwaffe* cliché is carved into a wood face.

This building located at *58 Blumenstrasse* in the Center of Solingen housed the Arthur Evertz edged weapon firm during 1933-45. Arthur Evertz was a brother-in-law of Paul Seilheimer. He was a grinder who founded his own company in 1925 at *58 Blumenstrasse* and purchased the real estate in 1929. Very little is known about this particular firm except for the fact that a number of SA daggers and dress bayonets have surfaced with their trademark. The *RZM* production number assigned to Arthur Evertz was *RZM M7/85.*

◀

Advertisement of the Arthur Evertz firm in Solingen appearing in the Trade Magazine, *"Die Klinge"* depicting one of their 1st Model *Luftwaffe* Daggers superimposed over a *Luftwaffe* Pilot. The Arthur Evertz, Solingen "AES" trademark is incorporated into the advertisement at the lower left.

▶

This small brick building located at *121-123 Schlagbaumerstrasse* housed the Carl Halbach firm during the period of the Third Reich. This firm manufactured a small number of party daggers. The Carl Halbach, Solingen trademark resembles a chess pawn and is illustrated on page 244 of **Volume I**.

The former *Gottlieb Hammesfahr* Buildings on *Focherstrasse* now house the huge, internationally-known *Krups* household appliance and coffee-maker factory. Dagger collectors/researchers know the *Gottlieb Hammesfahr* firm for their many 1933 SS daggers with their distinctive "pyramid" trademark. It is interesting to note that *Gottlieb Hammesfahr* manufactured blades (drop-forged) for many other Solingen manufacturers, as well as their own complete daggers. Pictured is the former *Gottlieb Hammesfahr* Head Office Administration Building of the complex, and this same building can be seen with SA men standing in front of it on page 10 of **Volume VI.** Note in both photographs the incorporation of the firm's trademark pyramids into the building motif. The large complex even includes a small cemetery and *Gottlieb Hammesfahr* is buried under a pyramid-shaped tombstone on the grounds.

Another view of the former *Gottlieb Hammesfahr* factory, which now houses the large German *Krups* household appliance and coffee-maker factory.

The J.A. Henckels *Zwillingswerk A.G.* as seen when driving west on *Grünewalder Strasse* from the City Center. Note the incorporation of the famous Henckels twins trademark not only on the roof of the building, but also in the original factory brickwork.

The J.A. Henckels' *Zwilling* (twins) logo has been intricately incorporated into the outside brick of the main Henckels factory building on *Grünewalder Strasse* in Solingen.

The Friedr. Herder Abr. *Sohn* factory (now closed) is located directly across the street from the J.A. Henckels *Zwillingswerk*. This manufacturing firm utilized the well-known crossed keys trademark and is best known for the manufacture of SA daggers during the 1933-1945 time period. Friedr. Herder holds the distinction of being the oldest of the Solingen firms, with a direct line back to 1727, when Peter Herder acquired the ownership of the spade trademark. In 1840, the firm acquired the crossed keys trademark. Large quantities of daggers and swords were produced by Friedr. Herder during the period of the Third Reich.

The H. Herder Edged Weapon Factory, Solingen, Germany. The H. Herder familiar trade-mark (a black spade inside a rectangle) is visible on the front of the company. This trade-mark had to incorporate the outer rectangle in order to distinguish it from the black spade trademark owned by the F. Herder firm in Solingen. The H. Herder Company is best known for the manufacture of SA daggers during the 1933-1945 timeframe using the *RZM* number *M7/111.* The company was founded in 1806 by a member of the F. Herder family and remains in operation today manufacturing tools and tableware. The "H" in the H. Herder company name is an abbreviation of Henrietta Herder and not the male name "Heinrich," as is commonly accepted.

The *Richard Abr. Herder* Company is located on *Rathausstrasse* in Solingen and is well-known among collectors. The firm is a branch of the Herder family and was formed initially to manufacture cutlery and tools. The Richard Herder company was active in both World War I and World War II in the manufacturing of sidearms for the German war machine and the commercial market. Their "four-pointed star" trademark is easily recognized by edged weapon collectors worldwide. The firm remains active today.

Another branch of the famous cutlery Herder family was Robert Herder whose firm, located at *Benratherstrasse 7* in Solingen-Ohligs, remains in business today. Robert Herder is known to have manufactured party-form dress daggers during the Third Reich, and collectors/researchers will readily recognize the company's "windmill" trademark. Two other commercial trademarks used by this firm are a "four-leaf clover" and an "eagle on a pillar." Robert Herder, like many of the other Solingen cutlery firms, is again making tableware and knives. The old plant can be seen on the right and the newer administrative building on the left.

The old *F. W. Höller* Building at *8 Sonnenstrasse* in the center of Solingen was the first *Waffenfabrik* that the author visited in 1960. At that time, the firm was still operational and had a large quantity of original parts and original catalogs available for sale. The last owner, *Herr* Grah, had switched the production to mainly flatware after the war. The *F. W. Höller* firm manufactured a full-line of dress daggers, swords, and bayonets during the period of the Third Reich, and collectors are very familiar with their "thermometer in a double oval" trademark.

The E. & F. Hörster Company was founded in 1850 and is located on *Katternberger Strasse*, Solingen. When founded in 1850, the company was registered for the production of, "swords, sabers, daggers, bayonets, foils, etc." The firm remains operational today and is engaged in manufacturing cutlery, ceremonial swords, daggers and nail & hair clippers. The name of the company, E. & F. Hörster *Waffenfabrik* (E. & F. Hörster Arms Factory) is emblazoned on the front of the building, and what appears to have been at one time a crest or a trademark can be observed directly under the roof line.

Advertisement of the E. & F. Hörster firm in Solingen appearing in the trade magazine, *"Die Klinge"* depicting the HJ *Fahrtenmesser* in wear. The E. & F. Hörster, Solingen trademark is incorporated into the advertisement at the lower left.

A large blade-grinding wheel still in operation in Solingen today. A steady stream of water passes over the rotating wheel in order to reduce heat. The technology of grinding blades in the edged weapon industry has remained the same for *two centuries*.

The small *Hubertus Schneidwarenfabrik* is located on *Wuppertalerstrasse* and was founded in 1932 by the well-known Solingen cutler Kuno Ritter. The firm remains operational today with Kuno Ritter's grandson-in-law, Henning Ritter, at the helm, and is well-known for superior hunting knives and pocket knives. The author had the privilege of meeting the late Kuno Ritter in early 1960, and receiving a handmade Navy dress dagger from him. Unfortunately, Herr Ritter passed away shortly thereafter.

The Robert Klaas *Waffenfabrik* is located on *Pfeilstrasse* in Solingen-Ohligs. The well-known Robert Klaas trademark of two kissing cranes was adopted in 1834, modified in 1935 to better adapt for metal stampings, and is visible on the front of the Klaas building. The Klaas firm manufactured a large quantity of daggers and dagger components during the 1933-1945 time period, and is still engaged today in the production of cutlery.

The small side street leading into the Robert Klaas factory has been named for the company, i.e., Robert Klaas *Strasse*.

This colorful green and white building on *Cronenbergerstrasse* was the 1933-45 site of the *Herm. Konejung A.G.* firm which Edged Weapons collectors/researchers know by the company's "spectacles" trademark. *Herm. Konejung* primarily manufactured party form daggers and a limited number of 1st Model *Luftwaffe* dress daggers. The present occupant of the building is an electrical handler for kitchen supplies.

Pictured is the large building on *Beethovenstrasse* that once housed the Peter Daniel Krebs firm, well-known for the manufacturing of the SS *Degen*. The building is presently occupied by a video parlor.

Current market prices for Third Reich dress daggers make the dollar prices on this reproduced November, 1967 invoice from the F.W. Höller firm in Solingen to the author seem almost comical, but this is what leftover Custom and Hunting daggers could be purchased for from the factory(ies) during the mid-to-late 1960s. ▶

The *Hugo Linder Deltawerk* firm is located at *16-18 Gas Strasse* near the huge J.A. Henckels complex in the center of Solingen. Although best known for their pocket-knives, the Hugo Linder firm manufactured SA daggers and dagger components during the period of the Third Reich.

This nondescript brown building located at *Schwertstrasse* (Sword Street) #6 is presently occupied by the Klesper Company which manufactures metal products, but housed the sizeable *P.D. Lüneschloss* factory during 1933-45. The *Lüneschloss* Company was founded to manufacture firearms, but later progressed to swords, bayonets, and sidearms of various types to include party form, *Wehrmacht,* and *Zoll* (Customs) dress daggers. *P.D. Lüneschloss* was one of the oldest Solingen edged weapons firms. The front of the *Lüneschloss* building was completely bombed out during World War II.

Located at *3-7 Bismarkstrasse* in the center of Solingen is the nondescript building which still houses today the *C. Lütters & Cie. Löwenwerk* firm. To date, the only known Third Reich edged weapons attributed to this firm are Hitler Youth knives and standard Army dress bayonets. The company's trademark of a couchant lion often appeared on blades without the firm's name.

Close-up of the *C. Lütters & Cie. Löwenwerk* brass sign. Note that the same couchant lion trademark is still used by the firm today in their manufacture of pocketknives.

◀

The Author located the well-known August Merten *Witwe* firm at # 7-9 *Schulte vom Brühlstrasse* in Solingen-Gräfrath. German dagger collectors/researchers know this firm for their prominent trademark (the letter "M" superimposed on two oak leaves). The same company trademark is visible on the front of their building today. The Merten firm produced a sizable number of SA daggers during 1933-45, and is presently engaged in the manufacture of *Bestecke* (tableware).

Close-up view of the advertising sign on the August Merten *Witwe* firm located at *#7-9 Schulte vom Brühlstrasse* in Solingen-Gräfrath. The *"Witwe"* on the sign translates as "Widow" in English. The identical "M" superimposed on two oak leaves trademark was utilized on the August Merten 1933 SA daggers. ▶

This private house located at *Merscheiderstrasse* #315 was the site of the *Robert Müller und Sohn Waffenfabrik* (Weapons Factory) during the 1933-45 timeframe. Herr Müller made numerous SA and NSKK daggers during the period and was assigned *RZM* number M7/32. The house is still occupied today by Müller's daughter.

Pictured above is the Old Ernst Pack & *Söhne* edged weapon factory located at *#61-69 Ritterstrasse* in the City of Solingen. As shown in Volume II of this reference series, the E. Pack firm offered a *vast* selection of quality edged weapons. A translated excerpt from the Third Reich era Pack catalog states, "The striking image a soldier makes is not complete until he is carrying an excellent sidearm . . . This edged weapon is a piece of jewelry in every respect and a sensible reminder of the enlistment period." Collectors are especially keen on the beautiful engraved bayonets from this firm.

The large *Pfeilring* (Ring of Arrows) factory is pictured in the Center City of Solingen. During the 1930s, this firm manufactured numerous SA dress daggers. To date, the author has not observed the company's distinctive ring of five arrows logo on any other Third Reich daggers or swords. The *Pfeilring* factory is known worldwide today for the manufacture of high-quality ladies and men's manicure sets.

The *Lauterjung & Sohn Puma-Werk* was located in this brick building at *9 Kanalstrasse* in Solingen. The *Puma-Werk* produced numerous dress daggers during the era of the Third Reich, although the firm's normal production consisted of hunting knives, razors, scissors, tableware and manicure articles. The firm utilized the famous "*puma* head profile in a diamond" trademark. The pictured *Puma* factory building was completely dismantled in early 1995.

The *Lauterjung & Sohn Puma-Werk* address sign was seen on one of the two concrete entrance columns on *Kanalstrasse*. The small, white device under the sign is the *Puma-Werk* doorbell.

The *Carl Schmidt Sohn* firm was located in this attractive building at *Kronprinzenstrasse 28* during the 1933-45 timeframe. The company manufactured only the party-form dress daggers and used a "church" trademark. The building is presently utilized as a bodybuilding center.

This photograph shows the present location of the *Carl Schmidt Sohn* building. Note the "church in a circle" logo at each end of the company sign. The firm today is a large manufacturer of *Bestecke* (tableware). The previous occupant of the complex was the *Heinrich Kaufmann und Söhne* firm.

This Stucco Building Located on *Burgstrasse* in the Center of Solingen Formerly Housed the Well-Known *Mulcuto-Werk,* Which was Owned by Paul Müller (not the famous swordsmith) and was one of the leading producers of body care instruments such as razors, scissors, clippers, etc. Adjoining this building to the left of the picture was the well-known *Stocker & Companie, Solingen Metallwarenfabrik (SMF).* Edged weapon collectors/researchers are familiar with the *SMF* firm for their manufacture of a preponderance of high-quality *Lutwaffe* sidearms.

The two-story white building in the center of the photograph is the site of the old Paul Seilheimer Firm at *12 Albrecht Strasse*. The Seilheimers were engaged in edged weapon production for several generations, serving the trade as swordsmiths and brass workers. Paul Seilheimer started his own business in 1917 in the building pictured. The Paul Seilheimer period catalog offers a wide variety of Third Reich edged weapons to include numerous Army sword and bayonet models, a complete line of *Luftwaffe* and Police side-arms, Army, Navy, SA, NSKK, HJ, and Customs daggers, as well as numerous Forestry and Hunting sidearms.

The original *Lauterjung & Companie, Tiger Stahlwaren- und Waffenfabrik* was housed in this building at *29 Gasstrasse* in Solingen during the Third Reich era. A manufacturer of all kinds of knives, scissors, manicure equipment and razors, *Lauterjung & Cie* produced many dress daggers during the 1933-1945 period, using their "tiger" trademark. The company is now out of business.

◄

The well-known Emil Voos engraved Army and 2nd Model *Luftwaffe* dress daggers with ivory grips were produced by Herr Voos in this small building on *Dingshauserstrasse* in Solingen. The building presently houses a *Kinderheim* (Children's Home).

►

37

This period photograph provides collectors/researchers with their first look at Emil Voos at work at his small workshop on *Dingshauserstrasse*.

During the Third Reich era, both the Paul and Max Weyersberg firms were housed in this building at *6 Olaf-Palme-Strasse* in Solingen. The old Weyersberg building is presently occupied by the H. RAUH *GmbH.*, a manufacturer of plastic articles and was receiving a facelift when this picture was taken during October 1994.

A "Foreign" Blade manufacturer which has operated a manufacturing firm in Solingen for many years is the famous British Firm (Wilkinson Swords). To paraphrase a British saying, the building of a blade factory in the city of Solingen is like "taking coals to Newcastle." However, it should be noted that the Wilkinson Swords plant in Solingen manufactures razor blades and not edged weapons. As a matter of fact, the building pictured used to be the production site of a large German manufacturer of safety razors, razor blades, and other cutlery related to barbers. The original owner's name was Osberghaus and his trademark was *"Fasan"* (pheasant).

The British Wilkinson Swords Company Sign and Logo of crossed swords is proudly displayed on one of the Main Streets in the *Klingenstadt* (Blade City) of Solingen.

The Anton Wingen, Jr. firm remained in business until 1995 and was located directly behind the huge J.A. Henckels Firm in Solingen on *Gasstrasse*. The Wingen firm was formed in 1888 and specialized in drop-forging. The company uses, in addition to their own "knight" logo, the tradename "Othello."

Original factory photograph from the now-defunct Anton Wingen, Jr. firm picturing from left to right, the Wingen Army Officer Dagger, 2nd Model *Luftwaffe* Dagger, Army Saber, SA Dagger and *RAD* Officer Dagger. This is one of the few source photographs to survive the Wingen firm.

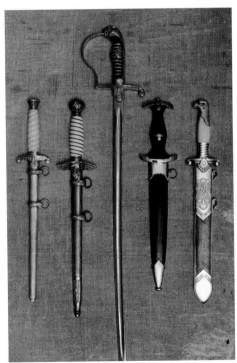

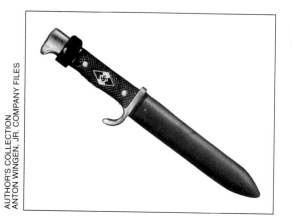

Actual catalog insert of the Hitler Youth knife manufactured by the Anton Wingen, Jr. firm.

RATHAUS

The present *Rathaus* (City Hall) building located in the center of downtown Solingen once housed the *Weyersberg, Kirschbaum & Companie (WK&C)*, which remained active from 1883 to 1930. Most likely Solingen's most famous cutlery firm, *WK&C* was the manufacturer of vast quantities (hundreds of thousands) of edged weapons during the period 1883-1918. The firm utilized the well-known "king and knight heads" trademark. When the *WK&C* firm went bankrupt in 1930, the three component parts of the company were auctioned to the highest bidder.

The WKC firm located on *Wittkuller Strasse* in Solingen remains in the Edged Weapons business today. The WKC firm was formed in 1930 and is one of three of the successors of the large *Weyersberg, Kirschbaum & Companie (WK&C)* which manufactured countless Imperial edged sidearms. When the WK&C firm went bankrupt in 1930, the three component parts were auctioned to the highest bidder. The WKC firm is best known among collectors for their productivity of high-quality Third Reich dress daggers (especially 2nd model Navy daggers) and numerous sword models. The old factory on *Wittkuller Strasse* received a "facelift" in the early 1990s when new windows, doors, and flooring were installed.

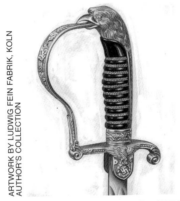

Source illustration from the WKC document files. This original factory illustration features a seldom-seen eagle head pommel Justice Official dress saber. The WKC model number 1702 is scribbled on the reverse side. Note the small open wing eagle on the obverse langet. The WKC sales catalog shows this same saber as Model number 1047. No explanation exists for the model number change.

Beautiful mirrored-glass advertising calendar from the WKC Firm. The calendar has windows for the day, date and month. The date was changed by turning the knobs on either side of the calendar to move the day, date and month which were printed on cloth belts. See pages 317 and 318 of **Volume VI** for more details on these WKC advertising calendars. Size is 9¹/₂" x 14¹/₄".

The *Ed. Wüsthof Dreizackwerk* was registered in Solingen during 1832 and remains in business today in a modern facility on *Kronprinzenstrasse*. *Ed. Wüsthof* (trident) kitchen knives and tools are known worldwide. The firm also manufactured dress daggers and dagger components during the period 1933-1945.

The large Aesculap firm was one of the major edged weapon manufacturing firms located outside the geographical area of Solingen. The Aesculap firm is located in Tuttlingen (80 kilometers east of Freiburg on the Danube River). The Aesculap firm in Tuttlingen and the Robert Klaas firm in Solingen were two of the few edged weapon manufacturers to produce the Red Cross dress daggers and hewers. Some of the primary goods still being manufactured in Tuttlingen are cutlery and surgical instruments.

Pictured above is the *Gebrüder Hartkopf* firm located on the *Bismarkstrasse* in downtown Solingen. The *Hartkopf* firm was responsible for semifinished and completed blade blanks which were hilted and sold by other firms. The company remains in operation today as a blade forge.

One of the largest crossguard manufacturers in Solingen was the sizeable Piel and Adley firm which remains in business today on *Lehnerstrasse*, operating as a very large and advanced caster of brass and German silver parts. This firm stamped their party-form internal crossguards with their initials "P" and "A."

One major source for *SA/NSKK/SS/NPEA/Feldherrnhalle* wooden grips in Solingen was housed in this building (presently an apartment house) on *Lehnerstrasse*. During the era of the Third Reich approximately six of the large party-form grip-making machines were housed in this building. These party-grip milling machines were not the same as the party-grip machine pictured on pages 55 & 56 of **Volume VI** of *Collecting the Edged Weapons of the Third Reich*. The sole function of the latter machine was to cut the rectangular slot in the party dagger grips.

The Oscar Jenisch *Schraubenfabrik* (Screw Factory) was one of the major suppliers of hilt and scabbard screws to the Solingen Edged Weapons industry. Although the Jenisch sign remains on the old factory building on *Schützenstrasse*, the firm has been sold to an automotive repair shop.

In 1938 the building pictured above housed the large *Ernst Köhnen Lederwarenfabrik* (Leather Goods Factory) which manufactured a large number of edged weapon leather accouterments for the Third Reich. The present occupant of the building is the Paul A. Henckels metal products firm.

Pictured above is the U.S. Army Military Government staff (Detachment H2 H2) assigned to the city of Solingen in April 1945. The detachment commander, Major John O. Hall from Texas, is pictured center front. What an opportunity these American soldiers had to acquire some edged weapon souvenirs!

Major John O. Hall, the U.S. Army Military Government detachment commander in Solingen, uses a Third Reich Army officer dress dagger to point out the location of Solingen on the world globe. The picture is dated April/May 1945.

◄

Again, Major John Hall selects a white-handle Army officer dress dagger to serve as a pointer to indicate the exact location of the U.S. Army Military Government detachment in the city center of Solingen.

►

Artist's concept of an *RLB Leutnant* (Lieutenant) in his greatcoat and wearing his first model *RLB* Officer's dagger, circa 1937.

Chapter 2

THE DRESS SIDEARMS OF THE *RLB*

"People could survive their natural trouble all right if it weren't for the trouble they make for themselves."
—Ogden Nash

During World War II, many a German civilian had the opportunity to observe the *Reichsluftschutzbund-RLB* (Air Raid Protection League) in action. As the Allies stepped up their bombing raids of major German cities and industrial areas, this organization stayed as busy as any of Hitler's minions.

The *RLB* organization was established by the Reich Air Ministry on 29 April 1933 from the existing *Deutsches Luftschutzverband* (German Air Protection League) by Hermann Göring's declaration that the *RLB* was to be the official air raid protection service of the state. This civil defense group became an official Third Reich State organization and was immediately renamed the *Reichsluftschutzbund* or *RLB*. The primary mission assigned to the renamed organization was to protect the German cities and population from hostile air attacks. Additionally, this group was charged with training the civilian population in civil defense matters and air raid precautions. With the exception of a small cadre of career *RLB* officers and officials, the vast majority of the members was composed of volunteers similar to the massive U.S. Defense Corps so evident during World War II. Every populated area in Germany, no matter how small, had its own *RLB* contingent drawn from local resident volunteers. Membership was achieved by application or by the conferring of honorary membership. One only has to review the organizational structure of the *RLB* to realize how deeply it penetrated the whole of German society and communities. The *RLB* was organized as follows:

(1) Presidency of the *RLB*
(2) *RLB* groups
(3) *RLB* district groups
(4) *RLB* local groups

(5) *RLB* community
(6) *RLB* auxiliary
(7) *RLB* blocks

Germany was all too familiar with the results of sustained Allied bomb-ing of German cities during the closing months of World War I when hun-dreds of German civilians were killed. With the advent of more modern bomber aircraft during World War II, the potential for disaster to the popu-lated areas was evident to Hermann Göring and other high-ranking *Luftwaffe* generals.

As head of all of the Third Reich Air organizations, the newly formed *RLB* fell under the purview of Hermann Göring who appointed *Luftwaffe* Lt. General von Roques as its first honorary president.

A little known fact is that the *RLB* was subdivided into two separate for-mations—the *Luftschutz* (Air Raid Protection) and the *Warndienst* (Air Raid Warning Service). After 1943, the *Warndienst* became a part of the German Order Police, although the organization still functioned as the Air Raid Warning Service of the *Reich*.

The *RLB* leaders wore distinctive and complete *RLB* uniforms similar to those of the *Luftwaffe*, while the millions of civilian volunteers were only issued *RLB* cloth armbands and steel helmets.

An interesting February 1937 letter from the Headquarters, Reichs Air Raid Protection League in Berlin to the large Carl Eickhorn firm in Solingen on the subject of *RLB* Enlisted daggers has been translated into English and is reproduced below. The original of this 11 February 1937 letter is on file at Johnson Reference Books (JRB).

Reichs Air Raid Protection League **Berlin W 35, 11th February 1937**
The Headquarters *(Präsidium)* **Rauchstrasse 14**
Fernruf: Nr. B5 Barbaroffa 9721

Firma Carl Eickhorn
Bruhler Strasse 55/57
Solingen

(1) In amendment of the agreement with your firm of 15 May 1936, starting the 1st of April 1937 no more payments will be made to the *RLB Präsidium* (Headquarters) and local groups. Additionally, only the agreed upon basic prices will be charged.

Starting from the above date no more statements of payments will be sent to jurisdictions and no copies of bills will be sent to the *RLB Präsidium* (Headquarters).

(2) The firm hereby promises, starting 1 April 1937, to only fill orders for groups of the *Reichsluftschutzbund* (Air Raid Protection League) for the following articles:

RLB Enlisted Men daggers   (only for the district groups of the
(crews)   *Reichsluftschutzbund*)

A list of these groups is available and is being kept up-to-date, with regulations being changed or added. The firm is ordered to disregard all orders coming from other organizations, local or district groups and forward them to the above official list without filling them and is obliged to destroy the order blanks.

(3) The stated price for *RLB* Enlisted daggers is 7.20 *Reichsmark*.

During May of 1940, a completely new and detailed regulation (ordinance) concerning the *RLB* was issued. This regulation has been translated into English and is reproduced in its entirety below:

1.1 Ordinance Concerning the German Air Protection Federation (RLB)

May 14, 1940

1

(1) The German Air Protection Federation *(RLB)* including its complete legitimate and non-legitimate formations and units are being transformed in a corporation of the public law; it is subordinate to the National Minister of Aviation and Commander-in-Chief of the Air Force.

(2) It is without liquidation the legitimate successor of its previous formations and units as well as the Danzig Air Protection Federation, corporation of the public law, which loses its own body corporate.

2

Leadership of the *Reichsluftschutzbund* *(RLB)*

(1) The President stands as the Head of the *RLB* legally and in all other affairs. He can further delegate his representation of authority.

Pictured (from left to right) is the newly named president of the *RLB*, Flak-Artillery General V. Schröder; the inspector of the civilian *RLB* in the State Air Ministry, Ministry Director, Dr.-Ing. (Phd in engineering with honors) e.h. Knipfer and the honorary President of the *RLB*, Lieutenant General v. Roques.

3

Duties and powers of the *RLB*

(1) Duties and powers of the *RLB* are in compliance with the Aviation Law of June 26, 1935 (RGBI. IS. 827) in the version of September 8, 1939 (RGBI. IS. 1762) as well as the enacted ordinances from the National Minister of Aviation and Commander-in-Chief of the Air Force, which are to be published in the State Law Gazette.

(2) The #1 section 3 of the Aviation Law finds no application for the *RLB.*

4

Membership in the Air Protection Federation

(1) Membership in the *RLB* is voluntary. It is achieved by application or by the conferring of honorary membership.

(2) Such members can be nominated for administrative positions of the *RLB*, who willingly declare themselves for acceptance as administrators in the *RLB*. The service of administrators is an honorable sacrificial assignment for the German community.

(3) The members of the previous *RLB* including its formations and units remain members of the *RLB* as a corporation of the public law.

5

Service dress and insignia

(1) The administrators of the *RLB* wear the service dress which is presented to them by the Minister of Aviation and Commander-in-Chief of the Air Force.

(2) The members of the *RLB* can wear in accordance with regulations for civilian dress the insignia of the *RLB*.

6

Relation(s) for service in the National Socialistic Movement

The representatives of the *Führer* decide in agreement with the National Aviation Minister and Commander-in-Chief of the Air Force to what extent the activity of *RLB* officials is being considered of the same activity of the members of the *NSDAP* and its formations.

7

Legal relations

The legal relations of the employees and workers of the *RLB* conform to those for the personnel of the administrations of the state active regulations.

8

Legal relations of honorary officials

Following regulations for the service of honorary officials of the *RLB* find suitable application:

(1) 14 of the first carrying-out ordinance for the Air Raid Protection Law of May 4, 1937 in the version of the proclamation of September 1, 1939 (RGBI. IS. 1630) as well as the law concerning the aid of the members of conscripted men and labor service workers (Family Relief Law) of March 30, 1936/modification regulation of May 14, 1940 (RGBI. 1936 IS. 327/1940 IS. 779) in connection with the regulation for completion and carrying-out of the Family Relief Law (Family Relief Carrying-Out Ordinance-Fu. D10-) of July 11, 1939/May 14, 1940 (RGBI. 1939 IS. 1225/1940 IS. 779).

(2) The regulation concerning the social insurance of the conscripted air-raid workers of November 11, 1939 (RGBI. IS. 2181) without #2, section 1.

(3) Of the first carrying-out ordinance for the Air Raid Protection Law provided that bearers of liability to repair is not the state, but the *RLB*.

9

To discharge obligation of the *RLB*, public contributions and fees for the state, the regional states, communities, local communities and corporations of the public law, the appropriate state regulations find application for the national state. The sec. 4 nr. 2 letter of the Land Tax Law (GrStG) of December 1, 1936 (RGBI. IS. 986) remains untouched.

10

Temporary regulations

The entries of previous formations and units of the *RLB* in the association records are to be cancelled officially free of charge, the entries in the land registers and other official public records are to be amended free of charge.

11

Financial policy

The financial policy of the *RLB* conforms itself to the law for the preservation and promotion of purchasing power of March 24, 1934 (RGBI. IS. 235)—paragraph 1 financial policy of the legal personnel of the public law and similar unions and organizations (contributions-law)—and the enacted regulations concerning financial policy in the *RLB* from the National Minister of Aviation and Commander-in-Chief of the Air Force in agreement with the National Minister of Finance.

12

Carrying-out—and supplementary regulations

The National Minister of Aviation and Commander-in-Chief of the Air Force permits the necessary legal regulations for carrying-out and completion of the directive as far as necessity in agreement with the authorized ministers.

13

Commencement

The directive goes into effect as of April 1, 1940.
Berlin, May 14, 1940
The President of the Cabinet Council for National Defense
Göring, Generalfeldmarschall

The State Minister and Head of the *Reichschancellory*
Dr. Lammers

1.2 Ordinance of the State Air Protection Federation of June 28, 1940

Upon the basis of article 3 of the ordinance concerning the *RLB* of May 14, 1940 (RGBI. IS. 784) I give the *RLB* the following ordinance:

1

Duties

(1) The *Reichsluftschutzbund (RLB)* has the duty to convince the German people of the vital importance of air protection and to gain the support for cooperation in self-protection.

(2) Furthermore, it is incumbent upon the *RLB* in the scope of regulations of air defense law, its carrying-out of ordinances and regulatory statutes.

1. The implementation of the organization of self-protection and the training of self-defense protection.

2. The advising of the population of the public and private agencies and businesses in self-protection and extended self-protection.

3. The cooperation of the clearing of attics, the acquisition of self-defense gear, the darkening and the makeshift construction of air raid shelters.

(3) The *RLB* furthermore has the duty in cooperation with the distribution of gas masks to the population.

(4) Further duties can be delegated by the National Minister of Aviation and Commander-in-Chief of the Air Force by regulations or administrative dispositions.

2

Organization

(1) The President of the *RLB* stands as Head of the *RLB,* below him is the Chief-of-Staff of the *Präsidium* of the *RLB.*

(2) The *RLB* is organized as follows:
a) Presidency of the *RLB*
b) *RLB* groups
c) *RLB* district groups
d) *RLB* local groups
e) *RLB* community
f) *RLB* auxiliary
g) *RLB* blocks

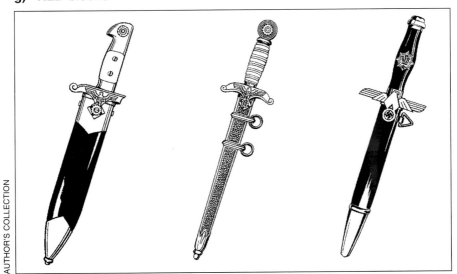

Original artwork from the Carl Eickhorn factory files.

THE *RLB* DAGGERS

BACKGROUND

As early as 1934 a sidearm was a component of the *RLB*-service dress uniform. During 1938, the *RLB* grip emblem was changed by direction of Hermann Göring, who designated a new flag and emblem for the *Luftschutz* in his capacity as National Minister of Aviation. A summary of official regulations for carrying the *RLB* sidearms was included in a 17 June 1939 *RLB* Ordinance. An English translation of these detailed regulations is provided below for the first time in a contemporary reference book.

Wearing Regulations of the *RLB* Sidearms:

7.3   The *RLB*-Sidearms

Since 1934 a sidearm was a component part of the *RLB* service dress uniform. In accordance with the rank-grouping, it was denoted with a dagger or hewer and distinguished themselves in importance by the way [they were] carried. In 1938, the grip emblem was changed. A summary of regulations for carrying the sidearm is included in an Ordinance of the *RLB Präsidium* of June 17, 1939.

7.3.1 Wearing Regulation of the *RLB*-Sidearms

The sidearm is a component part of the *RLB* service dress uniform. Therefore, it may only be put on when the official wears a complete and regulation service dress (uniform), or at least transitional (*RLB* Service dress without cloth coat).

RLB Dagger:
For wearing of the *RLB* dagger with carrying device only Officials of Leader Grade are qualified.

Method of wearing for the small (field) service uniform, small and large dress uniform: The *RLB* dagger is to be worn fastened under the cloth coat on the open loop (ring) of the lower belt, on the coat. The *RLB* dagger is to be worn out of the left coat pocket.

Method of wearing for the large (field) service uniform: The *RLB* dagger is worn on an open black leather loop or on the belt on whose lower end a ring is located. The loop is to be located on the belt so that the dagger is located on the wearer's left hip. In theaters and other buildings where generally headwear and outerwear are removed, the *RLB* dagger is also removed.

RLB hewer: For the wearing of the *RLB* hewer by the officials of rank-grouping 8-13 the regulations are in force in the provisions concerning the clothing-dress the *RLB*.

RLB DAGGER MODEL DESCRIPTIONS

1. **Type. First Model Subordinate Dagger**. Authorized for selected *RLB* subordinates on paid full-time duty (rank groups 5-10). *RLB* sidearms were distributed from the regional *RLB* groups to their lower offices. Commercial trade through normal retail outlets was not authorized.

2. **Year Adopted.** 1936.

3. **Description.** The pommel, crossguard and scabbard fittings are nickel-plated and contrast with the dark wood or ebony grip. The straight cross-guard features a large stylized national eagle and swastika. The oval pommel screws onto the tang of the blade, similar to the Army officer's, and secures the blade to the hilt. The early sunburst emblem of the *RLB* is affixed to the center of the wood grip. The straight, double-edged blade is found both with and without the manufacturer's trademark on the reverse side. The scabbard is pressed steel and is painted black with a nickel-plated lower fitting.

4. **Length.** 36 cms (14.2").

5. **Blade Motto.** None.

6. **Accouterments.**
    a. Hanger—black leather strap riveted to the carrying connector.
    b. Portepee—None.

7. **Collector Availability.** Scarce.

1st model *RLB* Subordinate Dagger by E. & F. Hörster—full length, obverse view. Note that the early, first pattern *RLB* sunburst emblem is affixed to the center of the dark wood or ebony grip.

Extreme close-up photograph of the obverse crossguard on the 1st model *RLB* subordinate dagger by E. & F. Hörster. The straight cross-guard features a large stylized national eagle and swastika. Note that the black leather single strap hanger is attached to the scabbard by four small nickel brads.

Extreme close-up view of the E. & F. Hörster trademark on the 1st model *RLB* subordinate dagger. This photograph also provides the reader with an excellent view of the reverse crossguard on the *RLB* subordinate dagger. A thin black leather blade buffer pad is barely visible in the picture.

Extreme close-up view of the *RLB* eight-pointed sunburst emblem on the 1st model subordinate dagger by E. & F. Hörster. The *RLB* monogram letters and minuscule swastika were finished in a dark blue enamel, and the background sunburst of the emblem was finished with a thin coat of silver plate.

◀

Excellent study of the 1st model *RLB* subordinate dagger black leather strap hanging device riveted to the carrying connector on the scabbard—obverse view. The original black scabbard paint is near perfect.

▶

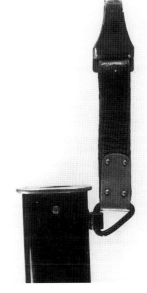

Excellent study of the 1st model *RLB* subordinate Dagger black leather strap hanging device riveted to the carrying connector on the scabbard—reverse view. Note that one of the four nickel rivets is missing.

◀

ARTWORK BY BRIAN MOLLOY, UNITED KINGDOM

Artist rendering of a *Reichsluftschutzbund (RLB) Luftschutz* (LS) *Truppmeister* wearing the 1st model (1936) subordinate *RLB* dagger. Because of the method of attachment to the scabbard, the leather hanger is often found missing from these daggers.

---

1.   **Type. First Model Leader's Dagger.** Authorized for *RLB* officials of officer rank in selected grades (rank groups 1-4 and the elite group).

2.   **Year Adopted.** 1936.

3.   **Description.** The basic design of this dagger is similar to the subordinate pattern. However, the leader's dagger features a black or dark blue leather wrap on the handle and scabbard and a flat raised oval pommel. The scabbard has two externally mounted silver-plated fittings. The grip insignia is identical to the subordinate model.

4.   **Length.** 39 cms (15.4").

5.   **Blade Motto.** None.

6.   **Accouterments.**
    a. Hanger—black leather strap riveted to the carrying connector.
    b. Portepee—None.

7.   **Collector Availability.** Rare.

A "complete" 1936 *Luftschutz* dagger (First Model *RLB* Leader's) with all of the proper accouterments.

A 1st model *RLB* Leader's dagger by Alexander Coppel (Alcoso) full-length—obverse view. During the period of the Third Reich, this firm used the Alcoso and the ACS "scales" trademark. The dagger is pictured with its accompanying black leather hanger and belt loop.

The obverse hilt of the 1st model *RLB* Leader's dagger by Alexander Coppel (Alcoso). Note the quality fit between the pommel and the top of the grip and the bottom of the grip and the crossguard.

◄

Close-up view of the reverse blade ricasso of the 1st model *RLB* dagger by Alexander Coppel (Alcoso). The "ACS" in the trademark represented <u>A</u>lexander <u>C</u>oppel <u>S</u>olingen. The remainder of the Alcoso trademark represented balanced scales.

►

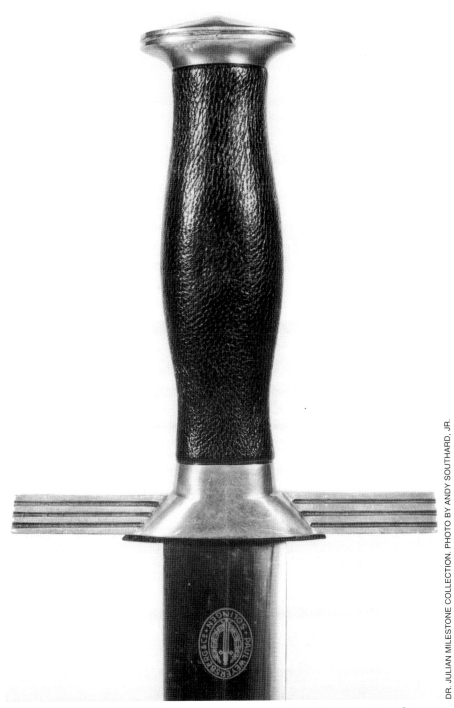

Close-up of the first model *RLB* leader's dagger by Paul Weyersberg—reverse view.

A 1st model *RLB* leader's dagger by Paul Weyersberg, full-length—obverse view. Note the minor difference in the crossguard eagle pictured and the one depicted on the *SMF* model dagger, also pictured in this chapter.

A 1st model *RLB* leader's dagger by *Solingen Metallwarenfabrik (SMF)*, full-length—obverse view. *RLB* sidearms by *SMF* are quite scarce, as the firm specialized in *Luftwaffe* sidearms.

◄

1st model *RLB* leader's dagger by *SMF* is pictured full-length—reverse view. Note the unusual method used by *SMF* of attaching the scabbard fittings by means of large "staples," in lieu of side-mounted screws.

►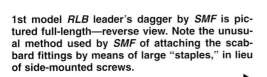

Unusual 1st model *RLB* Officer's dagger with a soft scabbard (no metal lining). Note the positioning of the manufacturer's logo (Rudolf Schmit, Solingen) close to the center of the obverse blade.

◄

Unusual factory customized 1st model *RLB* Officer's dagger by Ernst E. Witte. This original dress dagger was equipped with an *extra* upper scabbard fitting ring at the factory in order to accommodate a standard *Luftwaffe* "halfmoon" and teardrop sword hanger. The back of the hanger clip is "*D.G.R.M.*" and Assmann stamped.

►

2nd model *RLB* subordinate dagger by Paul Weyersberg & Co., full-length—obverse view. Authorized for selected *RLB* members on paid full-time duty in rank groups 5-10. This dagger is identical to the 1st model subordinate's dagger except for the incorporation of the revised 1938 *RLB* insignia, a black enamel swastika superimposed on a nickel-plated sunburst.

◄

1. Type. <u>Second Model Subordinate Dagger</u>. Authorized for selected *RLB* subordinates on paid full-time duty (rank groups 5-10). In 1938, the *RLB* experienced an insignia design change.

2. Year Adopted. 1938.

3. Description. This dagger is identical in all respects to the First Model Subordinate's dagger except for the incorporation of the revised *RLB* insignia on the grip, a black enamel swastika superimposed on a nickel-plated sunburst.

4. **Length.** 36 cms (14.2").

5. **Blade Motto.** None.

6. **Accouterments.**
   a. Hanger—black leather strap riveted to the carrying connector.
   b. Portepee—None.

7. **Collector Availability.** Scarce.

Close-up view of the obverse crossguard on the 2nd model *RLB* subordinate dagger by Paul Weyersberg & Co. The straight crossguard features a large stylized national eagle and swastika. ▶

▲

Close-up view of the reverse crossguard and Paul Weyersberg & Co. (Sword Within Wreath) Trademark. The straight double-edged blade on *RLB* subordinate daggers is found both with and without manufacturers' trademarks. A thin black leather buffer pad separates the blade and the crossguard.

Extreme close-up view of the lower scabbard fitting of the *RLB* subordinate dagger by Paul Weyersberg & Co.—obverse view. Note that the fitting is secured by two side-mounted recessed screws.

▶

The leather hanging strap on the 2nd model *RLB* subordinate dagger is identical to the one found on the 1st model subordinate dagger and is a single black leather strap riveted to the carrying connector on the scabbard.

◀

The black leather hanging strap on the 2nd model *RLB* subordinate dagger by Paul Weyersberg & Co. Note that the upper nickel/silver connecting clip is both *RZM* and *OLC* (manufacturer) stamped on the reverse.

▶

A member of the Air Raid Protection Association poses in front of the *RLB* banner. The sidearm being grasped is the 1938 pattern subordinate's dagger.

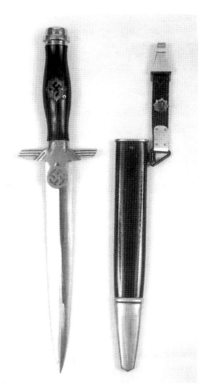

A 2nd model *RLB* subordinate dagger complete with an additional 1st model *RLB* insignia pinned to the leather strap hanger. Veteran purchased as pictured.

Highly unusual 2nd model *RLB* subordinate dagger by C. Gustav Spitzer modified to accept detachable, double strap hangers. Acquired by a WWII veteran during the war, "as is."

▶

1. **Type. <u>Second Model Leader's Dagger</u>.** Authorized for *RLB* officials of officer rank in selected grades (rank groups 1-4 and the elite group). In 1938, the *RLB* experienced an insignia design change.

2. **Year Adopted.** 1938.

3. **Description.** This dagger is identical in all respects to the First Model Leader's dagger except for the incorporation of the revised *RLB* insignia on the grip, the addition of a center scabbard band, and the provision for a double strap leather hanger.

4. **Length.** 39 cms (15.4").

5. **Blade Motto.** None.

6. **Accouterments.**
    a. Hanger—a double strap, detachable, dark blue or black leather hanger with oval buckles bearing oak leaves.
    b. Portepee—None.

7. **Collector Availability.** Scarce.

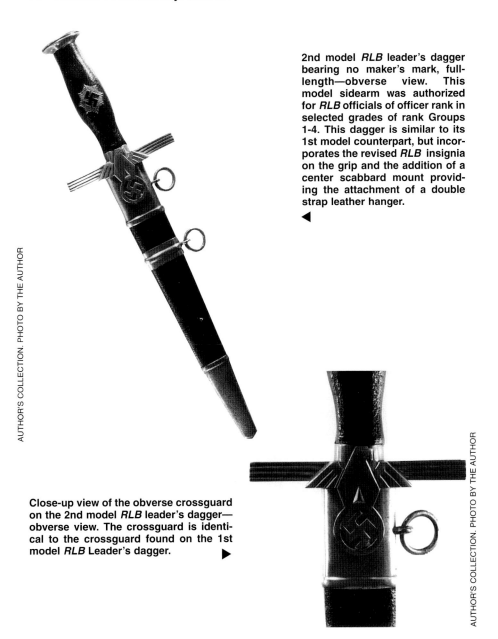

2nd model *RLB* leader's dagger bearing no maker's mark, full-length—obverse view. This model sidearm was authorized for *RLB* officials of officer rank in selected grades of rank Groups 1-4. This dagger is similar to its 1st model counterpart, but incorporates the revised *RLB* insignia on the grip and the addition of a center scabbard mount providing the attachment of a double strap leather hanger. ◄

Close-up view of the obverse crossguard on the 2nd model *RLB* leader's dagger—obverse view. The crossguard is identical to the crossguard found on the 1st model *RLB* Leader's dagger. ►

AUTHOR'S COLLECTION. PHOTO BY THE AUTHOR

AUTHOR'S COLLECTION. PHOTO BY THE AUTHOR

2nd model *RLB* Officer's dagger with *Soft* Scabbard by *SMF*. Pictured is an extremely rare *RLB* Officer's model dagger with a scabbard having no metal lining, and the scabbard hardware attached by two large "staples."

◀

Reverse view of the 2nd model *RLB* Officer's dagger with soft scabbard by *SMF*. Note the large "staples" attaching the upper and lower scabbard fittings to the soft leather scabbard.

▶

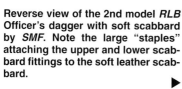

Extreme close-up view of the lower scabbard fitting of the *SMF* 2nd model *RLB* Officer's dagger with soft scabbard. The scabbard fittings are attached to the soft leather via a large metal nickel-plated "staple."

Close-up detail of a 1st and 2nd model *RLB* officer's dagger by Alcoso bearing Ordnance Stamps on one end of the crossguards.

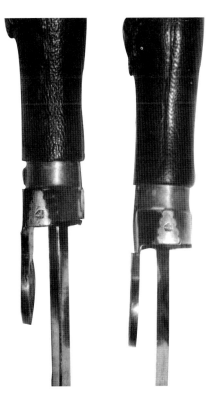

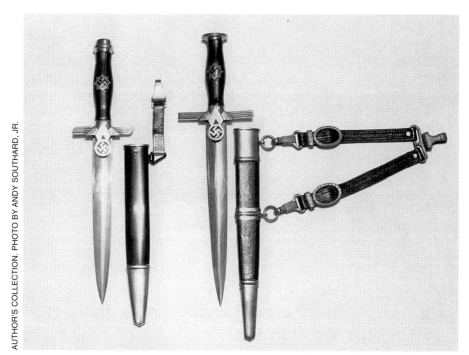

A"complete set" of the 2nd model *RLB* daggers and accouterments—obverse view.

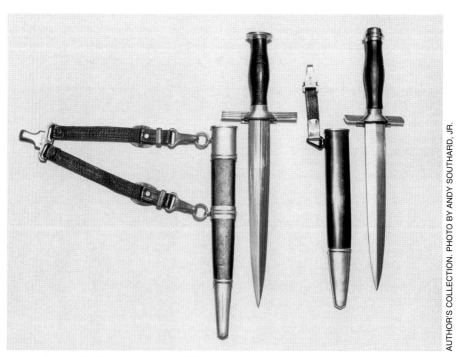

A"complete set" of the 2nd model *RLB* daggers and accouterments—reverse view.

Pictured is a complete set of 2nd model *RLB* leader dagger black leather hangers. The standard hangers for this model dress dagger consisted of a double strap, detachable, black leather hanger with silver hardware bearing oak leaves.

◀

2nd model *RLB* leader dagger hangers are pictured—reverse view. Note that the metal hanger hardware is both *RZM* and *D.R.G.M.* stamped.

◀

Close-up view of the pebbled upper connecting snap and correct belt loop for the 2nd model *RLB* leader dagger hangers—obverse view. The small belt loop is constructed of matching black leather.

Close-up view of the lower hardware fittings on the 2nd model *RLB* leader dagger hangers—obverse view. Note that the hardware is adorned with oak leaves, the buckles are oval in shape, and the lower clips are identical to the ones utilized on some Army and 2nd *Luftwaffe* hangers. ◀

Close-up view of the lower hardware fittings on the 2nd model *RLB* leader dagger hangers—reverse view. The "*D.R.G.M.*" stampings represent the German protection of patents. ▶

A *Reichsluftschutzbund (RLB) Stabsluftschutz-Führer* wears the 2nd model (1938) *RLB* leader's dagger with double strap, detachable, dark blue/black leather hanger suspended from the leather waist belt.

Second model *RLB* leader's dagger by Paul Weyersberg with unusual *Werkluftschutz* Eagle and Swastika emblem on grip. This is the sole example of this modification observed by the author to date.

◀

Extreme close-up view of the obverse crossguard and unusual *Werkluftschutz* emblem on the second model *RLB* leader's dagger by Paul Weyersberg.

▶

PERSONALIZED *RLB* DAGGERS

The author has personally observed a small number of *RLB* dress sidearms bearing engraved dedications on the reverse cross-guard, obverse upper scabbard fitting, or the obverse blade. While some aficionados are quick to question the authenticity of such personalizations, the following letter provided by Dirk Stefanski of Pattensen, Germany, dated 30 January 1940, and its accompanying English translation from *Luftschutz* General Schreiber, the leader of *RLB Gruppe XI* proves that such dedications did, in fact, occur. This letter also provides insight into the awarding of dress daggers to selected leaders in the *RLB* organization for meritorious service.

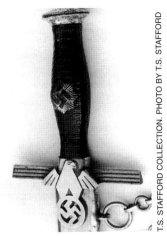

Unusual 2nd model *RLB* officer's grip with serrations in the leather. No explanation is available. Also, note the chain-link hanger attached to the upper scabbard ring.

Reichsluftschutzbund
Körperschaft des öffentlichen Rechts
Gruppe XI Niedersachsen

Hann.-Herrenhausen, den   30.1.1940
Burgweg 2, Fernruf 2 26 51/52

An den
    Luftschutzführer
    Franz Jennebach
    Hannover, An der Lister Kirche 2

Lieber Kamerad Jennebach!
    Als Zeichen meines Dankes für Ihre
Tätigkeit als mein persönlicher Adjutant
überreiche ich Ihnen den Führerdolch
des Reichsluftschutzbundes mit meiner
Widmung.
    Ich erwarte, dass Sie auch zukünftig mehr
als Ihre Pflicht tuen.

                Heil Hitler!

                General LS - Führer

The English translation of this letter follows:

Jan. 30, 1940

RLB Corporation of Public Justice
Group 11 Niedersachsen

Hann. Herrenhausen
Burgweg 2, Phone 22651/52

To the *RLB* Leader Franz Tennebach,
Hannover, *an der Lister Kurche 2*

Dear Colleague Tennebach!

As a symbol [sign] of my thanks for your work as my personal
Adjutant, I present to you the Leader's dagger of the *RLB* with my dedication.

I expect that you will also do more than your duty in the future.

Heil Hitler!
/ s / Schreiber
General LS—Leader

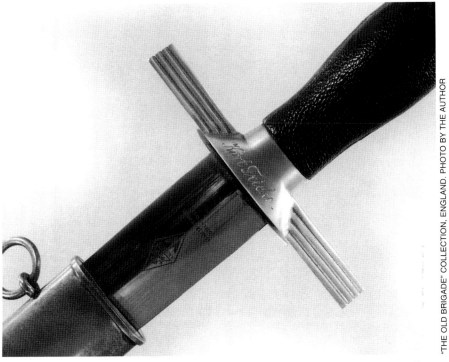

Pictured is an original personalized *RLB* 2nd model officer's dagger by Ernst Erich Witte,
Solingen. The owner's full name "Kurt Fricke," is professionally engraved on the reverse
crossguard. Personalized *RLB* edged weapons are quite scarce.

An example of an original *RLB* Leader's dagger bearing an engraved dedication on the reverse crossguard is pictured on the preceding page.

THE *RLB* BAYONET

At first, the various Third Reich organizations seemed perfectly content to merely attach their organizational emblem to the obverse grip of the standard *Wehrmacht* dress bayonet. For example, early examples of Hitler Youth, *RLB*, Postal, <u>and</u> Student League dress bayonets with the respective organizational insignia either pinned on or inset in the grip have been pictured in previous volumes of this series. An early *RLB* bayonet with the early *RLB* sunburst insignia attached to the obverse checkered grip plate is pictured in this chapter. The bayonet was manufactured in both a long and a short model, and conformed to the standard *Wehrmacht* Army dress bayonet in all aspects, except for the *RLB* grip emblem device found on the obverse surface of the black checkered grip. The ease of simply gluing an *RLB* emblem on the grip of a standard Army bayonet makes the early *RLB* bayonet an often counterfeited piece. An original model of the bayonet, like the one pictured, has the *RLB* emblem affixed to the grip plate by means of a retaining pin. An easy way to determine how the emblem is attached is to have the grip X-rayed from the side (see page 206 of **Volume V** for details).

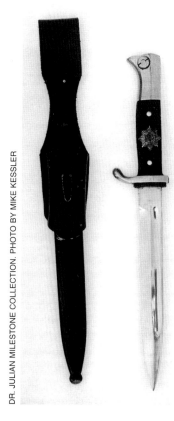

Evidently, the placement of organizational insignia on the obverse grips of edged weapons was commonplace during the period. The author had the opportunity during the mid-1960s to observe an accumulation (hardly a collection) of a large number of Third Reich edged weapons that had been assembled shortly after World War II in the late 1940s and early 1950s by a pawnshop in the state of Alabama. Although, regrettably, not a single item was for sale (then or now), the one dominant observation was that many of these untouched daggers and dress bayonets had emblems attached to the hilts, some organizational and some unidentified. Even a Red Cross Officer dagger featured an unusual small insignia on the obverse grip which resembled an Oriental flower. Present-day

RLB bayonet by Robert Klaas. A rare bayonet in its original state. The ease of simply gluing an RLB emblem to the grip of a standard Army bayonet makes the RLB bayonet an often counterfeited piece. An original model of this bayonet, like the one pictured left, has the emblem affixed to the grip by means of a retaining pin.

collectors are far too quick to criticize and condemn German sidearms with attached grip insignias, when many are, indeed, of original manufacture.

Detail of the obverse hilt of the rare *RLB* bayonet by Robert Klaas. An x-ray has verified that the specimen pictured has the *RLB* emblem on the obverse grip plate properly affixed to the grip with a retaining pin.

THE *RLB* PROTOTYPE BAYONET

During the late 1930s, it became obvious that the many different organizations of the Reich sought their own distinctive sidearm, and the numerous arms factories located in Solingen and elsewhere were ready and able to accommodate. Rather than merely mounting their unit insignia on the hilt of a "generic" dress dagger, sword, or bayonet, the leaders of the individual organizations wanted an edged weapon which was unmistakenly their own.

Evidently, the *RLB* was no different. As more and more of the numerous Reich organizations were awarded their own distinctive sidearm, the *RLB* wanted to follow suit. The first indication of a distinctive bayonet sidearm for the *RLB* was found by James P. Atwood on one of the early forays into the blade-producing city of Solingen (an entire chapter in **Volume II** of this series is dedicated to his Solingen visits). When Jim Atwood was provided the opportunity to review the complete 1933-45 files of the large Carl Eickhorn firm, he discovered the interesting black and white factory photograph shown for the first time on page 156 of **Volume III** and reproduced here. The original Eickhorn photograph remains on file at Johnson Reference Books. While the Eickhorn factory photograph is, unfortunately, not identified on the reverse, the sidearm most closely resembles the *RLB* dagger design. All indications are that this special model dress bayonet was being planned

An unattributed and badly corroded bayonet sidearm. The crossguard has the traditional eagle/swastika combination, but lacks any further identifiable features. Although it is an army-fashion eagle, the sidearm closest resembles the *RLB* dagger design.

▶

DR. JULIAN MILESTONE COLLECTION. PHOTO BY MIKE KESSLER

PHOTO COURTESY OF LTC (RET) JAMES P. ATWOOD

for the lower-ranking members of the *RLB*. A completely untouched specimen of the ultra-rare *RLB* Prototype dress bayonet recently surfaced in Germany and is pictured for the first time in this chapter. Compare this example to the photograph that Jim Atwood found in the Carl Eickhorn factory files in 1960 and provided the author for use in **Volume III**.

Since the specimen pictured is the only complete example of this model Third Reich bayonet known and was produced by WKC, one must wonder if both Eickhorn <u>and</u> WKC were attempting to introduce a new dress bayonet for the *RLB*, or was the piece pictured in the Eickhorn files actually a WKC bayonet, i.e., the blade in the Eickhorn picture is too far deteriorated to identify a company trademark. It appears that the two bayonets are <u>identical.</u> The overall length of the WKC *RLB* bayonet is 12-3/4 inches, and the scabbard is a standard black painted metal scabbard.

The WKC bayonet pictured is the sole specimen of this model bayonet known to the author. Its rarity places it in a category with the ultra-rare Diplomatic bayonet (only two originals are known to the author, to date) and the <u>one-of-a-kind</u> Red Cross dress bayonet which has been in the same collection for over twenty-six years and is pictured on page 215 of **Volume I.** Also, of note is the fact that the *RLB* Prototype bayonet was, obviously, worn, as both the bayonet and the scabbard show considerable wear. Hopefully, more details on these unique Third Reich sidearms will surface in the future.

A completely untouched example of the ultra-rare *RLB* prototype dress bayonet is pictured. Compare this example to the photograph that Jim Atwood found in the Carl Eickhorn factory files in 1960 and provided to the author for use in **Volume III** (see p. 156, **Volume III**). Since the specimen pictured is the only complete example of this model Third Reich bayonet known and was produced by WKC, one must wonder if both Eickhorn and WKC were attempting to introduce a new dress bayonet for the *RLB*, or was the piece pictured in the Eickhorn files actually a WKC bayonet, ie., the blade in the Eickhorn picture is too far deteriorated to identify a company trademark. The two bayonets appear to be *identical.* Also, of note, is the fact that the WKC specimen pictured was obviously worn and used based upon the condition.

▶

Reverse full-length view of the ultra-rare *RLB* prototype bayonet. The overall bayonet length is 12³/₄ inches.

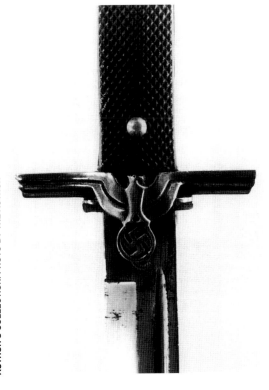

Close-up of the obverse cross-guard of the ultra-rare *RLB* prototype bayonet by WKC. The extreme top of the WKC Third Reich "knight head" trademark is visible directly under the swastika.

Close-up of the reverse cross-guard of the ultra-rare *RLB* prototype bayonet by WKC. Note the unusual indentations on the crossguard. The WKC "knight head" trademark is stamped on the *obverse* ricasso of the fullered bayonet blade.

THE *RLB* MINIATURE DAGGER

An exquisite 1st Model *RLB* Subordinate miniature dagger has recently come into the possession of the author. While little is known about the origin (other than the fact that it was purchased in England) and/or authenticity of this particular miniature, what can be said is that the quality is certainly of Solingen standards during the 1930s-40s. The miniature is 10-1/4 inches overall and can be completely disassembled into the identical component parts as the regulation size *RLB* Subordinate dagger. All fittings are nickel

The *RLB* 1st model subordinate miniature Dagger is pictured—full length, out-of-scabbard, obverse view. The overall length is only 10-1/4 inches and can be completely disassembled into the identical component parts as the regulation size *RLB* subordinate dagger. All fittings are nickel-silver, and the scabbard is equipped with the correct, single strap, black leather hanger, which is fully functional.

silver, and the scabbard is equipped with the correct black leather integral hanger, which is fully functional. The hanger is attached to the metal triangular keeper on the scabbard and held in place by four tiny rivets, as is the regulation hanger. The *outstanding* detail of this miniature is obvious in the accompanying photographs which will show the reader the miniature *RLB* dagger standing alone and compared to its regulation counterpart.

The *RLB* 1st model subordinate miniature dagger—reverse view. Note that the small black leather hanger is attached to the metal triangular keeper on the scabbard and is secured by four tiny rivets, as is the regulation subordinate hanger.

The *RLB* 1st model subordinate miniature dagger is compared to the regulation-size counterpart. The *outstanding* detail of this miniature is obvious in this comparative photograph.

RLB SIDEARM DISTRIBUTION

Although many current reference books (including this one) have reported that the *RLB* sidearms could not be privately purchased, it appears that by 1941, this regulation had been changed. Reproduced below is a 29 April 1941 inquiry from a uniform specialty store desiring to place an initial order for *RLB* daggers with a distributor in Göttingen.

Translation of this 29 April 1941 inquiry follows:

Firm Wilhelm Staufert, Göttingen/Fils.   **To: Firm WKC, Solingen-Wald**
A customer reminds you of our order from the 12th of March, 1940, for 40 pieces of Airforce Officer's daggers, model #1042.

Subject: Air Defense Daggers.
The Regional Defense Group for Air Protection *(RLB)* advises its members to purchase their daggers at the local specialty shops. Is a direct order possible right now? I am looking for an answer by return mail.

29 April 1941   **with German greetings,**
                                               / S /

The cover of an original sales catalog belonging to the Hermann Schellhorn firm in Offenbach (near Frankfurt) which specialized in fire department and *RLB* items.

HERMANN SCHELLHORN

| Luftschutz-Geräte und -Ausrüstungen Motorspritzen | Feuerwehr-Geräte und -Ausrüstungen **OFFENBACH AM MAIN** Spießstraße 30 / Fernsprecher 842 10 | Feuerwehrschläuche und Armaturen Tyfon-Brandalarmanlagen |

Feuerwehr-Ausrüstungen nach der neuen Bekleidungs-Ordnung.

Brandmeistermütze

Rockbluse
mit Koppel und Schulterriemen

Faustriemen
für
Mannschaften
Oberfeuerw.-
Leute und
Löschmeister

Koppel mit Schulterriemen

Faschinenmesser
für
Mannschaften

Faschinenmesser
für Brandmstr.
u. Wehrführer

Faustriemen
für Brandmstr.
u.Wehrführer

Säbel für höhere
Dienstgrade

Kragenspiegel
für Hauptbrandmeister
und Wehrführer

Kragenspiegel
für Brandmeister
u. Oberbrandmstr.

Kragenspiegel
für Oberfeuerwehrmann
Oberfeuerwehrm., Löschmstr.

| Wehrführer | Haupt-brandmstr. | Ober-brandmstr. | Brand-meister | Lösch-meister | Oberfeuer-wehrmann | Feuerwehr-mann |

Inside view of the single-page catalog of the fire department and *RLB* equipment/wares offered by the Hermann Schellhorn firm in *Offenbach am Main* (near Frankfurt).

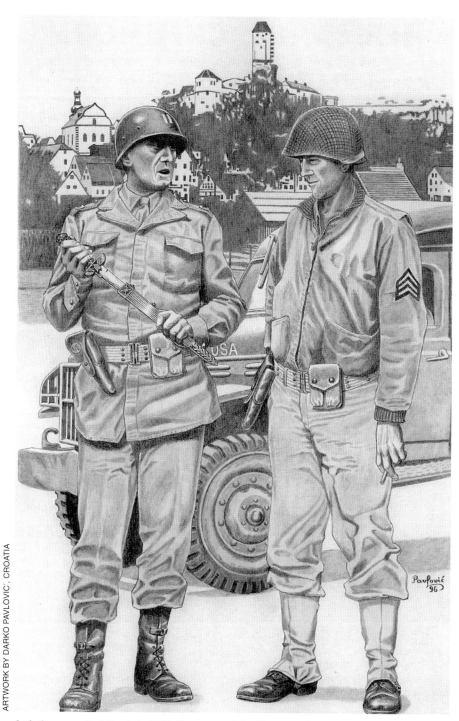

Artist's concept of the July 1945 discovery of the Hermann Göring *Reichsmarschall* dagger by American Forces. Pictured in the background is the *Schloss* (castle) Veldenstein where *Frau* Göring and her party were temporarily housed and the dagger was found during an unannounced inspection. Unfortunately, artist Pavlovic' was unaware of unique construction of the dagger, as explained and illustrated in this chapter.

Chapter 3

THE END OF THE HUNT FOR THE HERMANN GÖRING *REICHSMARSCHALL* DAGGER

By Ben Swearingen

"Where quality is the thing sought after, the thing of supreme quality is cheap, whatever the price one has to pay for it."
—William James

*(Author's Note: The majority of the readers of this reference series know the name of respected author/researcher Ben Swearingen of Lewisville, Texas. Ben is <u>easily</u> the most successful of all of the Third Reich treasure hunters, having both the Hermann Göring Hunting dagger (featured on the **Volume II,** 1st Edition dust jacket) and the Sepp Dietrich SS Honor sword (featured on the **Volume V,** 1st Edition dust jacket) to his credit, as well as countless other rare Third Reich artifacts that he has personally traced down. Ben is also the author of a best-selling, hardcover book published by Harcourt, Brace, and Jovanovich in 1985 entitled, **The Mystery of Hermann Göring's Suicide**. Additionally, Ben has served as a major contributor to my **Volume V** of **Collecting the Edged Weapons of the Third Reich** and **Volume II** of **World War II German War Booty**.)*

Blade collectors of the world may now call off their hunt for the Hermann Göring *Reichsmarschall* dagger. It has been found—at least, what is left of it. All that remains of the most sought-after Nazi dagger in the world are a few damaged pieces and a handful of gems.

The story of the fate of Hermann Göring's dagger will dash the hopes of all those who have dreamed of finding and adding this prize to their collection. Initially, I had no desire to write of its destruction. When Tommy Johnson first urged me to do so, I declined. "What's there to tell? It's gone!" However, when I later located the former Commanding Officer of the man who brought the dagger back to the United States, I found myself in the unique position of knowing not only what happened to the dagger after it was brought to the United States—as did several others in collecting circles—but also how the dagger was originally found and disposed of in 1945 in Germany. The latter knowledge only I possessed, and I realized that if I did not share it, the full story of the dagger would probably never be known and recorded.

In the summer of 1945, the 3rd Battalion, 359th Infantry of the 90th Infantry Division, under the command of Captain Orwin C. Talbott moved into the old German training area of Grafenwohr, near Nürnberg. Shortly thereafter, *Frau* Emmy Göring, *Reichsmarschall* Hermann Göring's wife, was transferred from *Schloss Fischhorn* in Austria to *Schloss Veldenstein* in Germany, the castle inherited by her husband in 1938, bringing her into the sector under Captain Talbott's command. "She did nothing to my knowledge in violation of our requirements, and appeared to be almost cowed by her sudden drop in status," recalled Talbott, now a retired Lieutenant General, in a letter to me. "But she was still a cause for concern because of her former high status as, in effect, 'the First Lady of the Third Reich.'"

The *Schloss Veldenstein* (Veldenstein Castle) as seen during 1945. This castle was where *Frau* Emmy Göring and her party were housed shortly after WWII ended and is where a member of the U.S. Army, reputedly, acquired the one-of-a-kind Hermann Göring's *Reichsmarschall* dagger.

Frau Göring and her party are pictured standing in front of an entrance to the Veldenstein Castle. From left to right are *Frau* Göring and daugher, Elsa Sonnemann; Elsa Kiuvina with son, Hans Kiuvina; Christo Gormans; Cilly Wachowiak; Martha Mader; Elsa Altmann; and Armin Rossius.
▶

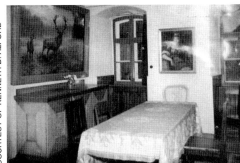

Pictured is a small dining area in the Veldenstein Castle as seen while occupied by *Frau* Göring and her party. Note the large hunting oil painting of a pair of German *Hirsch* (stag), characteristic of a Göring household.
◀

One of several out-buildings on the grounds of the Veldenstein Castle. In the foreground is a U.S. Army NCO. The date is 1945.
▶

One of the methods of enforcing the occupation in the first months after V-E Day was sudden and unannounced inspections for weapons and other contraband. In July of 1945, such an inspection was scheduled for the little town in which *Schloss Veldenstein* was located, "not because I was particularly suspicious of her," wrote General Talbott, "but because General Göring might have secreted something there." Though *Frau* Göring had asked for no special privileges, Talbott took care that she should be treated with consideration by the men under his command, and that her personal property would be protected. "In an officers' meeting beforehand, I very specifically ordered that an officer would be present in each room all the while her place was being searched to insure no looting or improper behavior was involved." One particular company under Talbott's command was given the job of conducting the search of the castle. A day or so after the search, *Frau* Göring informed Talbott that much material of importance to her was missing. He immediately drove to the castle, and with the aid of an interpreter became convinced that her complaint was valid. "That night, I assembled all officers and some senior non-commissioned officers, except those from the company which had been in *Schloss Veldenstein*. Very shortly after Taps, we 'raided' their barracks and searched for contraband." Part of the raiding party was stationed outside the barracks, in case contraband was thrown out the windows after the search began. This measure proved to be very wise, as many items were picked up outside the barracks by the waiting officers and NCO's. Numerous other "liberated" souvenirs were found in footlockers.

The next morning, Captain Talbott summoned the CO of the guilty company for questioning. "He had not at all obeyed my orders about having an officer in each room as it was being searched. Men were allowed to go to any room they desired without supervision necessarily being present, and stay as long as they desired." The result was that much looting had taken place, and among the items recovered during the raid was Göring's *Reichsmarschall* dagger.

The dagger presented a problem to Talbott. Unlike most of the other recovered items, it could not be returned to *Frau* Göring, as it was illegal at the time for Germans to possess any weapons. "An alternative I had in mind," recalled Talbott, "was to take the dagger to my Commander, and recommend it be forwarded to General Patton as a souvenir 'from' *Reichsmarschall* Göring via the 90th Division." However, for the time being, Talbott retained the dagger in his office.

A day or so after the raid, Lieutenant Wallace Stephenson, one of Talbott's officers about to return to the United States, came to the Captain's office, and asked to be given the recovered dagger. "He said that though for his entire adult life he had been in the Regular Army, he was going to get out, and wanted to buy a chicken farm, but did not have the means. He pleaded to be given the dagger, which he said he could sell and thereby get his farm." Lt. Stephenson's service record had been exemplary, and he had been in combat for two and one-half years and decorated three times for gallantry (Silver Star and a Bronze Star with oak leaf cluster), as well as being the recipient of two Purple Hearts. Talbott realized that this request "was not entirely 'kosher,'" but got "soft-hearted and finally said OK." Talbott admitted to me that he had had "several twinges of conscience over the years for that decision, even if it was not an earth-shaking one."

Talbott heard nothing more from Stephenson until they both attended a 90th Division reunion, perhaps around 1978 or so. Stephenson "had never been to one before, but had come to this one. He was very friendly, but made no mention of the dagger, nor did I."

It was probably only after I wrote to General Talbott, telling him that Stephenson's son was now in possession of the dagger, that he gave it

Artist's concept of *Reichsmarschall* Hermann Göring wearing his one-of-a-kind *Reichsmarschall* dagger and hangers. There is no photograph known to the author which shows this magnificent sidearm in wear.

The inside courtyard of the Veldenstein Castle is pictured during 1945. Evidently, the U.S. Army opened the castle to tourists and German school groups.

German laborers are pictured digging in the large courtyard of the Veldenstein Castle during 1945 under the direction of the U.S. Army Military Police.

another thought. "If the son still has the dagger," commented an obviously chagrined Talbott, "it was not sold as Lt. Stephenson had said was going to be the case!"

Lt. Stephenson's son did still have the dagger—again, at least what remained of it—and it was from him that I learned what had happened to the dagger after his father returned to the United States.

Lt. Stephenson evidently had an uneasy conscience about possessing the dagger. Other than to a few members of his family, he mentioned its existence to no one. In effect, it "disappeared," leaving behind only a few blurred pictures to excite the imagination of every collector of Third Reich daggers. Only many years later, long after Stephenson's death, did clues to its whereabouts begin to surface in collecting circles. As had been the case several times in the past when matters concerning Hermann Göring were involved, I became an active participant in the unfolding story.

I had just returned from the 1994 Militaria Antiques Xtravaganza (MAX) Show in Pittsburgh, and was sitting at my desk when the telephone rang. A gentleman identified himself as Mack Stephenson, saying he had read my book on Hermann Göring, and asking if he could avail himself of my knowledge of the subject. I agreed, and he began telling me the story of a dagger his father had brought back from the war. (At the time of our conversation, neither Stephenson nor I knew what had actually taken place in 1945, as later reported to me by General Talbott.) He said that his father, an Army officer, had gone to "one of Göring's homes," in 1945, where he found *Frau* Emmy Göring and her daughter in residence. Taking advantage of the opportunity, he asked if there were any weapons in the house. According to the story, *Frau* Göring then handed over to him an ornate and bejeweled dagger, which he eventually brought back to the United States.

From the brief description given me by my caller, I was fairly certain that Mack Stephenson's father had had the incredible good luck to have found the legendary *Reichsmarschall* dagger—and now I had found it! For a moment, my excitement was tempered by the suspicion that I was being "set up." It was too soon after the MAX Show, I thought, to be mere coincidence. However, as I talked with Stephenson, the more I became convinced of his sincerity—particularly after I finally understood that he no longer had the complete dagger, but only a few damaged pieces and the gems! No faker, I reasoned, would employ such a deception. In absolute dismay upon hearing even of the possibility that the *Reichsmarschall* dagger had been destroyed, I refused to identify it until I had more information. I asked Stephenson to sketch the pieces in his possession, and fax the drawings to me. The next morning, after the fax arrived, it was painfully obvious that the mangled pieces had once been part of the *Reichsmarschall* dagger. That moment was probably the most disappointing of my many years of pursuing war souvenirs!

The moment was made worse by the realization that I now had to inform Mack Stephenson that his father had destroyed an item of inestimable historical and monetary value. In a faxed letter accompanying the sketches he had made, he had written happily that he "couldn't possibly express in words my excitement about [the prospect of] finally identifying the object that has held my fascination and awe since childhood." I knew that what I now had to tell him would turn his excitement into dismay. Nevertheless, I wrote to him, telling him what I knew of the *Reichsmarschall* dagger, and sent photocopies of pictures of the dagger from the **Collecting the Edged Weapons of the Third Reich** series by LTC (Ret.) Johnson as it originally looked. In a few days, I had his reply. "It is unquestionably the same item," he wrote. "Simply cannot impart to you how I felt after I ripped open the envelope. Jeez . . . right there before my eyes, there it was." He handled the bad news much better than I would have done in his place, and only at the end of his letter did his disappointment show through, when he closed, "Thanks for making my day!"

In subsequent telephone conversations and letters, Mack Stephenson related to me the story of what happened to the dagger while it was in his father's possession. His father was evidently in constant fear that someone would try to take it away from him, and once back in the United States during a 45-day leave of absence at the end of the war, Stephenson did not even keep the dagger in his own home, but gave it to relatives for safe-keeping. "My father kept the object at my deceased uncle's house in Tennessee for many years after the war." According to Stephenson's son, having the dagger in his aunt and uncle's home made them miserable. "That dagger was the reason they had locks on their house, they finally buried it behind their house, and finally asked my father to come get his dagger." Once the dagger was back in his possession, Stephenson's fears evidently returned.

"I cannot picture anything other than fear (of what, I don't know) as being the driving force behind his decision to seriously compromise the integrity of the object," Mack Stephenson told me. He went on to relate a very strange incident that occurred during a family vacation to another state. "My Dad abruptly picked up and went home when he learned that some 'jeweler in Chicago' was looking for him." What precipitated the jeweler's interest in his father, the son never found out, but he was fairly certain that it had something to do with the Göring dagger. He also believes that it was shortly after that call that the dagger was destroyed.

Stephenson is not sure of the actual date—it may have been in 1961—that his father made the fateful decision to dismantle the dagger, and extract the jewels. Nor is he sure why his father decided to do so. But for some reason, his father, working with crude tools, and evidently not realizing that the dagger itself had any value, concentrated mainly on removing the gems. All that remains of the *Reichsmarschall* dagger today are the huge aquamarine that once topped the pommel, the damaged crossguard and the crushed throat of the scabbard, the loose diamonds and rubies (or garnets) which had been pried from them, and the diamond-studded body of an eagle. Saving only these few pieces and the loose jewels, Stephenson's father evidently disposed of the rest of the dagger and scabbard. (According to the relative who once had custody of the dagger, and "who probably held the real thing in her hands as many times as Göring had," Mack Stephenson said, the hangers were already missing.)

Mack Stephenson was kind enough to send me color photographs of the dagger's remnants (as seen in this chapter) and from them one can determine more precisely the original construction of the dagger. For example, if one looks at the photographs of the dagger in **Volume I** of Tommy Johnson's **Collecting the Edged Weapons of the Third Reich,** one would gain the impression that the jeweled eagle, swastika and crossed batons which comprise Göring's *Reichsmarschall* insignia are all part of the crossguard, and fit over the top of the scabbard. (Indeed, this is one of the mistakes made by a California dealer who commissioned a spurious "*Reichsmarschall* dagger" a number of years ago.) In fact, the photographs reveal that the entire insignia was at the top of the scabbard. The photographs also show that the eagle was not of one-piece construction; the head and body of the diamond-studded eagle—now detached, but undamaged—were separate from the wings, which were completely removed from their backing and stripped of their jewels. Only the bare outline of the eagle remains on the scabbard top.

The photographs also reveal a previously unknown and very curious aspect of the dagger's construction. When the dagger was sheathed, its crossguard was completely concealed under the outstretched wings of the *Reichsmarschall* eagle on the scabbard. The photographs show that the obverse of the crossguard was ornamented by a large, stylized *Luftwaffe* eagle, with its elongated wings and body studded with diamonds. Under each outstretched wing was a bough with diamond-studded leaves. This ornate insignia could be seen only when the dagger was withdrawn from its scabbard. The photographs show it to be undamaged, with the diamonds still in place, but with parts of the crossguard itself twisted and torn away, evidently in a futile attempt to remove the jewels.

OR DOES THE HUNT GO ON?

There was a time, shortly after I received the photographs from Stephenson, that some disturbing questions came to mind. If one closely examined the photographs of the remnants of the dagger in Stephenson's possession, comparing them with the pictures of the *Reichsmarschall* dagger in Tommy Johnson's book, there appeared to be minute differences. I called these differences to Tommy's attention, and he thought them significant. However, we eventually agreed that whatever differences we thought we saw probably could be attributed to photographic distortion. Still, the apparent differences bothered me.

I remembered that the first time I became aware of the existence of the *Reichsmarschall* dagger was in the very early 1960s, when I was at the University of Texas. I was looking through back issues of **"The Illustrated London News"** for November of 1945, and found a story about a horde of Göring's valuables seized by the Allies. I distinctly remembered that the article featured a photograph of the dagger. (This very picture was used by Tommy Johnson in **Volume I** of his dagger books.) I suggested to Tommy that it would be worthwhile to contact **"The Illustrated London News"** and learn the details of this vaguely remembered story. He did so, sending me xeroxes of the entire article. It was more extensive than I had recalled, and contained a real surprise.

Among the items photographed was "Göring's Marshal-of-the-Reich 'Dagger of Honor.'" It was described as "profusely ornamented with diamonds," and "made by academy students," which tallied exactly with what was known about the *Reichsmarschall* dagger. However, the surprising element—which I had forgotten over the years—was the fact that this dagger and the other items photographed were found in "an underground treasure-cave in the mountain-side at Koenigsee, near Berchtesgaden!"

This information gave rise to a real conundrum. If the dagger was found at Koenigsee, how could Stephenson have later obtained it after the search of *Frau* Göring's residence at *Schloss Veldenstein*? The only possible answer to this question, I thought, was that either Stephenson or one of his men had been at Koenigsee earlier, obtained the dagger, and it was later found during the barracks search conducted after the raid on Emmy Göring's residence. In other words, it had never been in *Frau* Göring's possession.

In order to check this theory out, I again wrote to General Talbott, asking if his unit had been in the Koenigsee area. In answer, General Talbott gave me his "<u>complete</u> assurance" that this could not have been the case. The unit came to Germany from Czechoslovakia and went directly to Grafenwohr in northern Bavaria, where it remained. Therefore, none of the men in his command could have obtained the dagger at Koenigsee. So much for that theory!

I immediately faxed Tommy Johnson General Talbott's reply, asking, "Well, what do you make of that?" His answer coincided with what was already going through my mind: "I make of it," he wrote, "the possibility of <u>two</u> *Reichsmarschall* daggers. The hunt goes on!"

As of this writing, "the hunt" is still on. Perhaps the last chapter in the hunt for the Hermann Göring *Reichsmarschall* dagger is still to be written!

MADE IN GERMANY: OSTENTATIOUS TREASURES FROM GOERING'S "ALADDIN'S CAVE"; PRODUCTS OF BERLIN TECHNICAL ACADEMY.

A U.S. SERGEANT EXAMINING ONE OF MANY ORNATE "WORKS OF ART," MADE IN BERLIN TECHNICAL ACADEMY FOR GOERING AND FOUND IN HIS PRIVATE HOARD IN A MOUNTAIN CAVE. ANOTHER PHOTOGRAPH SHOWS THE BOX IN DETAIL.

DESIGNED AS A CHURCH SHRINE, THIS HEAVILY GILT SILVER CABINET WAS USED BY GOERING AS A COCKTAIL CABINET. IT IS LINED WITH MIRRORS.

THIS BOX, NEARLY 14 IN. LONG, MADE BY STUDENTS OF BERLIN TECHNICAL ACADEMY, HAS AN ORNATE KNOB OF SILVER-GILT AND AQUAMARINES.

AN INTERESTING DESK STAND USED BY GOERING. THE "INKWELL" ON THE LEFT HOUSES A SECRET DICTAPHONE, WHICH COULD TELL MANY STRANGE TALES.

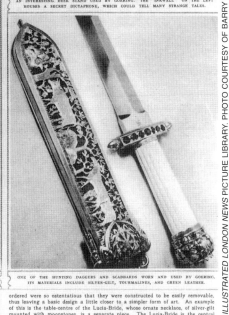

ONE OF THE HUNTING DAGGERS AND SCABBARDS WORN AND USED BY GOERING. ITS MATERIALS INCLUDE SILVER-GILT, TOURMALINES, AND GREEN LEATHER.

Among the many treasures of Goering's hoard, of which examples have already appeared in our pages, there has been found a number of pieces specially designed and produced for him by the Berlin Technical Academy. Made by students of the Higher Class of the Academy, to the design of its director, Professor Herbert Zeitner, who himself put the finishing touches to many of them, they reflect the crude tastes of their former owner. In some cases, indeed, the decorations ordered were so ostentatious that they were constructed to be easily removable, thus leaving a basic design a little closer to a simpler form of art. An example of this is the table-centre of the Lucia-Bride, whose ornate necklace, of silver-gilt mounted with moonstones, is a separate piece. The Lucia-Bride is the central figure of a Swedish custom on the festival of St. Lucia (December 13), when the daughter chosen for this honour, wearing candles in her hair, awakens the

Reproduction of the 24 November, 1945 article appearing in *The Illustrated London News* showing a collage of treasures taken from Hermann Göring's "Aladdin's Cave" near Berchtesgaden. The hunting dagger pictured on the bottom right is the one Göring is shown wearing on page 298 of Volume III of this series.

(ABOVE.) THIS GREEN LEATHER BELT, WITH ITS GILT CLASP AND DECORATIONS, ON WHICH ARE MOUNTED PRECIOUS STONES, WAS WORN BY GOERING WITH ONE OF HIS EXTRAVAGANT HUNTING SUITS.

(LEFT.) ANOTHER PRODUCT OF ACADEMY STUDENTS TO GOERING'S ORDERS: A BOX IN WHICH SILVER-GILT, GOLD, PEARLS AND PRECIOUS STONES ABOUND, WITH ORNAMENTS MOUNTED ON IVORY PLAQUES.

A LARGE SILVER-GILT TABLE-CENTRE, DECORATED WITH PRECIOUS STONES. IT REPRESENTS THE LUCIA-BRIDE—THE CENTRAL FIGURE IN SWEDISH CELEBRATIONS OF THE FESTIVAL OF ST. LUCIA.

GOERING'S MARSHAL-OF-THE-REICH "DAGGER OF HONOUR" IN ITS SCABBARD. PROFUSELY ORNAMENTED WITH DIAMONDS, IT WAS MADE BY ACADEMY STUDENTS.

A DETAIL VIEW OF THE TABLE-CENTRE SEEN ABOVE. THE NECKLACE IS REMOVABLE, AS ARE THE MORE CRUDE FEATURES OF SOME OTHER PIECES.

household and distributes food. She is addressed only as "Lucia-Bride" on that day, and not by her own name. This figure was one of the designs of Professor Zeitner, who, before becoming director of the Higher Class in the Academy, was director of gold and silver crafts at Berlin High School, and who, while carrying out the orders of his political masters, at the same time strove for basically sound art structure. In several of the pieces illustrated, this "pure" design is visible

beneath the trappings. Of the other pieces illustrated, the decorations in general are a reflection of Goering's notoriously vulgar ostentation, and the hunting accessories in particular of his hankering after the barbaric splendours of the Middle Ages. One other aspect of Goering's character is revealed in the innocent-looking desk-stand, whose concealed dictaphone could record the words of his visitors and guests.

Continuation of the 24 November, 1945 article appearing in *The Illustrated London News.* The Göring *Reichsmarschall* dagger is pictured on the bottom left.

100

**Three Key Collectibles Taken by U.S. Allied
Troops from Hermann Göring's "Aladdin's
Cave" Near Berchtesgaden during 1945.**

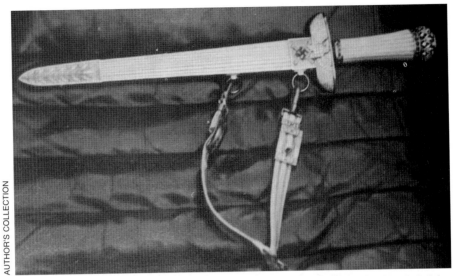

Pictured above is one of only two known actual photographs of Göring's *Reichs-marschall* dagger. It is shown here with original hangers attached, lying on the seat of Göring's Mercedes-Benz automobile. This rare photograph was discovered recently in a grouping of Göring photos taken by his personal driver.

Artist's concept of the Hermann Göring *Reichs-marschall* dagger hangers. A detailed description and drawing of these one-of-a-kind gold and silver fabric hangers can be found in the following source document, *Uniformen-Markt*, 1940, Number 22, page 175. An English translation of the 1940 German text describing the hangers is as follows: "Dagger Hanger of the *Reichsmarschall*. At the end of October, 1940, the special model of the dagger hanger for the *Reichsmarschall* was also completed. It consists of, as customary, two light weight white cloth straps which vary in length. They are 2mm thick with silver 20mm wide braid trimming. The latter is interwoven with two small circa 5mm wide gold stripes. The braid straps hang closely side-by-side at the top in a divided, long, rectangular loop, gilt trimmed buckle. The braid straps themselves are the same."

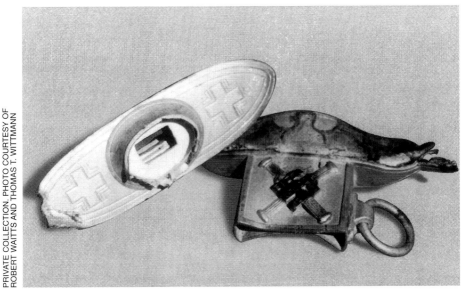

The damaged top of the crossguard and the upper scabbard fitting featuring the *Reichsmarschall* eagle, crossed batons, and swastika.

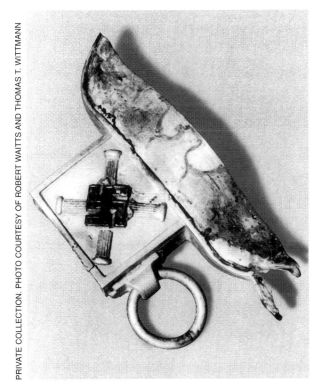

Close-up view of the severely damaged upper scabbard fitting featuring the *Reichsmarschall* eagle, crossed batons, and swastika. Note that all of the diamond chips have been removed from the body and wings of the eagle. The interior crossguard of the *Reichsmarschall's* dagger fits inside the top of the part shown.

Pictured for the first time is the obverse crossguard of the Hermann Göring *Reichs-marschall* dagger. The obverse crossguard features a large, stylized *Luftwaffe* eagle, with its elongated wings and body still studded with diamond chips.

Pictured is the diamond-studded body of the *Reichsmarschall* eagle which has been removed intact from the obverse upper scabbard. An American Roosevelt dime has been included in the photograph for size comparison. Three loose diamond chips are visible to the left of the eagle. To the best of knowledge to this author, none of the remaining parts of the dagger, i.e., pommel, grip, blade, remainder of the scabbard, etc., still exist.

PRIVATE COLLECTION. PHOTO COURTESY OF
ROBERT WAITTS AND THOMAS T. WITTMANN

Pictured together are the damaged obverse crossguard on the left and the upper scabbard fitting on the right. Visible between the two are a number of the many precious stones removed from the Göring dagger. Note the severe damage to the upper scabbard fitting.

PRIVATE COLLECTION. PHOTO COURTESY OF
ROBERT WAITTS AND THOMAS T. WITTMANN

The majority of the precious stones removed from the Göring *Reichsmarschall* dagger are visible in the photograph of this Ziploc plastic bag. A humble existence to what, undoubtedly, would be the most desirable German edged weapon of them all!

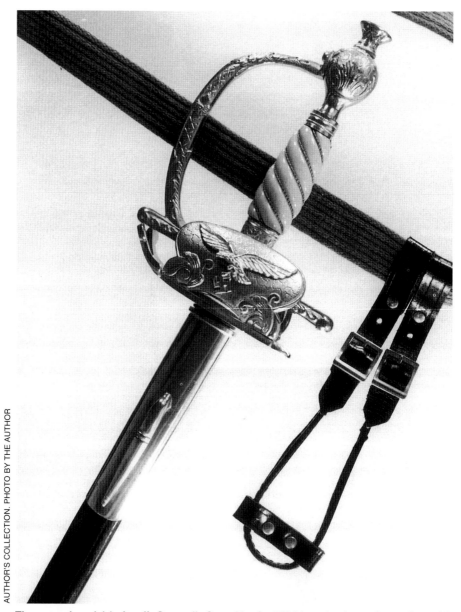

The second model *Luftwaffe* General's Sword by Carl Eickhorn is pictured complete with the correct fabric inner belt and black leather hanging device.

Chapter 4

THE RARE AND UNUSUAL BLADES OF THE REICH

"We do not expect people to be deeply moved
by what is not unusual."
—*Middlemarch,* 1871-2

Again, as with all preceding seven volumes of **Collecting the Edged Weapons of the Third Reich**, the subject matter of this chapter on the rare and unusual blades of the Reich lends itself more to pictorial than narrative coverage. Since the publication of **Volume VII** in 1994, numerous rare and unusual Third Reich edged weapons have been discovered and are pictured for the first time in any contemporary reference. The demise of communism and the opening of the former East Germany, as well as other Eastern European countries, have brought many previously "unseen" German and Axis Power edged weapons to light. Several of these sidearms are pictured in this reference book for the first time and should prove to be of utmost interest to the serious edged weapon collector/researcher. As the values of these sidearms continue to escalate, more effort and funds are expended each and every year in ferreting out the remaining pieces. Other rare edged weapons featured in this chapter have appeared in previous volumes of this series, but time has allowed the production of much better and more detailed photography for the reader to enjoy. On that subject, many collectors who have kindly provided quality photographs of edged weapons or edged weapons in wear may be disappointed by the absence of their respective pictures in this book. The reason for this omission is simply one of space, as a lot of material had to be deleted, and the decision was made to cut photographs as opposed to text. However, a follow-on **Volume IX** of this series is being considered by the author, and the vast majority of deleted materials from **Volume VIII** may see print in a **Volume IX** of this ongoing series. The final sections of this chapter will be devoted to the updating of several pertinent sections found in the first seven volumes, to include manufacturer proofmarks, detailed prices by selected year, and current valuations.

HERMANN GÖRING'S PROPENSITY TO LOSE
HIS PERSONAL DRESS DAGGERS

The charismatic individual who is best remembered for his gargantuan love of exotic sidearms was Hermann Wilhelm Göring. A little-known fact is that Göring evidently had a difficult time keeping up with his prized possessions! The author is aware of <u>two</u> different times when Göring actually lost daggers, once in 1935 and again in 1938.

The 14 June 1935 "**New York Times**" reported that Göring dropped his "dagger of honor" overboard during a sea excursion from Dubrovnik. The dagger was presented to Göring by Adolf Hitler and efforts to recover it were unsuccessful. A close reading of the original "**New York Times**" article indicates that the dagger in question was, most likely, an Unground Röhm SA dagger. A copy of the original newspaper article was provided to the author by Courtney S. West of Altavista, Virginia, and is reproduced in its entirety below:

Goering's Dirk of Honor Is Reported Lost in Sea

Wireless to THE NEW YORK TIMES.
BELGRADE, Yugoslavia, June 13.—It is reported here that General Hermann Wilhelm Goering, German Air Minister, during a recent sea excursion from Dubrovnik, lost his "dagger of honor," presented to him by Reichsführer Adolf Hitler. The dirk dropped overboard, and, although efforts were made to recover it, they proved vain, to General Goering's deep disappointment.

It is recalled that it was about a year ago that Captain Ernst Roehm, chief of the Nazi Storm Troops, also stayed at Dubrovnik wearing such a dirk of honor. After Roehm and others had been shot on June 30, all the dirks of honor throughout the Storm Troops had to be handed in to have the name of Roehm erased from the blade.

A short three years later, the small German newspaper, "**Der Sylter Zeitung**" ("**The Sylt Island Newspaper**") reported in their 25 July 1938 edition that Göring had lost another dress dagger while taking a walk. Sylt is a popular resort island in the North Sea where the Görings often vacationed. An accurate English translation of the German newspaper article reads:

A DAGGER IS LOST—Field Marshal Göring has lost a dagger during the evening of Tuesday, 25 July, about 2030 hours, while taking a walk in the immediate vicinity of the restaurant Rosse at Morsum Cliff (35-40 cm. in length, 4 cm. wide, with red moroccan leather scabbard and a gold handle). The finder is kindly asked to return it to the hotel "Crownprince," Wenningstedt (Telephone 303) for a reward.

Evidently, this dagger was recovered and returned to Göring, as it is obviously the unique Hunting dagger presented to him by his brother-in-law, Count Eric von Rosen. The dagger is pictured on page 263 of **Volume I** of this series and is presently on display at the United States Military Academy Museum at West Point. The original copy of this article was provided to the author by collector/researcher Dirk Stefanski of Pattensen, Germany, and is reproduced in its entirety.

Herr Generalfeldmarschall Göring hat am Dienstag, 25. Juli, abends gegen 20.30 Uhr, auf einem Spaziergang in unmittelbarer Nähe des Restaurants Rösse beim Morsumcliff

einen Dolch verloren

(35-40 cm lang, 4 cm breit, mit roter Saffian-Scheide und vergoldetem Griff).

Finder wird gebeten, ihn gegen Belohnung im Hotel zum Kronprinzen, Wenningstedt abzugeben (Telefon 303)

UPDATE ON THE SEPP DIETRICH SS-HONOR SWORD

The prestigious Sepp Dietrich SS-Honor Sword was acquired from a veteran source in 1983 and first publicized in **Collecting the Edged Weapons of the Third Reich, Volume V**. At that time, it had not been possible to identify the Damascene smith who had handcrafted the Damascus blade of this magnificent weapon. Recently, the sword has been disassembled (for only the second time in sixty years), and close-up photography of the blade tang has provided further clues to the identification of the blade's creator.

The photograph which accompanies this article displays the phrase, "*Damascene . . . C.W.*" in two lines. There is the remains of another word above "*Damascene*," but the characters are faint and broken up. In all probability, it is the word, "*Echt.*" This, in English translation, would complete the phrase, "Genuine Damascus C.W." which is a known tang mark used by Carl Wester who was one of six Damascene smiths acknowledged by the Solingen Chamber of Commerce and Industry in the year 1938. Carl Wester created several important blades during the Third Reich period, to include the blade of the Victor Lutze Army Honor Dagger.

The tang of the Sepp Dietrich SS-Honor Sword displays another set of initials—"*H.G.*" This stamp is inverted to the "*Damascene C.W.*" phrase, is deeper cut and of a differing lettering style. In 1983, when the sword was first disassembled, the "*C.W.*" initials were overlooked and research centered upon the identity of "*H.G.*" as being the blade's creator but the initials "*H.G.*"

This close-up photograph pictures for the first time the internal stampings on the blade tang of the one-of-a-kind Sepp Dietrich SS Honor Sword. The "C. W." initials obviously belonged to Solingen Damascus smith Carl Wester. The identity of the "HG" initials remains unknown to date.

did not correlate with the six Solingen Damascus smiths. The identity and/or function of "H.G." remains an unknown. It is possible that "H.G." was employed by the Adolf Braun firm, who was responsible for overall production of the sword, in which case it is again possible that "H.G." denotes that an overall quality inspection had taken place before final assembly of all components, "H.G." being the inspector's stamp. Additional research in Solingen by LTC (Ret.) Thomas M. Johnson has revealed that there was a 1930s-40s Solingen Damascus smith of some renown whose last name was Grasser. Every attempt is being made to ascertain the first name, as perhaps he was the "HG" involved with the Dietrich SS-Honor Sword in a possible collaborative effort with Carl Wester, which might also explain the dual stamping.

At a recent German antiques fair an original *LAH* photograph album surfaced containing a photograph of Sepp Dietrich wearing his one-of-a-kind SS-Honor Sword. That photograph is reproduced with this article and the actual tie of the portepee can be discerned, as well as the sword hanger in use. The portepee as tied by Dietrich differs to the present weave, probably because the portepee was removed at some point after 1945 and subsequently re-tied. In the original *LAH* photograph the horizontal weave of the strapping passes behind the reverse hilt. In all post-war photographs it passes in front of the obverse hilt. Ordinarily a minor point of detail, but with a weapon of such outstanding historic importance it rivals an archeological

PHOTO COURTESY OF BARRY BROWN, ENGLAND

This enlarged photograph provides the serious collector/researcher with the first look at the type of hanger employed by Sepp Dietrich for suspending his SS Honor *Degen*. The hanger appears to be a standard teardrop form with either a silver brocade or white leather facing to match the *LAH* parade dress accouterments. This is one of several source photographs showing the magnificent Dietrich sword in wear.

find. The source photograph also provides evidence that the type of hanger employed by Dietrich for suspending this sword was of standard teardrop form, but with silver brocade or white leather facing, to match *LAH* parade dress accouterments.

Probably the most visually stunning aspect of the Sepp Dietrich SS-Honor Sword is the reverse blade displaying 105 names of the *LAH* Officer Corps. It was noted in **Volume V** that this roster was not in alphabetical order. Research confirms it as being in order of seniority as of May 1936, commencing with the three Battalion Commanders and concluding with several Junior Officers recently graduated from the SS Officer Cadet Schools at Bad Tolz and Braunschweig. Two of these newly-commissioned young Officers, Karl Brohl and Jochen Peiper, were delegated to present the Honor Sword to their Commander, Sepp Dietrich. One can only speculate on their emotions. The wartime exploits of the *LAH* are legendary and most of the 105 Officers named on the sword blade figure large in the history of the *LAH* and its sister *Waffen-SS* divisions. However, there was a darker side to the battlefield achievement of this remarkable unit which can be personified by the career of Jochen Peiper who won the Knight's Cross, Oakleaves and Swords. In 1946 he was convicted and sentenced to death for being the Commander of SS troops who shot down unarmed American POWs at Malmedy Crossroads. His devotion to the person of Adolf Hitler was undiminished, his only regret . . . "that at the end of the war when the *Führer* needed his *Leibstandarte* the most, fate had separated us from him."

The Sepp Dietrich SS-Honor Sword remains what is arguably the most beautiful and desirable of all Third Reich edged weapons. However, inevitably it shares the tarnished escutcheon of the super-elite unit whose name is forever inscribed on its blade—"*Leibstandarte SS Adolf Hitler.*"

(Author's Note: The above update narrative is based on original research conducted by well-known collector/researcher Barry Brown, England, and the author.)

UPDATE ON THE EDGED WEAPONS OF THE GERMAN RAILWAY

Recently the contemporary reference books on the subject of Third Reich edged weaponry, including this series, have been challenged on the subject of the 1935 (First Model) Railway dress daggers. One popular theory is that all of the reference books are incorrect and that this model sidearm is, in fact, nothing more than an Army Officer dress dagger with a variation dark purple or black grip manufactured exclusively by one or two Solingen manufacturing firms. What follows should, once and for all, put the matter to rest and prove that the reference books and not the dagger "pundits" are correct. The author has in his personal collection a First Model Railway and a Second Model Railway *(Bahnschutz)* dagger which were both worn during the Third Reich era by the uncle of the wife of a German friend of the author. The uncle gave his niece his three personal WWII Railway sidearms—a nondescript Third Reich-era service bayonet, a First Model Railway dagger, and a Second Model *Bahnschutz* dagger. All three pieces, when presented to his niece, were complete with all accouterments and provide the reader with an exacting study of both model Third Reich Railway dress daggers, complete with their accompanying Railway accouterments in an "as issued, unaltered state." Detailed professional photographs of the pair are shown in this chapter.

The original wearer of the three German Railway sidearms mentioned was a *Herr* Hermann Benz, who served during the Third Reich as a Railway official with the upper-railway line in the city of Düsseldorf, Germany. *Herr* Benz was born in 1910 in Düsseldorf, and joined the German Railway System in the early 1930s, at the age of twenty.

The *Bahnschutz* (Railway Special Protection Force) was established during 1933 and was responsible for the protection of the German railroads in the time of war and/or civil disorder.

For the first several years of service, Hermann Benz wore the nondescript service bayonet mentioned in the first paragraph. Benz's first dress dagger was obviously given to him by a fellow railway official, as the original owner's initials, "*H.St.*," are etched on the reverse crossguard of the Model 1935 Railway dagger, as seen in the accompanying photographs. Most likely, the donor was a retiring Düsseldorf railway official. This model dagger is identical in all respects to the standard, more common Army Officer's dress dagger, except for the addition of a distinctive dark purple or black *Trolon* grip. The grip on the Benz Model 1935 Railway dagger appears to be black, and the maker is Alcoso. It should be pointed out that *Herr* Benz had absolutely no association with the German *Wehrmacht* at any time during his career and, thus, would not have come into contact with an Army Officer dagger. Additionally, his niece is positive that her uncle personally wore all three of the Railway sidearms mentioned above.

In 1937, Hitler brought the entire German Railway System under complete Third Reich national control. The following year, a search began for a distinctive model dress dagger for the German Railway officials. The Railway Leader's *(Bahnschutz)* dagger was adopted in 1938 for senior members because of the stated lack of distinctiveness between the existing 1935 Model dagger and the standard Army Officer's dagger. This time, *Herr* Benz, who had been promoted to Railway Leader with the senior rail management in Düsseldorf, was authorized and received his own personal Railway sidearm, an aluminum 1938 *Bahnschutz* dagger.

Another theory laid to rest by the Benz *Bahnschutz* dagger is the subject of the manufacturer. Many contemporary dagger "pundits" maintain that only two Solingen manufacturers, Carl Eickhorn and E. & F. Hörster, produced the *Bahnschutz* model dagger. The trademark on the Hermann Benz dagger is Paul Weyersberg. This is of special interest to the author, as he personally witnessed several very experienced edged weapons dealers reject a "walk in" original 1938 *Bahnschutz* dagger complete with accompanying hangers and portepee at the 1995 MAX Show in Pittsburgh, Pennsylvania, because of a Paul Weyersberg trademark (once again proving that there is always something new to learn in this hobby)!

The reader should pay special attention to the dress hangers and portepees pictured with the two Railway daggers belonging to *Herr* Benz, as all of the accouterments pictured are undeniably original and accompanied the daggers when presented to his niece during the mid-sixties. Both portepees even remained tied in the original wrap as when the niece received the daggers. However, it should also be pointed out that other style Railway hangers and portepees, e.g. as described and pictured in **Volume I** of this series, pages 119-123, are also correct for these two model sidearms. For example, compare the *Bahnschutz* hangers accompanying the Benz dagger in this section with the rectangular-buckle set shown on pages 122 and 123 of **Volume I**. Both variations are original period production dress hangers. Additionally, other variation Railway dress hangers have been observed by the author bearing slightly different hardware, backings, etc.

Hermann Benz remained with the *Bahnschutz* organization in Düsseldorf until the war ended in 1945, and passed away in 1968.

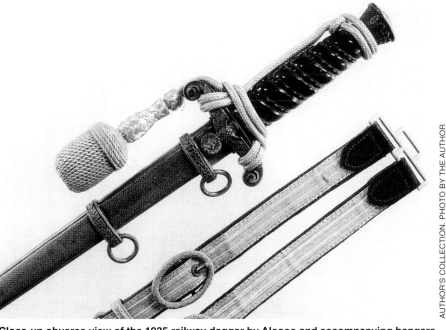

Close-up obverse view of the 1935 railway dagger by Alcoso and accompanying hangers as worn by German rail official, Hermann Benz.

Detail of the reverse crossguard of the model 1935 railway dagger by Alcoso. An explanation of the "H. St" etched on the reverse side is explained in the text accompanying these photographs. Note the distinctive Alcoso "scales" trademark.

Pictured is the black thread "dot" on the bottom of the portepee acorn attached to the Hermann Benz 1935 railway dagger. Note that the portepee cord is void of any black interwoven thread. However, it is known that some portepee manufacturers did utilize a purple or black interwoven thread in the cord and acorn stem. ▶

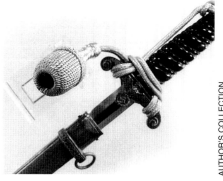

Pictured is the black thread "dot" on the bottom of the portepee acorn attached to the Hermann Benz *Bahnschutz* Dagger. ◀

114

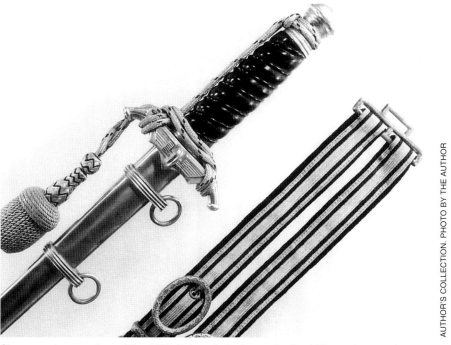

Close-up obverse view of the 1938 *Bahnschutz* dagger by Paul Weyersberg and accompanying hangers as worn by German rail official, Hermann Benz.

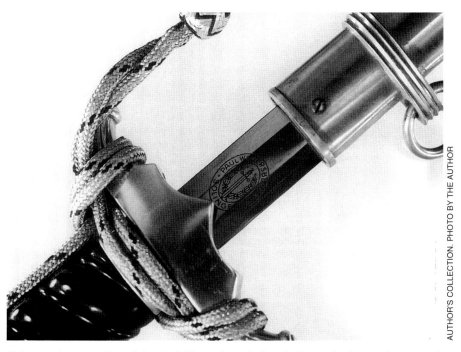

Extreme close-up view of the Paul Weyersberg & Co., Solingen double oval trademark on the 1938 *Bahnschutz* dagger worn by Hermann Benz.

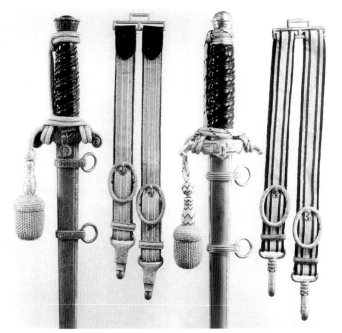

Both of the railway dress daggers and accompanying fabric dress hangers and portepees worn by Hermann Benz are pictured side-by-side for comparative purposes.

The fabric dagger hangers of the two railway official dress daggers belonging to Hermann Benz are pictured side-by-side for comparative purposes—full-length, obverse view. The 1935 1st model railway hangers are pictured on the right and resemble a set of standard Army officer hangers. The railway hangers have aluminum bullion fronts in the style of Army hangers but with slight differences in the woven background and the placement of the woven bullion stripes. The latter *Bahnschutz* dress hangers are shown on the left and feature aluminum bullion fronts with two black stripes and standard Army-style fittings. Note the similarity of hardware with the exception of the lower clips.

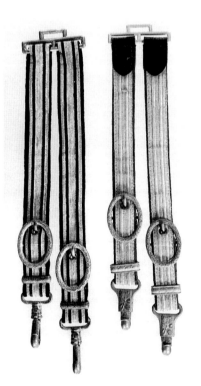

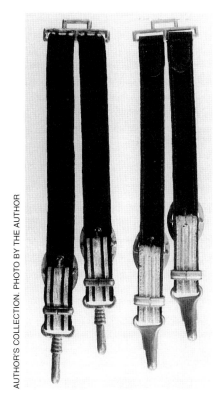

The fabric dagger hangers of the two railway official dress daggers belonging to Hermann Benz are pictured side-by-side—full-length, reverse view. The 1935 1st model railway hangers are pictured on the right and feature backings of a dark green (almost black) velvet and are complete with black leather tabs. The *Bahnschutz* hangers are shown on the left and feature black velvet backings.

◀

An example of an SS Roman numeral stamped sideways. The "II" Roman numeral on this early 1933 SS dress dagger by Robert Klaas is definitely an off-center strike, as mentioned in the text.

UPDATE ON THE ROMAN NUMERAL STAMPINGS APPEARING ON 1933 SS DAGGER REVERSE LOWER CROSSGUARDS

The Roman numeral stampings appearing on the reverse lower crossguards of early 1933 SS daggers have been the subject of debate among German edged weapon collectors/researchers for several years. Many contemporary dagger reference books simply avoid the issue since a source document verifying and explaining the meaning of these stampings has not been located to date. Other reference books, including this ongoing series, have indicated that these numbers, most likely, indicated the SS group or district of the dagger wearer, similar to the *Gau* stampings found on the reverse lower crossguards of SA and NSKK daggers (see pages 250 and 251 of **Volume I**). However, there was a total of eight (8) *SS-Gruppen* in 1934 and expanded to ten (10) SS main districts with some thirty (30) sub-districts in 1935. Since the only known numerals are I, II, and III, the SS group and/or district theory appears to fall short, i.e., early SS daggers would logically be stamped from I to VIII (or to X or even to XXX).

A totally new theory has been recorded by Alain Taugourdeau of France which seems to be perfectly logical to this author. Monsieur Taugourdeau reports in the November 1995 U.K. issue of "Militaria" magazine. . . . "The most recent explanation, and the most likely, is that the numerals correspond to the three principal distribution and equipment control centres for the SS: Munich (I), Dresden (II) and Berlin (III). This may also explain why these markings are often poorly applied (stamped too lightly or at an angle): manufacturers would have taken more care, whilst the distribution centres would have done things more hastily." The logic of this new theory is difficult to refute and seems to solve a long-standing mystery within the hobby. Additionally, the logic is in keeping with the explanation provided in the chapter on SS daggers in **Volume V** of this series. The author of this chapter, Thomas T. Wittmann, states on pages 6 and 7 of **Volume V**, "The reverse of the lower crossguard will be hand-stamped with a Roman numeral. Although in the past it has been stated that this numeral will be found with digits as high as XXI, as a practical matter, crossguards are only encountered with a I, II, or III. These numerals were probably affixed outside of the blade factories, as it is hard to imagine that the Solingen craftsmen could have been responsible for such haphazard number positioning and off-center strikes. In fact, many daggers have been observed with the numerals stamped sideways—certainly not a factory specification!"

UPDATE ON LONG AND SHORT MODEL FIREMAN DRESS BAYONETS

Just as pertinent information can be gleaned from a single original factory letter or even postcard, an advertisement from the 1933-45 period can also enlighten the serious edged weapon collector/researcher and provide factual answers to longstanding questions. For example, collectors have mused for years over the different lengths of dress bayonets. The various lengths of German dress swords can be directly attributed to the individual height of the wearer, and this fact is well known among collectors. However, the same rationale, obviously, does not apply to dress bayonets, and, yet, several model Third Reich dress bayonets were issued in different lengths, as well. Speculation for these different bayonet lengths centered on the wearer's individual preference or, perhaps, the wearer's rank. Reference books in the past have simply referred to dress bayonets as "long and short models."

One tremendous advantage to this continuing series of reference books is that it provides to the collecting community new information as it becomes available. Now, a single page 1930s advertisement from the *Hermann Schellhorn* firm in *Offenbach am Main* (by Frankfurt) tells the real story and puts the matter to rest. The *Schellhorn* firm specialized in providing official uniforms and equipment to the *RLB* and Fire Departments. Note that in the reproduced *Schellhorn* advertisement appearing on page 87 both the long and the short Fireman dress bayonets are pictured and identified. The long model appearing on the left was definitely designated for *Mannschaften* (crew members, lower ranks), while the short model bayonet appearing on the right was designated for the Fire Brigade leaders and investigators (Senior NCOs and Officers). It is also interesting to note that the familiar red

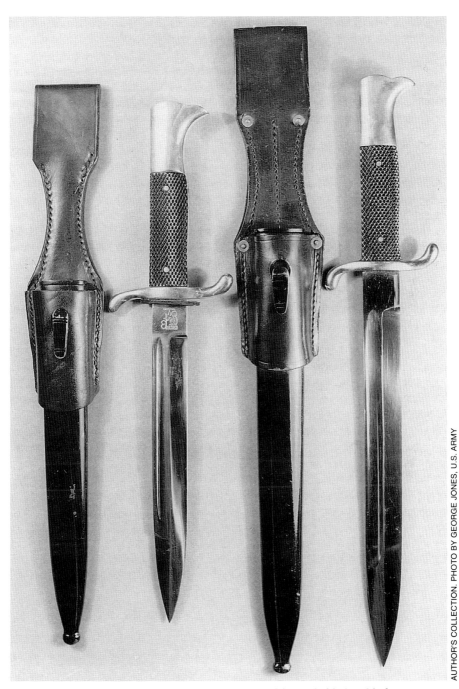

The two different length Fireman dress bayonets are pictured side-by-side for compara-tive purposes. The short model bayonet on the left was designated for the Fire Brigade leaders and investigators (Senior NCO's and Officers) while the long model bayonet on the right was designated for the Fire Department *Mannschaften (*crew members and lower ranks).

and silver *Faustriemen* (bayonet knots) designed for the Fire Departments were designated for Junior and Leader ranks of the Fire Department units charged with extinguishing fires and that a second style standard bayonet knot was correct for other Fire Department leaders (Senior NCOs and Officers). How many bayonet collectors have removed a standard grey bayonet knot with silver strap braid from a Fireman dress bayonet thinking that the combination was a mismatch?

Although the author is unable to provide, to date, source documentation on some of the other Third Reich dress bayonets, a logical conclusion to draw is that a similar rank designation would apply to the other models as well, i.e., a long model sidearm for the Junior grades and the short model being designated for the Senior NCOs and Officers. The page from the period Max Weyersberg sales catalog reproduced on page 271 confirms this theory. However, when one considers the Police edged sidearms, an anomaly exists. A review of page 184 in **Volume I** of this series will show three different lengths for the Police bayonets. Additional research is needed to ascertain the designation of the medium length Police sidearm. As is often the case with this intriguing hobby of collecting the edged weapons of the Third Reich, when one question is answered, another question appears!

UPDATE ON *TENO* LEADER HANGERS

Page 51 of **Volume VII** described in detail the three types of hangers correctly associated with the *TENO* Leader dagger—the standard black and silver fabric dress hangers, the black leather service hangers, and the rarer reddish-brown leather service hangers. In May of 1996, the author received a letter from dagger collector Tony Ward of England who had acquired an unusual, genuine *TENO* Leader's dagger from a private source complete with the accompanying accouterments. What is unusual about the ensemble is the fact that the accompanying service hangers are dark blue leather (see photograph appearing in this section). To the best of knowledge of Mr. Ward and the author, this is the first time that a set of blue leather *TENO* hangers have been found. A careful inspection of the hangers leaves little doubt about their authenticity. Additional research will, hopefully, reveal the purpose and use for the different colors of leather utilized with the *TENO* Leader's dagger.

PHOTO COURTESY OF
TONY WARD, ENGLAND

The *TENO* leader's ensemble belonging to collector Tony Ward of England which is complete with unusual dark *blue* leather service hangers.

Unusual set of dark *blue TENO* leader service hangers. ▶

THIRD REICH DRESS DAGGERS

Double-engraved Army officer dagger by Emil Voos. Pictured is one of the highly desirable Voos engraved dress daggers. Although several other Solingen firms offered a double-engraved blade pattern, it is the Voos model which has won the greatest acceptance among German edged weapon collectors—most likely due to the exceptional blade etch and plating by Emil Voos. The superb double-engraved Voos Army and 2nd model *Luftwaffe* daggers are legendary in the edged weapon collecting community. ◀

Close-up view of the obverse blade of the Emil Voos double-engraved Army officer dagger. Note the meticulously embellished obverse blade etch which incorporates an outstretched-wing Third Reich eagle and swastika above two oak leaves. ▶

Close-up view of the reverse blade of the Emil Voos double-engraved Army officer dagger. The Emil Voos trademark, a snake wrapped around a tree stump within an oval, is clearly visible stamped into the reverse ricasso. Herr Voos, who worked in a very small workshop on *Dingshauserstrasse* in Solingen, obviously took considerable pride in his workmanship. Of note is not only the high quality blade etch, but also the exceptional detail to the grip ferrule.

▲ Early nickel-silver 1st model *Luftwaffe* dagger with engraved reverse upper scabbard fitting—full length, reverse view.

Detail of the engraving on the upper scabbard fitting of the early nickel-silver 1st Model *Luftwaffe* dagger. The reverse upper scabbard fitting on this dagger is professionally engraved, *"Für Bestleistungen, H.F.S., September 1937."* While both the owner of this dagger and the author acknowledged that the dagger was awarded during September of 1937 for the "best performance," it took the Director of the *Geheimes Staatsarchiv* in Berlin to finally decipher the meaning of the *"H.F.S."* These three initials were extracted from *"Herbstflugschau"* (autumn air show), and the pictured dagger was awarded for the best performance at the show.

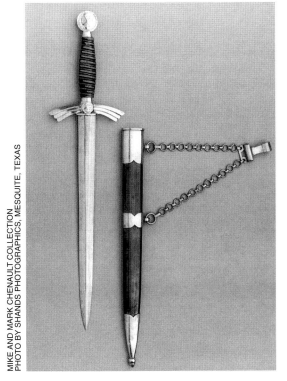

MIKE AND MARK CHENAULT COLLECTION
PHOTO BY SHANDS PHOTOGRAPHICS, MESQUITE, TEXAS

Unusual 1st model *Luftwaffe* dagger by *Gebrüder* Heller/Marienthal—full-length, out-of-scabbard, obverse view. This dagger is outfitted with a special bronze hilt. The end of the bronze crossguard is stamped with a government property stamp eagle and the number "73." Additionally, the hilt metal parts are considerably smaller than those found on a standard 1st model *Luftwaffe* dagger.

MIKE AND MARK CHENAULT COLLECTION
PHOTO BY SHANDS PHOTOGRAPHICS, MESQUITE, TEXAS

Reverse Hilt of the unusual 1st model *Luftwaffe* dagger by *Gebrüder* Heller/Marienthal. Although not obvious in this photograph, the hilt metal parts are made of bronze and are considerably smaller in size than those found on a standard 1st model *Luftwaffe* dagger.

BAVIN J. LANE COLLECTION, ENGLAND
PHOTO BY BAVIN J. LANE

***Luftsport (DLV)* leader dagger by SMF, *Solingen*—full-length, out-of-scabbard, obverse view. This dress dagger served as a transitional model between the early 55 cm. *DLV* Flyer's dagger and the standard 1st model *Luftwaffe* dagger adopted in 1934.**

The *Luftsport (DLV)* Leader dagger by SMF is pictured—full-length, reverse view. The scabbard of this model dagger has no metal base, and the external scabbard fittings are mounted with large oval nickel-silver "staples."

Extreme close-up detail of the SMF, Solingen trademark stamped on the reverse blade ricasso of the *Luftsport (DLV)* Leader dagger. Note that a small eagle *Waffen Amt* acceptance stamp has been stamped below the SMF trademark.

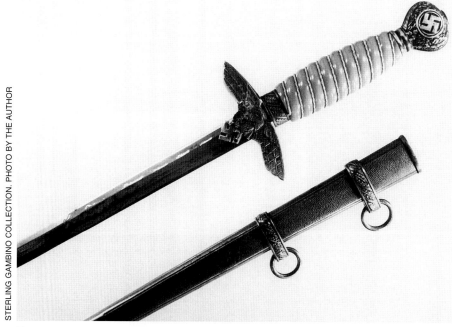

Rare 2nd model *Luftwaffe* dagger featuring an obverse blade etch depicting five German aircraft flying over a village. This unusual *Luftwaffe* dagger was a direct WWII veteran purchase from New Jersey. There is no maker's mark evident on the blade. The author is unaware of another specimen bearing this unusual blade etching.

Close-up, detailed view of the obverse blade etch on the unusual 2nd model *Luftwaffe* dagger. The unique etching clearly depicts five German *Luftwaffe* aircraft flying over a small village and neighboring mountains.

Reverse blade etching on the rare 2nd model *Luftwaffe* dagger with the obverse blade depicting five German aircraft. Note that no manufacturer's trademark appears on the reverse blade ricasso.

2nd model *Luftwaffe* dagger with unusual brown grip by E. & F. Hörster. This dagger features a previously unseen dark rust *brown*-colored *Trolon* grip. Dagger is complete with its 23-centimeter *Luftwaffe* portepee.

125

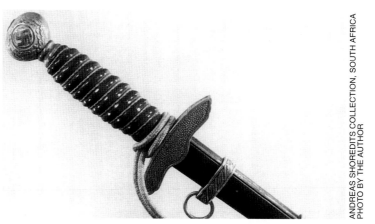

2nd model *Luftwaffe* dagger by E. & F. Hörster with unusual *brown* grip is pictured—reverse view. Although the solid *Trolon* grip photographs almost black in this black-and-white photograph, the true color is a dark rust *brown*.

Close-up view of the reverse crossguard and engraved blade of the Emil Voos engraved 2nd model *Luftwaffe* dagger. The Emil Voos trademark (snake wrapped around a tree stump) is clearly visible stamped into the reverse blade ricasso. Complementing the blade is a handsome genuine ivory grip which is superbly crafted.

Custom-made 1st model Navy dagger with unique crossguard by WKC. The standard Navy crossguard has been personalized with the addition of a red and green stone (representing port and starboard) beautifully inset into each crossguard finial. The dagger is pictured complete with a near-mint nylon portepee with nice age toning in a correct "reef" knot tie.

▶

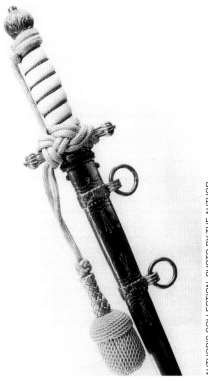

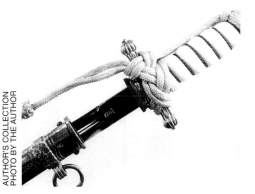

The WKC trademark on the custom-made 1st Model Navy Dagger with unique crossguard is pictured. Note that the stamped WKC knighthead trademark is considerably smaller than normally seen.

◀

Close-up view of the green glass stone factory inset into the crossguard finial of the custom-made 1st model Navy dagger by WKC.

▶

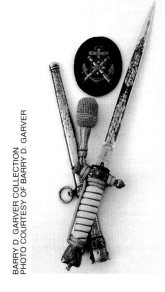

2nd model navy dagger by E. Pack & *Söhne*—full-length, reverse view. The E. Pack firm, evidently, manufactured few Navy daggers, as this trademark is quite scarce on this model dagger. The example pictured features a "sailing ship" motif on the reverse blade displayed on a blued panel. Also of note is the celluloid grip on the Pack model which is slightly longer than Navy grips on other manufacturers.

◄

Personalized 2nd model Navy dagger complete with Damascus steel blade and ivory grip. This high-quality, special order Navy dagger belonged to Naval Officer Kurt Ambrosius, who served in the German Navy during both WWI and WWII. Deeply stamped into the obverse blade ricasso is a facsimile of the German Iron Cross with the date "1914" above and "1939" below (indicating service in both wars). The owner's last name, "Ambrosius" is professionally engraved on the upper portion of the brass scabbard.

▼

Close-up view of the obverse blade ricasso of the personalized 2nd model Navy dagger belonging to Kurt Ambrosius. Of interest in this detailed photograph are the genuine white ivory grip, the beautiful hand-forged genuine Damascus steel blade (small rosebud pattern) and the original owner's engraved name on the scabbard.

2nd model Navy dagger with a *U-Boat* marked blade. The obverse ricasso has a 3/8" x 5/8" frosted panel with the raised inscription, "U41" (U-Boat #41). It is quite rare to find a Navy dagger designed for use by a U-Boat member.

Close-up detail of the "U41" designation engraved on the obverse ricasso of the 2nd model Navy dagger belonging to a *U-Boat* member during World War II.

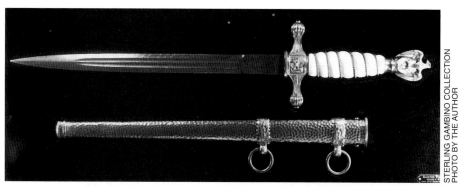

Rare 2nd model Navy dagger with genuine ivory grip and Damascus blade in original presentation case. This exceptional combination was recently acquired by the author in northern Germany. The Damascus pattern of the blade on this stunning showpiece is the seldom-seen "peacock" pattern. The original black leatherette case is recessed to accommodate the dagger and scabbard and still bears a small metal plate advertising the case manufacturer or the distributor's name and address.

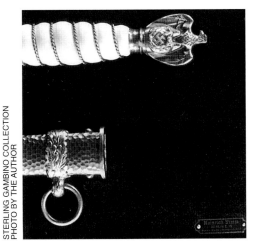

Close-up view of the rare 2nd model Navy dagger with ivory grip and "peacock" pattern genuine Damascus blade. Note the custom-made presentation case is complete with the case manufacturer's or distributor's name and address, "Heinrich Timm, Berlin C-19" followed by the street address. The padded blue velvet interior is neatly recessed to accommodate the dagger and the scabbard.

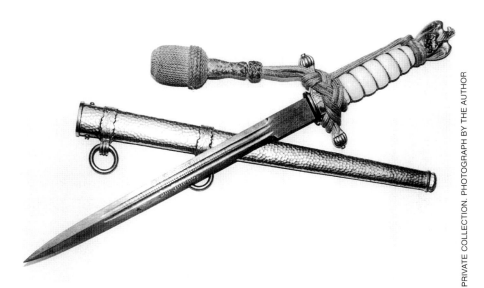

2nd model Navy (*Kriegsmarine*) presentation dagger from Solingen. This unique dagger features a genuine ivory grip and a beautiful "maiden hair" pattern Damascus blade with the word, "Damast" stamped into the tang. A raised gold inscription on the obverse blade features in Gothic script the following presentation: *"Gewidmet von der N.S. Marinekameradschaft — Solingen Im Juli 1942."* An English translation of the German blade presentation is as follows: "In Dedication from the National Socialist Naval Comradeship — Solingen, July, 1942." This beautiful dress dagger was crafted by the Carl Eickhorn firm in Solingen, and is complete with a hammered scabbard and gold Navy portepee.

A *rare* combination of the 2nd model Navy honor dagger and the accompanying award document presented to Admiral Willy von Nordeck by *Grossadmiral* Raeder on 31 August 1942.

Rare SA Marine (Naval) standard Service dagger by Carl Eickhorn, Solingen. This model dagger is identical to the standard 1933 SA dagger except for gilt-plated cross-guards and scabbard fittings. Due to the extremely small size of this element of the SA and the short duration of wear, this model SA dagger is extremely rare. Note the unusual brown leather vertical carrying device, complete with retaining strap.

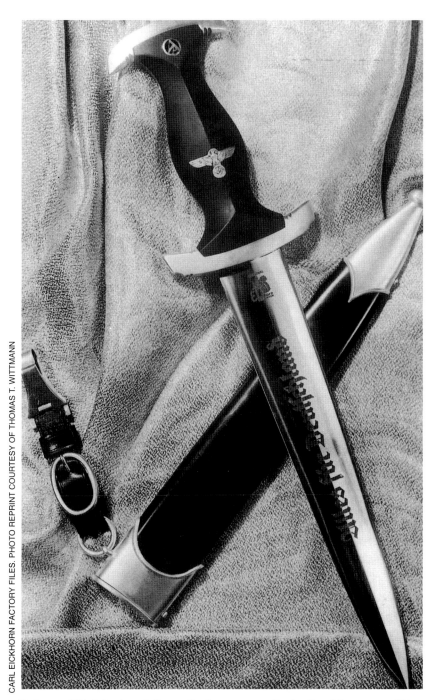

Volume VII introduced the collecting community to the *Obergruppenführer* Heinrick Knickmann/Krefeld Bridge SA presentation dagger by Carl Eickhorn. Confirming the original existence of this extraordinary presentation dress dagger are two period photographs from the 1930s Carl Eickhorn factory files. Complete details on this rare artifact are available on pages 87-91 of **Volume VII**.

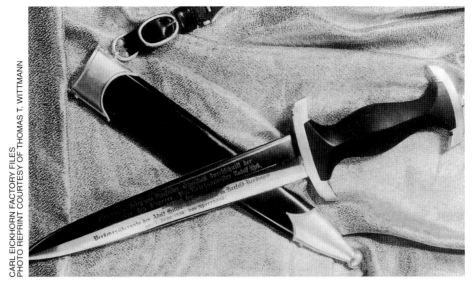

The Krefeld Bridge SA presentation dagger by Carl Eickhorn—full-length, out-of-scabbard, reverse view. On 7 June 1936, the Adolf Hitler Bridge over the Rhein River was dedicated in the city of Krefeld-Uerdingen and a special SA presentation dagger was presented by Nazi Party Deputy Rudolf Hess. Two black and white photographs of this prized dagger were found in the Eickhorn factory 1930s files.

An original SA dagger showing the post-war addition of a "Field Day Germany 1945" acid etch inscription on the obverse. The reverse blade engraving shows soldiers in combat. This, most likely, was the idea of an enterprising dagger manufacturer who customized existing stocks of daggers and sold them to military occupied forces as trophies for Field Day sporting events. What better way to raise some post-war needed funds and at the same time eliminate some (at the time) totally worthless stock.

Pictured on the right is a photo reprint of a 1930s Period Carl Eickhorn factory photograph depicting the ultra-rare SA presentation dress dagger with eagle heads on the crossguard. Like a number of other authentic pieces, this model dagger has been attacked by numerous dagger "pundits" as being a total fake. This photo reprint unquestionably documents the existence of this model dagger during the period.

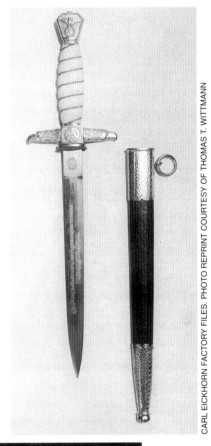

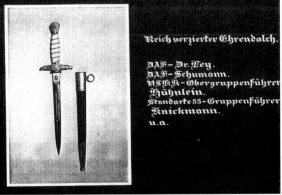

Reich verzierter Ehrendolch.

DAF — Dr. Ley.
DAF — Schumann.
NSKK — Obergruppenführer
Hühnlein.
Standarte 53 — Gruppenführer
Knickmann.
u.a.

On the page from the Eickhorn factory files showing the original photo of the ultra-rare SA presentation dress dagger with eagle heads on the crossguard is a listing (or partial listing) of the recipients of this honor dagger.

SA High Leader's dagger by F. Dick, Esslingen. While common acceptance among German edged weapon collectors is that the Carl Eickhorn Company in Solingen was the sole producer of the SA High Leader daggers, here is proof that at least one other firm produced this model. Long-time collector Carter Jennette of North Carolina purchased the pictured dagger directly from the wife of a deceased WWII veteran in his hometown of Elizabeth City. Obvious differences in this F. Dick model and the Eickhorn version are the plain nickel-silver crossguards and scabbard fittings, plain nickel blade and metal scabbard shell on the F. Dick model.

Extreme close-up view of the reverse blade ricasso and obverse chain suspension hanger on the SA High Leader's dagger by F. Dick. Under the F. Dick (arrow), Esslingen trademark is the original owner's name and unit, "A. Lenk, 1/R 153." The reverse lower crossguard is SA group stamped "Sw" (Sudwest). Note the excellent grip-to-crossguard and blade-to-crossguard fit.

The Wilhelm Bruckner SA honor dagger is pictured outside its scabbard—obverse view. Note that this honor dagger is fitted with plain nickel blade and not the typical genuine Damascus blade. Plain nickel blades were utilized by the Carl Eickhorn firm on both SA and SS Honor daggers.

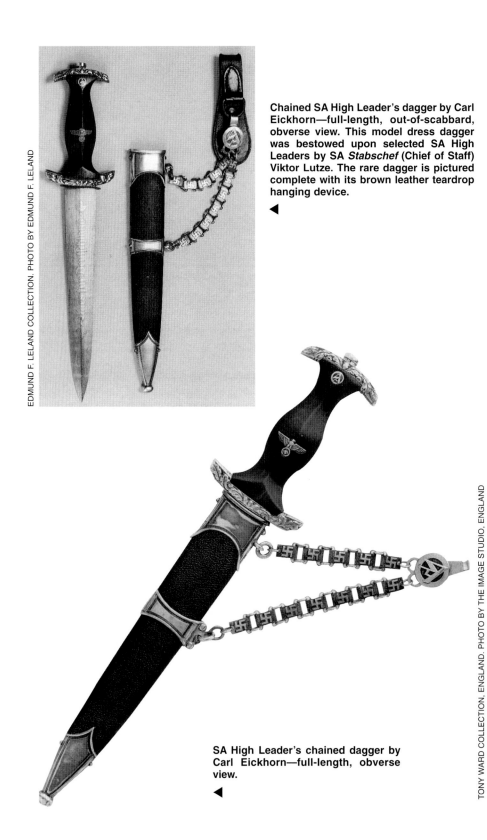

Chained SA High Leader's dagger by Carl Eickhorn—full-length, out-of-scabbard, obverse view. This model dress dagger was bestowed upon selected SA High Leaders by SA *Stabschef* (Chief of Staff) Viktor Lutze. The rare dagger is pictured complete with its brown leather teardrop hanging device.

◄

SA High Leader's chained dagger by Carl Eickhorn—full-length, obverse view.

◄

1933 NSKK dagger by Hugo Linder with light wood grip. This early dress dagger features the solid nickel-silver fittings with the reverse lower crossguard being group marked, "Ns" (*Niedersachsen*). The beautiful light wood grip is made of *Eiche* (oak). This hard, durable wood exhibits deep striations along its surface, which are its large vessel lines, making it quite distinct in appearance. The black NSKK scabbard is a possible period repaint.

Close-up of the obverse hilt of the 1933 NSKK dagger by Hugo Linder. Notice the dark striations of the light wood oak grip. The Hugo Linder trademark stamped on the reverse ricasso incorporates an oak leaf within a triangle.

Unissued 1933 NSKK dagger by *RZM M7/12* (Max Weyersberg). The dagger is complete with the rarely-seen Max Weyersberg (WMW) issue tag, a riveted *RZM* triangular issue tag, and a WMW paper issue bag (not shown). Note the <u>perfect</u> original black scabbard paint.

◀

Unusual NSKK Leader's dagger by Jacobs & Co., Solingen. This model dagger was evidently a transition piece prior to the introduction of the NSKK chained dagger in 1936. Note the unusual scabbard with larger than normal scabbard rings and the accompanying black leather dress hangers, similar to Hitler Youth Leader hangers. This dagger was veteran purchased, as is, complete with the accompanying hangers.

▶

Early 1933 SS dagger with an extremely rare Ed. Gembruch (fish) trademark—full-length obverse view. Attached to the scabbard is a unique early vertical hanger, which features a leather strap which extends around the upper scabbard fitting. This strap is notched on the side and has been factory-fitted over the scabbard ring.

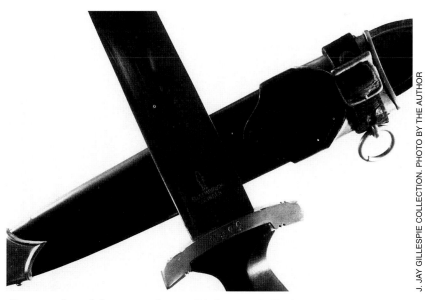

Close-up view of the extremely rare Ed. Gembruch (fish) trademark on an early 1933 SS dagger. The original owner's SS serial number, "5640," is deeply stamped on the reverse lower crossguard.

1933 SS Dagger by Gottlieb Hammesfahr with unique stamping on the reverse upper scabbard fitting. This classic '33 SS dagger was veteran purchased in Scotland complete with the black leather vertical hanger and original 23cm portepee in the correct "tie" for the SS Officer dagger.

◄

AUTHOR'S COLLECTION. PHOTO BY THE AUTHOR

Close-up study of the reverse upper scabbard fitting on the 1933 SS dagger by Gottlieb Hammesfahr. The leather vertical hanger has been loosened in the photograph in order to reveal the jeweler-engraved SS runes and the original owner's SS serial number, "216007." The lower reverse crossguard is stamped "III," and the early nickel-silver clip on the vertical hanger is both Assmann and D.R.G.M. stamped.

►

AUTHOR'S COLLECTION. PHOTO BY THE AUTHOR

1933 SS dagger by Robert Klaas, complete with unusual black leather vertical hanger. Note the near-perfect grip-to-crossguard fit. The early vertical hanger features a leather strap in lieu of the normally seen buckle. Dagger is complete with both its original vertical hanger and black leather belt loop.

◀

Early 1933 SS dagger with motto exclamation point by the Jacobs & Co.—full-length, obverse view. While 1933 SS daggers with the Jacobs & Co. *RZM* number and motto exclamation point are scarce, the early models bearing the Jacobs & Co. trademark are extremely rare. The specimen pictured is one of only three known to the author.

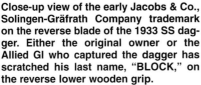

Close-up view of the early 1933 SS motto exclamation point by the Jacobs & Co. This was the sole edged weapon manufacturing firm to place an exclamation point after the obverse blade SS motto and the reason remains a mystery.

Close-up view of the early Jacobs & Co., Solingen-Gräfrath Company trademark on the reverse blade of the 1933 SS dagger. Either the original owner or the Allied GI who captured the dagger has scratched his last name, "BLOCK," on the reverse lower wooden grip.

Unissued 1933 SS dress dagger by Gustav C. Spitzer (*RZM* 7/80) is pictured full-length in the scabbard—obverse view. This mint-condition dagger is pictured complete with its triangular stock paper *RZM* issue tag which has never been removed from the scabbard ring. Note the *RZM* stampings on both the black leather hanger and the belt loop metal "D" ring. The *RZM* number on the cardboard tag "No. 009432" was a unique number assigned to this single dagger from Gustav Spitzer. The author of this reference had the privilege of meeting Gustav Spitzer's son in Solingen in 1961.

Exceptional condition 1936 Chained SS dagger by Robert Klaas with serial number on crossguard and the original owner's silver SS ring attached to chain cloverleaf clip. This superb example was purchased from the original owner's niece and is in untouched condition. The lower crossguard is deeply stamped with the owner's SS number, "138526," on both the obverse and the reverse. The dagger is complete with its original period portepee in unusual "tie."

Close-up view of the *RZM* stamping on the reverse blade ricasso of the Gustav C. Spitzer (*RZM* 7/80) which matches the manufacturer's code on the issue tag. Also of note is the fact that this marking identifies a previously unknown SS alternate *RZM* code for the G. Spitzer firm, i.e., "*RZM* 1197."

Close-up view of the exceptional-condition Robert Klaas 1936 Chained SS dagger. Note the unusual method of attaching the portepee, the original owner's SS number, "138526," stamped on the obverse lower crossguard, and the owner's silver SS ring attached to the cloverleaf chain clip. The silver ring features the typical SS skull and crossbones.

Close-up reverse view of the 1936 chained SS dagger with the original owner's silver ring attached. It is interesting to note that the owner's SS number, "138526," is stamped on both the obverse and the reverse lower crossguard. Barely visible in the photograph is the Robert Klaas "kissing cranes" trademark on the reverse blade ricasso. The original blade buffer pad is still intact. The silver SS ring is unusually large and is hallmarked on the inside. The owner's niece stated that her uncle served with the SS/Police in the city of Berlin.

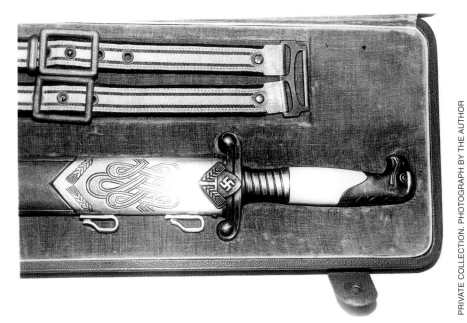

Close-up of the RAD officer's dagger and special fabric dress hangers by the Ed Wüsthof firm, Solingen.

Exterior of the red RAD officer's leatherette case. This high-quality case features the RAD emblem on the center of the top lid, as well as four "NS" National emblems.

Of special note to German edged weapon collectors is the 1930s Austrian Air Force dagger. As mentioned in the Introduction of this volume, Canadian author Kurt Glemser intends to show in his **Volume III** of a **A Guide to Military Dress Daggers** period photographs which will prove that the Austrian Air Force dagger model pictured was worn during the Third Reich period (after the 1938 *Anschluss*) by Austrians in German *Luftwaffe* uniforms. The dagger is shown complete with its rare accompanying accouterments. The maker is "Zeitler, *Wien* (Vienna)." ▶

◀ Pictured is the obverse hilt of the WWII Austrian Air Force dagger complete with accompanying accouterments. The rare dress hangers pictured feature a blue material sewn to red leather and were authorized for junior, noncommissioned officers (NCO's). Attached to the upper clip of the hangers is an original, rare brown leather belt loop with protective leather backing.

Unusual *Deutsches Jungvolk* (DJ) knife with brass swastika inset on the obverse grip plate by Robert Klaas.

◀

The reverse blade of the small DJ knife is stamped with the Robert Klaas, Solingen "kissing cranes" trademark.

Unissued Hitler Youth knife by Paul Seilheimer—full-length obverse view. This near-mint condition *HJ* knife is complete with the original red and gold Paul Seilheimer paper quality tag. The mint blade is the model without the HJ motto. The leather scabbard hanger is stamped on the reverse with "L" and "F" and oak leaves.

Unusual Hitler Youth knife complete with a leather scabbard located on Iceland. The overall length is 10-1/4 inches. Note the different style blade on this Youth knife, compared to the standard model.

◀

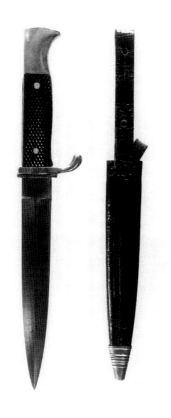

The unusual Hitler Youth knife complete with a leather scabbard is pictured—full-length, reverse view. Note that the knife is void of a maker's mark and/or an *RZM* number.

◄

Close-up view of the obverse hilt of the unusual Hitler Youth knife complete with a leather scabbard. The black leather scabbard is complete with a single leather retaining strap. ►

The 1935 *Reichsparteitag Nürnberg* souvenir party knife—full-length, out-of-scabbard, obverse view. It is believed that a large number of these souvenir knives were sold commercially to the public during the 1935 Party Day held in Nürnberg. The colorful crest on the blade is the Nürnberg city coat of arms.

Hitler Youth knife with unusual motto. This unusual *HJ* knife reflects no maker's mark, but a most unusual motto, "Ver es Becsulet!" on the obverse blade.

Extremely rare Spanish Civil War *Carlist* Youth knife. Attached to the obverse grip is a yellow/red/yellow Hitler Youth (*HJ*) style painted diamond. The upper obverse scabbard is fitted with a black and silver metal *Carlist* insignia. This knife is patterned after the German *HJ* knife but is of heavier construction.

◄

Close-up view of the reverse blade of the rare Spanish Civil War *Carlist* Youth knife. The reverse blade ricasso is stamped, "SEAM 1936/8" and a "flaming grenade" trademark. The plated blade is thicker than those found on German *HJ* knives.

►

Disassembled hilt components and scabbard of an unusual Government Official's dagger by Carl Eickhorn. Note the rotating pommel nut which is void of the characteristic two small holes and features a single slot designed for a normal screwdriver. *All* internal parts, including the tang *and* pommel nut, are stamped "42." The entire dagger is undeniably genuine. No explanation is available for the different style pommel nut, but the author is aware of more than one of these.

Top view of the unusual Government Official's dagger by Carl Eickhorn. The *slotted* rotating pommel nut is clearly visible in this photograph. *All* internal parts, including the tang *and* pommel nut, are stamped "42."

The obverse hilt of the Gilt Railway Water Protection Police leader's dagger by Carl Eickhorn. Note the exquisite detail to the national eagle on the obverse crossguard.

Water Protection Police dagger complete with grip insignia by Alcoso—full-length, out-of-scabbard obverse view. This rare dagger was authorized for wear by officers and administrative officials of the *Wasserschutzpolizei* (Water Protection Police).

The obverse hilt of the rare Water Protection Police dagger complete with grip insignia by Alcoso. This model dagger is *identical* to the pre-1938 1st model Navy dagger except that the wood grip is wrapped in a dark blue leather bound with a gold wire wrap. On a small number of the daggers, a gilt metal Third Reich Police badge is affixed to the obverse leather grip.

Royal presentation hunting *Hirschfänger* by ACS. Ornate gilt-over-brass hilt fittings feature a large Royal crown pommel and a unique oak leaf embellished crossguard with a clamshell depicting three deer in a forest. Attached to the stag grip is a gilted circular band engraved, "1931." This rare one-of-a-kind *Hirschfänger* was presented by Friederich August for the shooting of *1000 Rehbock* (small deer) and is a magnificent example of the edged weapons manufacturer's art. ◄

Close-up view of the obverse hilt of the Royal presentation hunting *Hirschfänger* by ACS. in addition to the gilted circular band engraved with the date, "1931," two oak leaves with acorns are pinned to the stag grip. Note the lavishly embellished straight crossguard. Although not visible in the photograph, the polished blade is double-etched with hunting scenes. A matching skinning knife is also present. ►

Close-up view of the reverse upper scabbard fitting on the Royal presentation hunting *Hirschfänger* by ACS. The reverse upper fitting is engraved with a Royal crown, the initials, "FA" (Friederich August, the last King of Saxony) and *"1000er Rehbock"* (deer), *5.9. 1925"* (5 September 1925). ◄

Ornate hunting/skinning knife with a hand-carved stag grip by the Schratinger firm. The beautiful stag grip features a hound dog carved in relief with the dog's head and paws extending through the butt of the grip. The small leather sheath is hand-sewn on the reverse.

◄

Detail of the hand-carved stag grip on the ornate hunting/skinning knife by Schratinger. This outstanding carving skill would be difficult to duplicate to-day.

►

Hermann Göring presentation Forestry dagger handmade by Professor Zeitner, Berlin—full-length obverse view. This ornate, handcrafted Forestry dagger was presented by Hermann Göring on Christmas 1938. An example of one of these *ultra-rare* Göring daggers in wear can be seen on page 279 of **Volume V**. Hilt fittings are .835 fine silver. The dagger is pictured complete with its integral silver suspension chain hanger.

◄

Close-up view of the Hermann Göring presentation Forestry dagger—obverse hilt. The .835 fine silver hilt fittings show light wear with age toning to the oak leaf pommel and recurved cross-guard. The top of the pommel cap is malachite stone, and the grip is genuine ivory.

Extreme close-up view of the reverse crossguard and upper scabbard of the Hermann Göring presentation Forestry dagger. Note the detailed engraving of the facsimile of Göring's signature and *"Weihnachten* (Christmas) 1938." Although not seen in the photograph, the scabbard throat is also stamped ".835, Zeitner, Berlin," followed by the Zeitner trademark.

The obverse hilt of the deluxe subordinate Forestry dagger by E. & F. Hörster is pictured. The gilted brass hilt fittings are beautifully detailed with an oak leaf motif on the knuckle-bow and crossguard. The clamshell features a large German *Auerhahn* (a rare bird which resembles a wild black turkey).

◀

Rare subordinate presentation Forestry official's cutlass by WKC. An English translation of the four-line raised dedication on the beautifully "frosted" obverse blade reads, "Honor Award of the Shooting Association of the Municipal Senior Forestry Office *Saarlpuis-Werzig* (location) for the shooting match conducted on 21 September 1929." The top of the WKC "knight head" logo is barely visible directly under the clamshell.

◀

Deluxe senior Forestry cutlass by *Clemen und Jung*—obverse view. Here is a stunning showpiece with lavishly embellished upper and lower scabbard fittings. All fittings, including the fluted clamshell, retain almost all of the original fire gilting. The grip plates are genuine ivory, and the cutlass is shown complete with its original Senior Forestry silver bullion with green stripes portepee.

▶

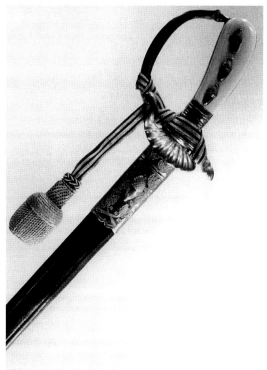

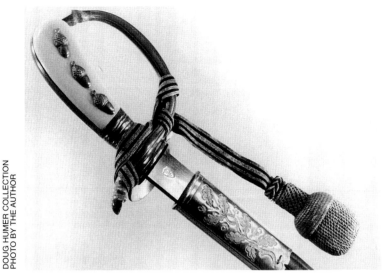

The deluxe senior Forestry dagger by *Clemen und Jung*—reverse view. The manufacturer's "Z" inside a shield trademark is clearly visible stamped on the reverse blade ricasso. Note that three identical acorns without oak leaves decorate the reverse ivory grip plate. Both of the scabbard fittings are stamped "11" on the reverse under the retaining pins. This photograph offers the reader an excellent view of the correct portepee "tie" for this model sidearm.

Senior Forestry cutlass complete with national emblem on the ferrule. This deluxe Forestry cutlass was manufactured by E&F Hörster, Solingen, and features a bellowing stag on the clamshell. The specimen pictured is complete with its accompanying original accouterments, i.e. a green leather v-shaped frog hanging device and a gold and green Senior Forestry portepee. ▶

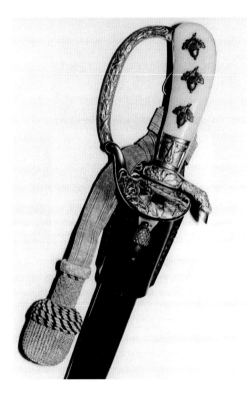

THIRD REICH MINIATURE EDGED WEAPONS

Outstanding ensemble of a large-scale miniature Army dagger by Alcoso in its original Alcoso factory issue box and complete with the quality control tag. This rare set would be the highlight of any advanced German miniature dagger collection.

▶

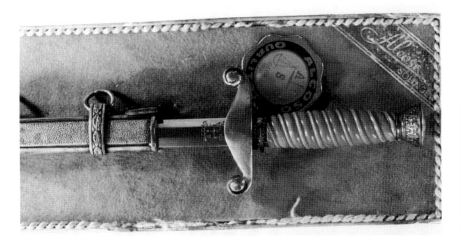

Close-up view of the large-scale miniature Army dagger by Alcoso in its original Alcoso factory issue box. The "Alcoso 'scales' Solingen" trademark is clearly visible on the reverse blade ricasso. An Alcoso factory quality control tag is still tied to the grip ferrule.

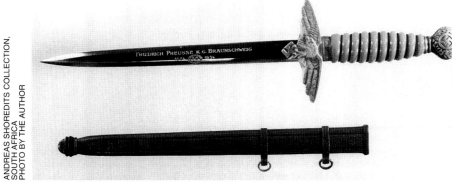

A miniature 2nd model *Luftwaffe* dagger by SMF commemorating a 50th anniversary of a firm in Braunschweig. The obverse blade is deeply etched, "Friedrich Preusse K.G. Braunschweig, 1884," "50" in a wreath, and "1934." This miniature dress dagger was, obviously, given as a 50-year anniversary gift.

Close-up view of the obverse blade etching on the miniature 2nd model *Luftwaffe* dagger by SMF.

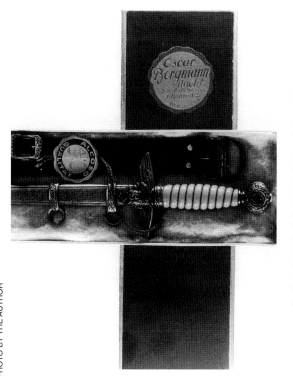

Close-up view of a 2nd model *Luftwaffe* miniature dagger by Alcoso in its original issue box and complete with original leather hangers and Alcoso quality control tag. This is the sole example observed by this author, to date, of a 2nd model *Luftwaffe* miniature dagger, complete with miniature leather hanging straps. The same model miniature dagger, complete with miniature fabric *Luftwaffe* hanging straps, can be seen on page 196 of **Volume V** of this series.

◄

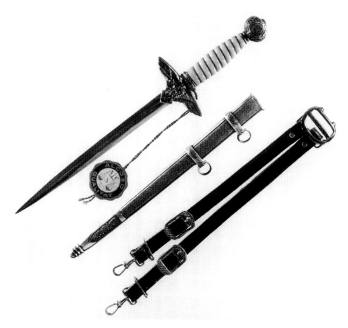

The unissued 2nd model *Luftwaffe* miniature dagger with original Alcoso quality control tag and brown leather hanging straps is pictured out of its issue box. This is the large size Alcoso salesman sample miniature, and the quality approaches its full-size counterpart.

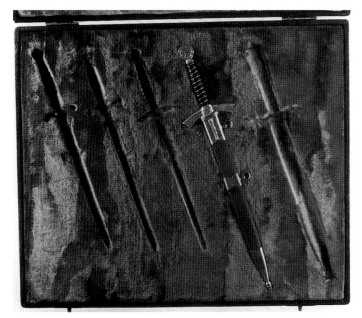

An original dagger salesman sample kit case by the E.&F. Hörster firm. The case is pictured open with the 1st model *Luftwaffe* miniature intact. Recesses are also provided, from left to right, for the miniature Army dagger, 2nd model Navy dagger, 2nd model *Luftwaffe* dagger, and, on the far right, the miniature hunting dagger. Although the case is not marked, the Hörster miniatures are the only ones that perfectly fit the recesses in this case.

Luftwaffe Sword Salesman Sample by Paul Weyersberg, Solingen, full-length, out-of-scabbard, obverse view. Note the rounded blade tip and the custom-designed scabbard. This shortened sword version was much easier for a factory salesman to carry and display at the various military installations.

▶

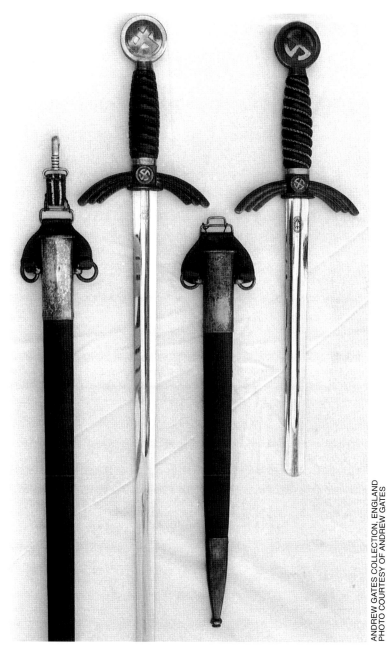

The *Luftwaffe* sword salesman sample by Paul Weyersberg compared to a regulation *Luftwaffe* sword by Carl Eickhorn. Note the "customized" fabric hanging device consisting of a short section and aluminum snap of a 2nd model *Luftwaffe* dagger hanger attached to the Eickhorn leather sword hanger.

165

THIRD REICH PERSONALIZED EDGED WEAPONS

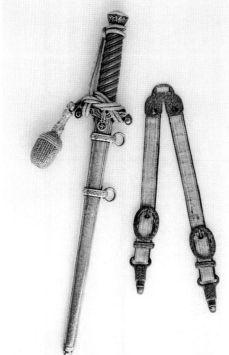

Personalized Army Officer's Dagger and Hangers by Gustav Spitzer belonging to *Baron* von Osten—Full-length, obverse view. The accompanying dress hangers are the ornate "horseshoe" variety.

◄

Detail of the reverse crossguard of the *Baron* von Osten personalized Army officer's dagger by Gustav Spitzer. The original owner's monogram of the letter "O" under a coronet is professionally engraved on the reverse crossguard.

Close-up view of the reverse crossguard of a personalized Army officer dagger by Alcoso. The reverse crossguard is professionally engraved, "*Dein Schwert dem Führer dein Herz der Frau deine Seele Gott!*," which translates, "Your sword for the leader, your heart for the wife, your soul to God." The grip is a dark orange *Trolon*.

Army 0fficer dagger with number "80" unit marking by Robert Klaas. This is a typical Robert Klaas production dress dagger which has asterisks on the side of the scabbard bands. The reverse crossguard has a gilted number "80" professionally applied, complete with small pins which fold down on the back of the crossguard.

Pictured is the Personalized *Generalfeldmarschall* Gerd von Rundstedt Army officer dagger with double-etched blade. This rare dagger was acquired in 1995 by bid from the Hermann Historica Auction House in Munich, Germany. The dagger was placed in auction by a doctor from the Munich area, along with a number of other military belongings of *Generalfeldmarschall* von Rundstedt.

▶

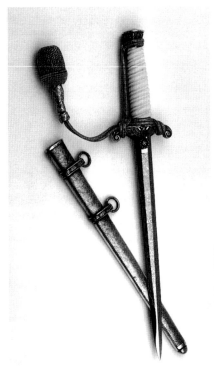

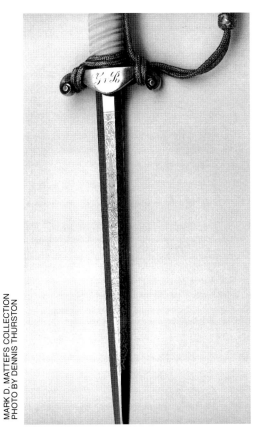

The reverse blade of the *General-feldmarschall* von Rundstedt Person-alized Army Officer Dagger. While the blade is not maker-marked, the etch pattern appears to be from Emil Voos. *Generalfeldmarschall* von Rundstedt's initials, "G. v. R." are professionally engraved on the reverse crossguard. The white grip is genuine ivory, and the dagger is pictured complete with its accompanying silver portepee.

Personalized Army officer dagger by Carl Eickhorn. The dark orange *Trolon* grip appears nearly black in this black and white photograph. The reverse crossguard is uniquely jeweler engraved with the original owner's rank and last name, "*Obltn*. Adolph" (1st Lieutenant Adolph). This desirable dress dagger is complete with its original portepee (in a correct Army "tie"), standard Army officer dagger hangers, original clover-shaped leather belt attachment, and the brown waist belt with leather tongue and nickel-silver roller buckle.

▶

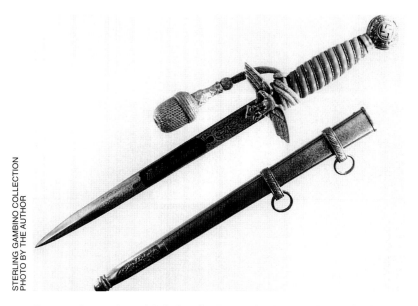

Presentation 2nd model *Luftwaffe* dagger by Robert Klaas—full-length, obverse view. The obverse blade is nicely etched featuring a floral pattern with the owner's full name, "Wilhelm Brittendorf," on a raised inscription in the center of a blued panel.

Close-up view of the obverse blade etching on the presentation 2nd model *Luftwaffe* dagger by Robert Klaas. The original owner's full name, "Wilhelm Brittendorf," appears in a raised signature facsimile on a blued panel. Presentation *Luftwaffe* daggers bearing the owner's full name are quite rare and highly desirable.

Extreme close-up view of the blued panel and floral etching appearing on the obverse blade of the Wilhelm Brittendorf presentation 2nd model *Luftwaffe* Dagger by Robert Klaas.

Detailed view of the Robert Klaas "kissing cranes" trademark on the reverse blade ricasso of the Wilhelm Brittendorf presentation 2nd Model *Luftwaffe* dagger. A beautiful floral etching decorates the reverse blade. ▶

Personalized 1933 SA dagger belonging to Oskar Lemke. This superb personalized SA dagger bears an unattributed "R&K" within a crown trademark. The early nickel-silver lower cross-guard features a sunwheel swastika deeply engraved on both sides and the original owner's full name, "Oskar Lemke," beautifully jeweler-engraved in the center. Although not visible in the photograph, the reverse upper scabbard fitting is engraved with, "*Treue um Treue*" and "St. 2/1."

◀

Another example of a presentation inscription located on the reverse upper scabbard fitting of an SA dagger. This dagger bears *RZM 7/49*, which indicates that it was manufactured by the Friedrich Herder Company in Solingen. The presentation reads *"Wettkampfe der SA-Gr. Südwest 1938."* This translates in English as "Competitions of the SA Group Southwest 1938." Note the consistency of the "S" (*Schlesien*) group mark and the *RZM* stamping on the leather hanger.

Excellent example of a personalized RAD officer's dagger by Ernst Erich Witte. Both the reverse crossguard and the reverse upper scabbard are personalized with the monogram of the original owner whose initials are "LH."

Excellent example of a personalized RAD officer's dagger by Ernst Erich Witte. Both the reverse crossguard and the reverse upper scabbard are personalized with the monogram of the original owner whose initials are "LH." The Ernst Erich Witte firm utilized a "crown over 'W' inside a diamond" trademark which is visible on the reverse ricasso of the blade.

◀

Close-up view of the rear crossguard and rear upper scabbard "LH" monogram on the personalized RAD officer dagger by Ernst Erich Witte.

▶

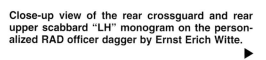

THIRD REICH DRESS SWORDS

Rare Third Reich double-engraved presentation sword. This deluxe Eickhorn *Scharnhorst* pattern saber features pink jewel-like eyes and a closed-wing Army eagle/swastika on the langet. This example features a rare double-engraved Third Reich period blade. The obverse blade is engraved with a floral panel with a Third Reich helmet and crossed rifles within a wreath of oak leaves and a two-line raised presentation to the original owner, *Feldwebel* Georg Schmidt. The saber is pictured with its original sword knot in a correct "tie."

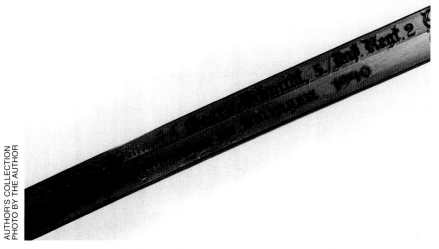

Extreme close-up of the two-line raised presentation appearing on the obverse blade of the Georg Schmidt double-engraved Third Reich presentation sword. The raised two-line presentation is translated, "To *Feldwebel* Georg Schmidt, 5th Company, Infantry Regiment 2. A Souvenir of Solingen 1940." More than likely, the original owner was an employee in one of the numerous Solingen edged weapon factories.

The reverse blade of the Georg Schmidt double-engraved Third Reich presentation sword features a floral panel with a closed-wing Army eagle/swastika. In the center of the reverse blade is a German motto which translates, "To be German is to be called a fighter."

Unusual lion head saber with Silver Eagle/Swastika on the crossguard by Richard Herder. The crossguard on this sword is quite unique in that it features a silver-plated eagle, which is an integral part of the langet. The short-winged, political-style eagle shows nice definition with the swastika in its talons surrounded by oak leaves and acorns. ◀

Extreme close-up view of the reverse crossguard and langet of the unusual lion head saber with silver eagle/swastika on the obverse crossguard. The R. Herder, Solingen trademark is clearly visible on the reverse blade ricasso. ▶

Extremely rare Richard Herder Model number 1017 Army officer sword. This quality sword is considered by many German edged weapon collectors to be the most ornate model Army sword produced under the Third Reich. Note that the celluloid grip on this unusual sword has only seven grooves for wire wrapping, whereas the majority of Third Reich swords feature ten grooves. The hand-chiseled, ornate lion head pommel features swirls and a raised motif which appears to emulate a sea serpent. A highly stylized closed-wing Third Reich eagle is prominent on the obverse langet. ▶

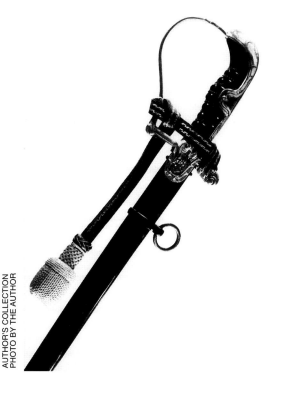

Rare unattributed Richard Herder Army officer sword. The specimen pictured is the *sole* example of this rare sword model observed by this author to date. A similar Richard Herder model featuring a panther head hilt was used on the cover of one of the Herder Company 1930's sales catalogs and is pictured on page 144 of **Volume I.** The crossguard features a highly stylized closed-wing *silver* eagle/swastika.

◀

Close-up view of the obverse hilt of the rare unattributed Army officer sword by Richard Herder. Note the highly unusual crossguard and backstrap. The highly stylized closed-wing *silver* eagle/swastika are an integral part of the crossguard. The celluloid grip features a triple wire wrap with an extended area near the base. Almost 100% of the original factory gilting remains on the hilt.

Close-up view of the reverse hilt of the rare unattributed Army officer sword by Richard Herder. The extended area at the base of the celluloid grip is clearly visible in this picture. The Richard Herder 4-pointed star is stamped on the reverse blade ricasso.

Unissued *"Prinz Eugen"* Field Marshal sword by Carl Eickhorn. This unique condition saber is in its factory new, unissued condition and is still complete with the original red metal Eickhorn quality control tag and Eickhorn protective paper wrap on the metal scabbard. The *"Prinz Eugen"* model number, "Nr. 1765," can be observed between the Eickhorn squirrel trademark and the Third Reich eagle/swastika on the paper scabbard wrap.

The unissued *"Prinz Eugen"* Field Marshal sword by Carl Eickhorn is pictured atop its original felt issue bag. This unique condition saber is in its factory-new, unissued condition and is still complete with the original red metal Eickhorn quality control tag and Eickhorn protective paper wrap on the metal scabbard.

▶

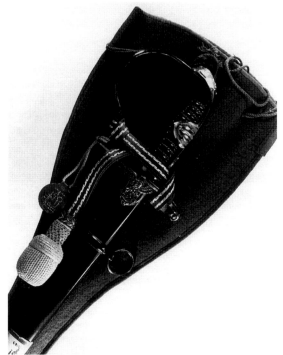

Close-up obverse view of the Eickhorn factory scabbard protective paper wrap on the unissued *"Prinz Eugen"* Sword. The *"Prinz Eugen"* model number, "Nr. 1765," is positioned between the Eickhorn "squirrel holding sword" trademark and the Third Reich eagle/swastika. The diagonal colored band reads (translated), "Original Eickhorn Model *Prinz Eugen* from our Field Marshal Series."

◀

The General Dietrich von Criegern 2nd model *Luftwaffe* dagger is pictured in color—obverse view. The General's last name is engraved in an oval between the two scabbard bands on the reverse side of the scabbard. The blade is artificial Damascus. For complete details on this personalized dagger refer to Appendix 1 in this volume.

The chained SA High Leader's honor dagger belonging to collector William Laret is pictured out of the scabbard—obverse view. The blade, like all of the SA High Leader pieces, is "maiden hair" pattern genuine Damascus steel which features a raised gold SA motto with a single gold oak leaf at each end. This high-quality color photograph provides an outstanding view of the SA High Leader chained hanger, brown leather scabbard, and belt loop.

Although SA dagger examples are occasionally encountered still with factory issue tags, it is rare to see NSKK examples. The original riveted triangular tags are secured around the upper portion of the grips. The reverse tags bear a purple rubber-stamped code, "M7/37," indicating manufacture by the Robert Klaas factory. Pictured behind the two daggers is the original packing tissue.

Outstanding color photograph of the reverse blade of an SS Himmler dedication dagger by Carl Eickhorn (Sole Manufacturer). Details on this rare model dagger are available on pages 20-22 of **Volume V.** The top quality example pictured was acquired by the late Lindsey Wilson from a WWII Army veteran residing in Colorado, along with the SS officer's sword pictured on page 166 of **Volume I.** Both sidearms were "liberated" by the veteran from the same SS officer's quarters during 1945. Note the gold tint barely visible in the Himmler inscription and the yellow-toned scabbard fittings (observed on several other original Himmler daggers).

A 1936 chained SS dagger complete with the original owner's SS Number "314532" stamped on the obverse crossguard.

Undoubtedly, two of the most desirable SS edged weapons to have survived World War II are the unique, silver SS honor sword presented to Sepp Dietrich (the subject of Chapter 7 in **Volume IV** of this series) and the SS honor dagger with raised oak leaves and acorns on the hilt and scabbard fittings, formerly reposing in the internationally known Dr. Julian Milestone collection.

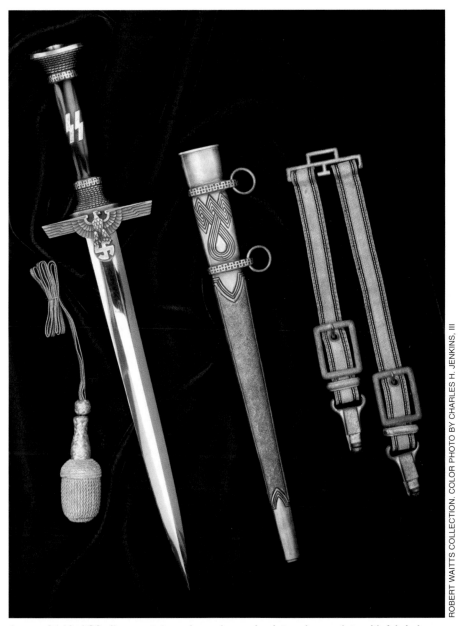

A one-of-a-kind SS silver prototype dress dagger is pictured, complete with fabric hangers and portepee. The maker of this unique piece was the large Alcoso firm in Solingen. A similar SS prototype dagger from the same firm was covered in detail on pages 266-268 of **Volume II** of this series.

Color photograph of the RAD officer's prototype dagger by Richard Herder which was featured on pages 207 and 212 of **Volume I.** This hewer utilized the standard 1937 RAD leader's dagger as its basic pattern, but incorporated mother-of-pearl grip plates and a very distinctive variation eagle and swastika crossguard. While many have labeled this unique dagger a reproduction, the author does not believe this to be true.

Pictured for the first time in a contemporary reference work is a cased Hitler Youth leader's dagger, hangers, and beltloop belonging to the author. The maker of the dagger is E. & F. Hörster (*RZM M7/36*).

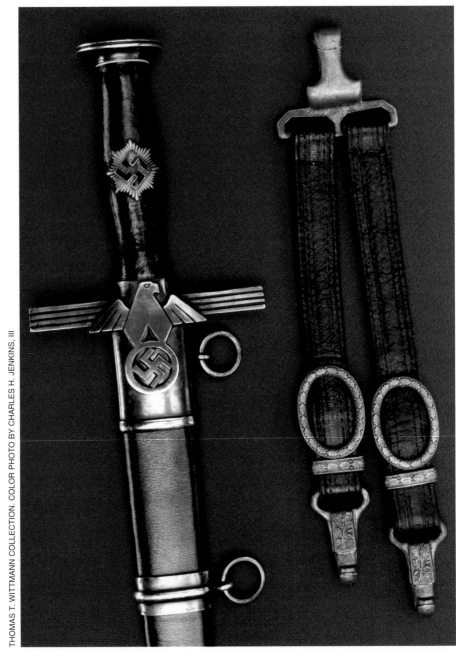

The 2nd model *RLB* leader's dagger and hangers are pictured in color—obverse view. See chapter 2 of this volume for complete details on the *RLB* sidearms.

ROBERT WAITTS COLLECTION. COLOR PHOTO BY CHARLES H. JENKINS, III

A complete set of the four standard issue *RLB* dress daggers in exceptional condition is pictured. From left to right are the 1st Model Leader, the 1st Model Subordinate, the 2nd Model Leader, and the 2nd Model Subordinate.

191

A 1938 *Bahnschutz* (Railway Leader) dress dagger is pictured, complete with accompanying black and silver fabric dress hangers and portepee. Note that the hangers feature the rectangular style buckles.

Beautiful close-up study of the one-of-a-kind Hermann Göring jeweled hunting dagger discussed in Chapter 3. Although this spectacular sidearm has been covered in detail in the previous volumes of this series, this is the first time that the reverse scabbard has been shown. This richly decorated hunting dagger, presented to Göring by his brother-in-law, Count Eric von Rosen, features numerous precious stones and period photographs of Göring wearing the dagger are available on pages 298 and 307 of **Volume III**.

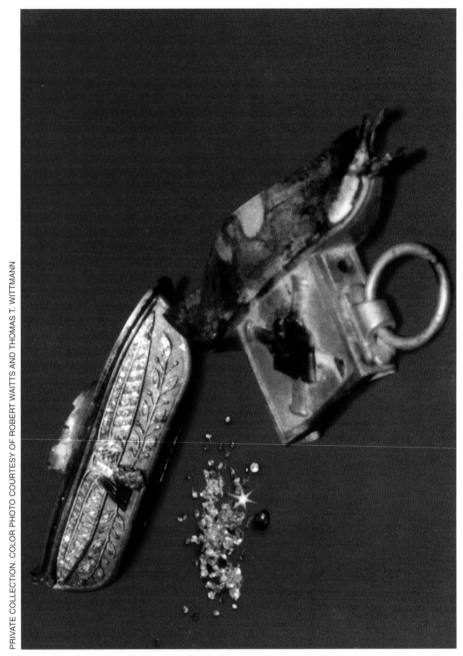

PRIVATE COLLECTION. COLOR PHOTO COURTESY OF ROBERT WAITTS AND THOMAS T. WITTMANN

Practically all that remains of the priceless Hermann Göring *Reichsmarschall* dress dagger can be seen in this color photograph. Pictured together are the damaged obverse crossguard on the left and the upper scabbard fitting on the right. Visible between the two damaged parts are a number of the many precious stones removed from the Göring dagger. Note the severe damage to the upper scabbard fitting. Consider what "might have been" by comparing this color photograph to the other bejeweled Göring hunting dagger appearing on the preceding page! Complete details on the capture and destruction of this one-of-a-kind valuable artifact are available in Chapter 3 of this reference.

Obverse and reverse views of an original 2nd model Navy honor dagger pommel with 17 rose-cut diamond chips inset in the Swastika. A number of these original Naval honor pommels were acquired from *Herr* Helmut Eickhorn by James P. Atwood circa 1960's. A letter exists in the files of Johnson Reference Books from *Herr* Eickhorn verifying the authenticity of these leftover Naval honor pommels.

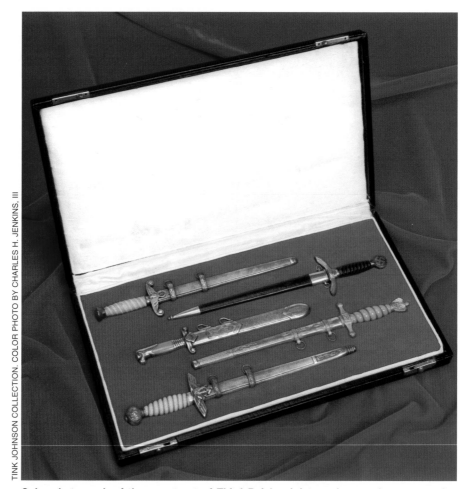

Color photograph of the rarest set of Third Reich miniature daggers known to exist. Pictured is an original Alcoso firm salesman sample kit of large miniature Alcoso sidearms. The kit includes an Army officer's dagger, a *Luftwaffe* sword, a RAD officer's dagger, a 2nd model Navy dagger, and a 2nd model *Luftwaffe* dagger.

Pictured for the first time in a contemporary reference book are the six portepees correctly worn with the *TENO* Enlisted Hewer. They are identified from left to right as Standby Service Enlisted, Stand-by Service NCO, Technical Service NCO, Technical Service Enlisted, General Service NCO, and General Service Enlisted. Note that the color combinations remain the same for the NCO and EM services.

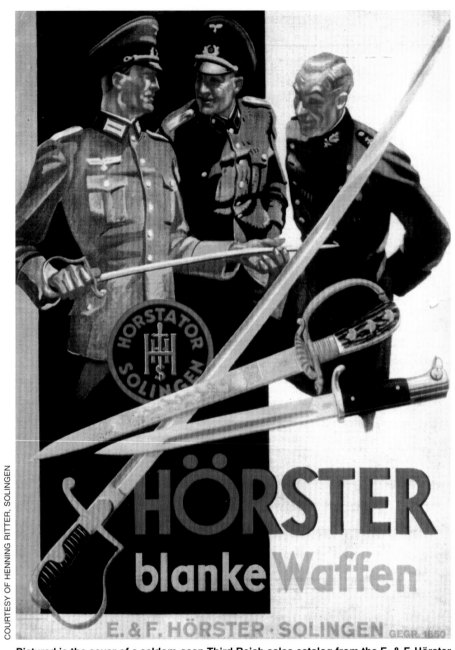

Pictured is the cover of a seldom-seen Third Reich sales catalog from the E. & F. Hörster Firm in Solingen. A complete copy of this rare catalog is on file at Johnson Reference Books.

Third Reich Fire Police lion head presentation sword. This rare sword, located by the author in the former East Germany (DDR), features outstanding definition to a silvered aluminum lion head hilt complete with red glass eyes. The black celluloid grip has its triple-twisted wire wrap intact. The obverse crossguard is complete with a Third Reich eagle/swastika with outstretched wings. The obverse blade features a floral motif with the center panel having a three-line engraved presentation. Sword is complete with its original red and silver Fire Police sword knot.

◀

Close-up view of the obverse engraved blade of the rare Third Reich Fire Police lion head presentation sword. The three-line engraved presentation appearing on the center blade panel translates, "To R. Treen from the Comrades of the Fire Police, the City of Hennickendorf." This town is located southwest of Berlin in the former East Germany (DDR). Pictured alongside the obverse blade is the red and silver acorn of the original Fire Police sword knot.

Puma Salesman lion head sword sample. This specimen is complete with red glass eyes and still retains the original metal Puma quality control tag. The same trademark on the quality control tag is also stamped on the reverse blade ricasso. An excellent write-up on sword hilt salesman samples is available in the June 1991 *MAX Gazette*, pp. 12-15.

▶

Outstanding Major Julius Liebrecht Damascus *Luftwaffe* presentation sword by Alcoso. The genuine Damascus steel blade features a three-line raised dedication on the obverse positioned between two raised *Luftwaffe* eagles.

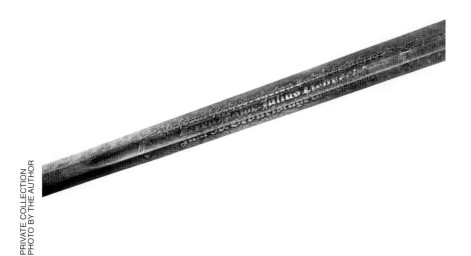

Close-up detail of the three-line raised dedication on the Major Julius Liebrecht Damascus *Luftwaffe* presentation sword. This beautiful presentation sword was presented to Major Liebrecht on his 50th birthday.

The ornate pommel on the Major Julius Liebrecht *Luftwaffe* presentation sword is encircled with gilted oak leaves and acorns.

◄

Positioned on the reverse blade ricasso of the Major Liebrecht Damascus *Luftwaffe* presentation sword is a raised Alcoso "scales" Solingen trademark.

►

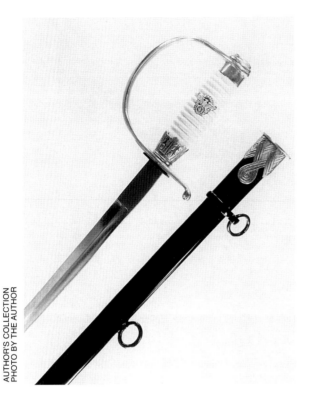

Unusual Police NCO *Degen* with a *White* Grip. This side-arm was acquired, as is, in Czechoslovakia after the fall of the Berlin Wall. The white grip paint is very old, and it is doubtful that this change was made after World War II. Most likely, this Police NCO sword accompanied the German delegation to Japan during 1938. The scabbard paint is a professional repaint.

◄

Double-etched presentation Police NCO *Degen* by Peter Daniel Krebs. This extremely rare sword was veteran acquired in the state of North Carolina by advanced collector Carter Jennette. Both the scabbard throat and the bottom of the crossguard/knuckle-bow are SS stamped.

►

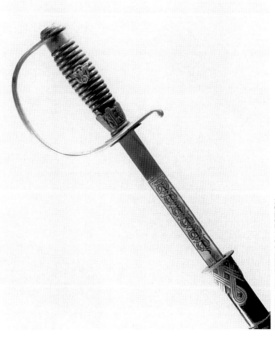

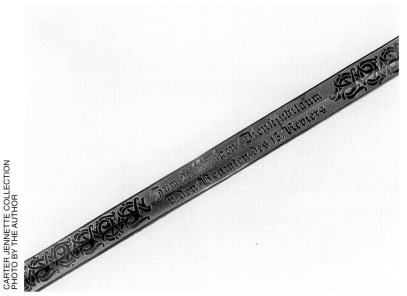

Close-Up View of the Raised Dedication Appearing on the Obverse Blade on the Double-Etched Presentation Police NCO *Degen* by Peter Daniel Krebs. The raised dedication reads, *"Zum 25 Jährigen Dienst-Jubilaum V. Den Beamten Des 13. Reviers"* (For the 25th Year Service Anniversary from Officials of the 13th Precinct). Presentation Police swords are extremely rare.

Detail of the Peter Daniel Krebs "crayfish" trademark on the double-etched presentation Police NCO *Degen*. Note the quality of the stunning blade etch. The SS stamping on the scabbard throat is also barely visible in this photograph.

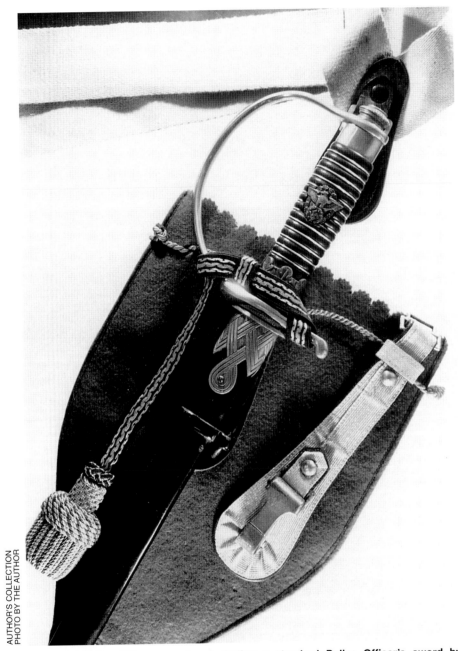

Complete Police Officer grouping including a standard Police Officer's sword by Hermann Rath, a black leather teardrop hanger, an alternate silver bullion teardrop hanger, an over-the-shoulder cloth hanging device, and an original felt carrying/storage bag. This entire assemblage was purchased in Germany from its original owner.

Personalized SS/Police NCO *Degen* by F. W. Höller. The original owner of this sword was Helmut Kordts, *Sturmbannführer*, 4th SS/Police Grenadier Division. The pommel cap is complete with raised SS runes. Deeply etched into the obverse blade is the SS motto, "*Meine Ehre heisst Treue.*" It is interesting to note that Kordts is listed in the 1944 SS ranklist as a *Sturmbannführer* and had not been presented an SS *Degen*. Thus, the Police Officer *Degen* was the correct sword for him to carry.

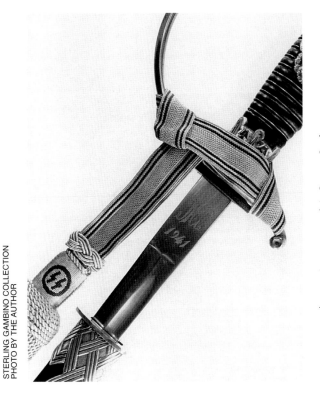

The obverse blade ricasso of the personalized SS/Police officer *Degen* by F.W. Höller. Professionally engraved in shadowed script are the owner's initials, "H.K." and the date, "1941". Although not visible in the photograph, both the underside of the cross-guard and the scabbard throat are stamped with SS proofmarks.

◄

Extremely rare double-engraved SS officer candidate sword complete with SS officer sword knot.

►

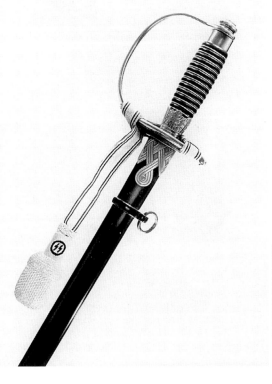

206

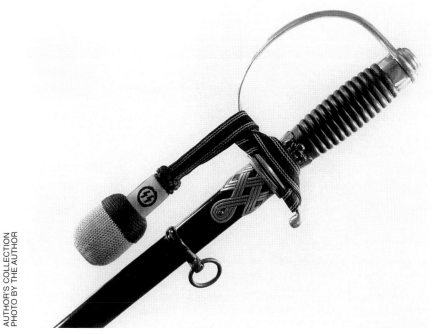

SS NCO *Degen* **by Peter Daniel Krebs—obverse view. Attached to the crossguard and ferrule is the original SS NCO sword knot featuring two thin tan lines on each side of a black cloth strap. The off-white stem has SS runes within a circle on both the obverse and the reverse. The flat nickel pommel cap is decorated with convexed runes within an oval with a black background.**

The SS NCO *Degen* **by Peter Daniel Krebs—reverse view. The original cloth** *RZM* **control tag can be seen sewn on the inside of the portepee strap. The overall condition of the specimen pictured is near mint.**

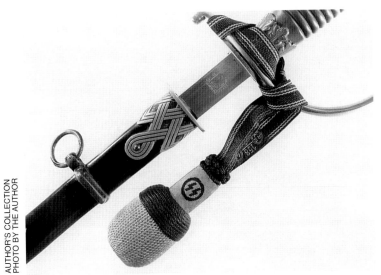

Close-up view of the SS sword knot and manufacturer's trademark on the SS NCO *Degen* by Peter Daniel Krebs. Inside the sword knot strap is the original cloth control tag which is "*RZM* 158 35" marked with SS runes in a circle. The white leather SS sword buffer pad is visible under the crossguard. The Peter Daniel Krebs "crayfish" trademark is stamped on the reverse blade ricasso.

Early brass SS lion head sword by WKC, Complete with black leather hanger and early SS Silver and Black Sword Knot. The original owner's initials, "FC," are stamped on the reverse langet. The Army-style lion head pommel is embellished with red glass eyes.

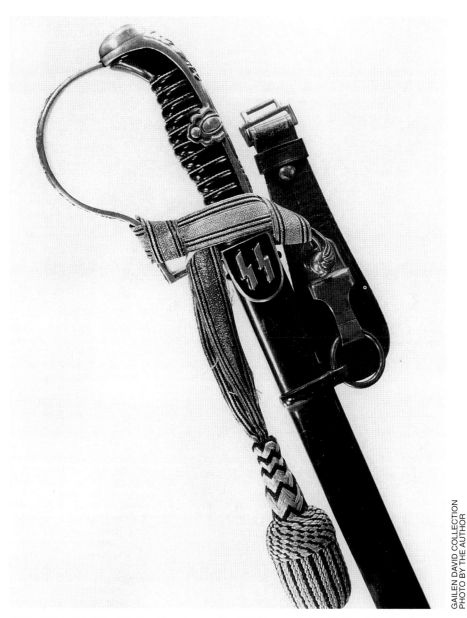

Ultra-rare early silver SS dove head sword by WKC, complete with black leather hanger and early SS silver and black sword knot. This seldom-seen early SS saber model is the WKC model number 1013. This model SS sword is shown in the equally rare early WKC sales catalog with the *gold* knight head on the cover. The leather hanger is *"D.R.G.M."* stamped on the metal fastener.

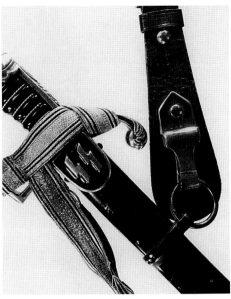

The ultra-rare early silver SS model number 1013 by WKC is pictured—reverse view. Note the overall superior condition to include the accouterments. A truly exceptional grouping.

Extreme close-up view of the WKC model Number 1013 Early Silver SS Sword. Note that all of the black enamel on the obverse langet remains intact. The "*D.R.G.M.*" stamping on the leather hanger metal fastener is clearly visible in this close-up photograph.

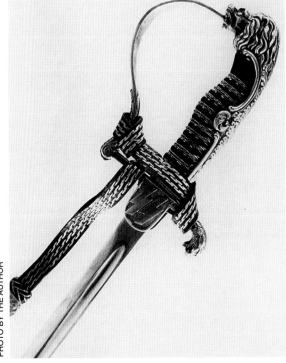
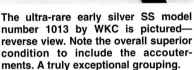

Early silver SS officer Saber by Malsch & Ambronn. Pictured is an example of an early SS sword manufactured in the village of Steinbach located in the former East Germany (DDR). A chapter was devoted to Steinbach "The Other Solingen" manufacturers in **Volume VII** of this series. The nickel-silver lion head pommel is accented with green glass eyes. The obverse langet features raised, gilted SS runes on a stippled background. The underside of the crossguard is SS proofmarked.

◀

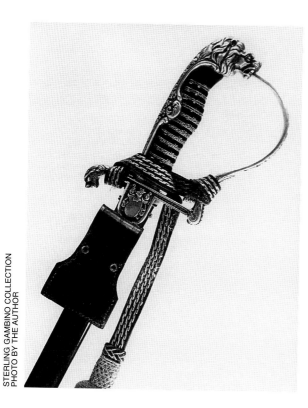

The early silver SS officer saber by Malsch & Ambronn is pictured—reverse view. Note the superb detail on the lion head pommel, oak leaf knuckle-bow and lion head crossguard quillion. Also of interest are the crest on the reverse langet and the unusual black leather belt attachment.

◄

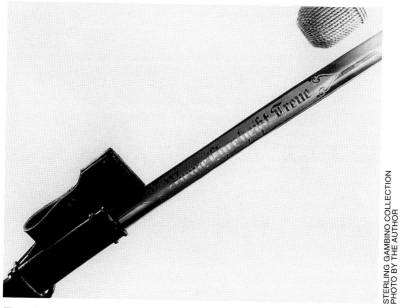

The obverse plated blade on the early silver SS officer saber by Malsch & Ambronn is beautifully etched with the SS Motto, "*Meine Ehre heisst Treue*" (My Honor is Loyalty) in raised Gothic letters on a deeply etched and frosted panel background.

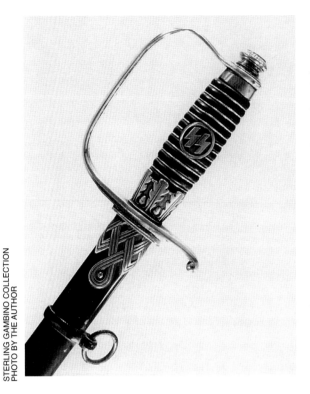

SS honor sword presented to *SS Obergrüppenführer* Wilhelm Reinhard—obverse hilt. All hilt and scabbard fittings are .800 fine German silver. Wilhelm Reinhard was born on 18 March 1869 in the town of Lutau on the German-Polish border. He was awarded the *Pour Le Merite* (Blue Max) during WWI. On 11 November 1941 he was promoted to *SS Obergrüppenführer* and assigned to the staff of *Reichsführer SS* Heinrich Himmler. In addition to the SS honor sword, Reinhard was also awarded the Golden Party badge and the *SS Totenkopf* honor ring.

◀

The Wilhelm Reinhard SS honor sword—reverse hilt. This ultra-rare sword surfaced in the state of California during 1994. As evident in this close-up photograph, the condition is exceptional. Note the superb quality of the handcrafted silver hilt fittings.

▶

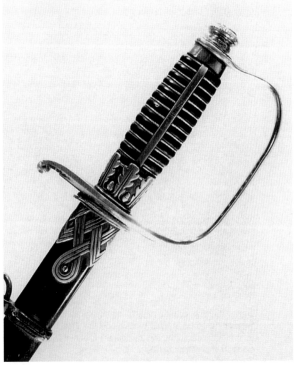

The obverse blade of the Wilhelm Reinhard SS honor sword. The obverse Turkish Damascus blade bears the dedicated presentation to Wilhelm Reinhard in raised letters, with Himmler's signature in facsimile, with the whole of the inscription flanked by two swastikas. Paul Müller handcrafted all of the SS honor sword blades in the Turkish Damascus pattern, which was acknowledged to be the most difficult to create and, therefore, the costliest. The Müller blades consisted of four *Tortieren* horizontal levels of Damascus steel, and these four levels are visible in this close-up photograph.

The SS honor *Degen* and original sword knot presented to Werner Lorenz by the *Reichsführer*-SS, Heinrich Himmler.

A very unusual personalized Army-style SS Saber by Carl Eickhorn, complete with unique crossguard and artificial Damascus steel blade. The original wearer of the saber was Kurt Göritz and his full name appears in raised gold letters on the obverse blade.

Detail of the unique (and unidentified) crest on the obverse crossguard langet. Note the discreet SS runes superimposed over the left wing of the eagle. Also of interest is the fact that the hilt fittings are in a gold and not a silver wash.

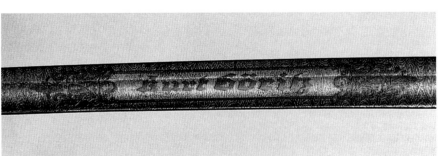

The obverse artificial Damascus steel blade on the unusual Army-style SS saber by Carl Eickhorn features the original owner's full name, Kurt Göritz, in raised gold letters. Although not visible in this photograph, the Eickhorn trademark on the blade is the "squirrel holding sword" mark.

Detail of the hilt backstrap on the unusual Army-style SS saber by Carl Eickhorn. A unique eagle and swastika is centered on the backstrap.

◀

Rare Water Customs sword complete with correct accouterments. An edged weapons distributor's trademark, "A. Luneburg, Kiel," is stamped on the blade ricasso. This rare model Third Reich sword has not been pictured or described in any current reference material. The gilt hilt features a stylized lion head with red and green glass eyes, an oak-leaf embellished flat knuckle-bow and an angular-shaped langet with open-wing eagle. The sword is pictured complete with the accompanying double-strapped black leather hangers with lion head buckles and a black leather sword knot with triple silver bullion lines.

▶

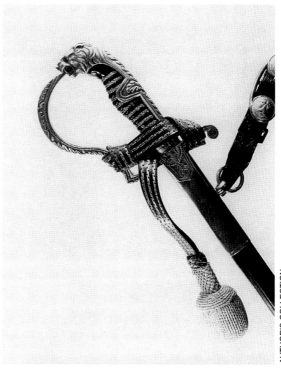

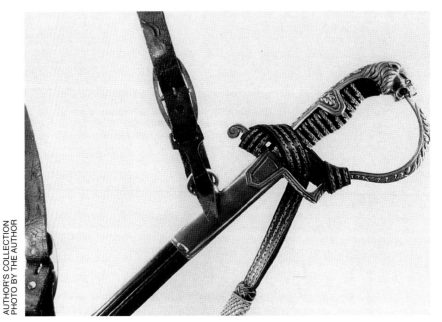

The rare Water Customs sword complete with correct accouterments—reverse view. The black leather scabbard is fitted with three plain brass scabbard fittings attached with brass "staples." Although not visible in the photograph, the silver sword knot acorn "dot" is black to match the scabbard leather and the sword knot leather strap.

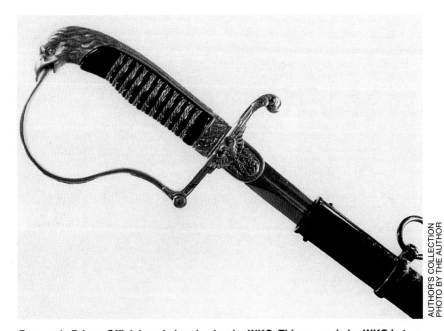

Rare early Prison Official eagle head saber by WKC. This example by WKC is typified by the distinctive design of the brass eagle head pommel. The obverse crossguard langet features a Third Reich eagle with outstretched wings with a swastika in its talons.

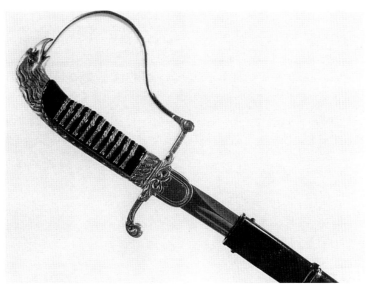

The rare early Prison Official eagle head saber by WKC—reverse view. The black celluloid grip is complete with a triple wire wrap. The WKC "knight head" trademark is stamped under the reverse langet.

High-quality Prison Official saber by Carl Eickhorn, complete with original *Wehrmacht* (Army) sword knot—obverse hilt. The saber pictured belonged to Karl Hoffmann, *Heeresgefangnis Der 4 Armee* (Army Prison of the 4th Army).

Pictured is the reverse hilt of the Karl Hoffmann Prison Official saber by Carl Eickhorn. Note that the reverse hilt is an exact "mirror image" of the obverse hilt.

THIRD REICH DRESS BAYONETS

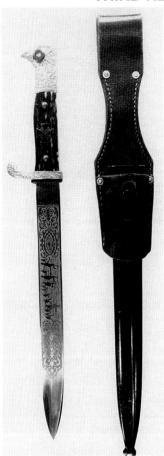

Gilted deluxe shooting award presentation bayonet by Carl Eickhorn—full-length, obverse, out-of-scabbard view. This rare presentation bayonet was presented by the 11th Infantry Company headquartered in Düsseldorf. The obverse blade etch features rushing infantry troops.

◄

Close-up view of the obverse blade on the gilted deluxe shooting award presentation blade by Carl Eickhorn. An English translation of the three-line raised dedication reads, "For the best marksman of our Tradition Battalion's (unit used for parades and ceremonial occasions) 11th Company *Reichsbund* (literally Empire organization/association), formerly the 99th registered society, Düsseldorf."

Detail of the exquisite blade etching and the stamped Carl Eickhorn "squirrel holding sword" trademark on the gilted deluxe shooting award presentation bayonet.

▼

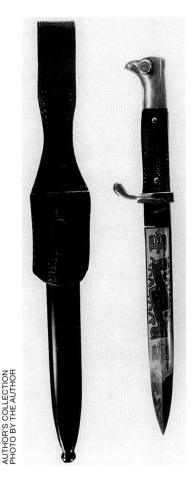

Rare Carl Eickhorn single-engraved Army dress bayonet model number 3219. This desirable short model Army dress bayonet was purchased from WWII veteran Richard Gulick who served as a Lieutenant in the 17th Airborne Division. The bayonet features a beautiful engraved "frosted" panel with a Third Reich closed-wing Army eagle at each end. The raised ribbon bearing the standard, "In Remembrance of my Service Time" (translated), has a *blue/green* background. The bayonet is complete with a quality black pigskin leather hanging frog.

◄

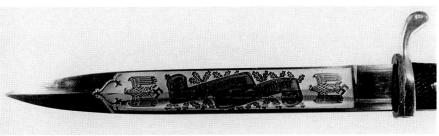

Close-up of the obverse blade of the rare Eickhorn single-engraved Army dress bayonet model number 3219. The scroll bears the standard, "In Remembrance of my Service Time" (translated), on an unusual *blue/green* ribbon with a frosted background panel. This exact blade engraving motif is pictured in the Carl Eickhorn *Kundendienst* catalog.

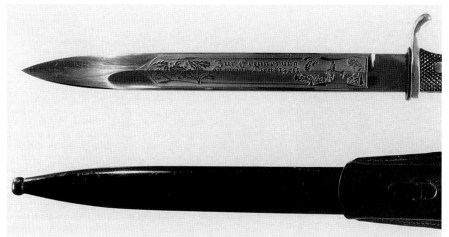

Single-engraved long model *Luftwaffe* dress bayonet by E. Pack & *Söhne*. The obverse blade on this E. Pack dress bayonet features a beautiful frosted panel with the standard service, "In remembrance of my service time" motto, a German biplane, oak leaves and acorns. Note the offset lower grip lug which was characteristic of the E. Pack firm. The black metal scabbard is shown complete with its original dark brown leather frog.

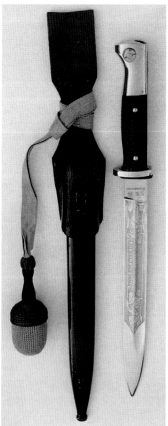

Army pioneer dress bayonet with single-etched blade by E. Pack & *Söhne*—full-length, obverse view. Note that in addition to the standard Pack infantry etch, the obverse ricasso is etched, "I.R. 24 Braunsberg, OSTP." Another interesting feature is the absence of the typical offset spanner nuts and rivets used by the E. Pack firm.

▶

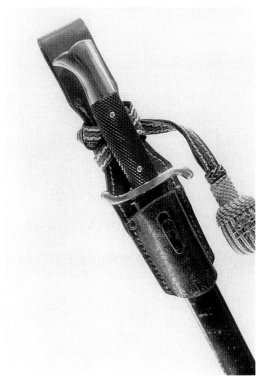

Long model fireman dress bayonet complete with hilt stamping and unusual bayonet knot. The reverse blade ricasso is deeply stamped, *"HORST WOLFF, G.M.B.H., LEIPZIG CI"* (most likely a distributor and not a manufacturer). This sidearm was veteran purchased in Atlanta, Georgia, complete with the pictured black leather frog and original Police NCO knot with a unique Fireman's metal emblem attached to the portepee ball.

◄

Long model fireman dress bayonet complete with hilt stamping and unusual bayonet knot—reverse view. The stamping on the reverse blade ricasso is, *"HORST WOLFF, G.M.B.H. LEIPZIG CI."* The reverse of the original black leather frog is stamped, "RF NR. 0/0494/0008."

►

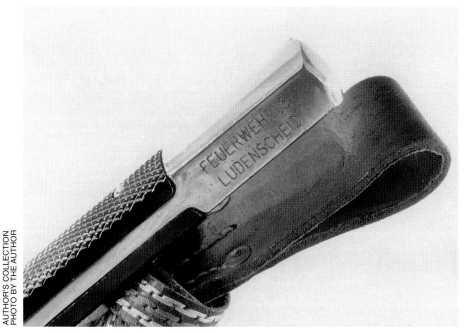

The flat portion of the hilt backstrap of the long model fireman dress bayonet from Leipzig is stamped with the Fire Department's number and location, *"FEUERWEHR 3 LUDENSCHEID."* The town of Ludenscheid is well-known to German blade collectors as it is nearby Solingen and was to dagger accouterments what Solingen was to dagger blades.

Extreme close-up photograph of the highly unusual bayonet porte-pee on the long fireman dress bayonet from Leipzig. The original Police NCO bayonet knot attached is the standard green/silver ball with a red/silver/black leather strap. A metal Fireman's emblem featuring a gilted Fire/Police helmet with crossed axes and ladder is attached to the bayonet knot ball.

▶

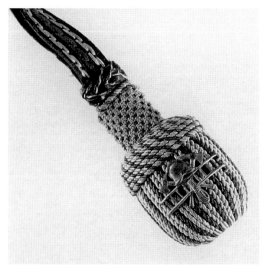

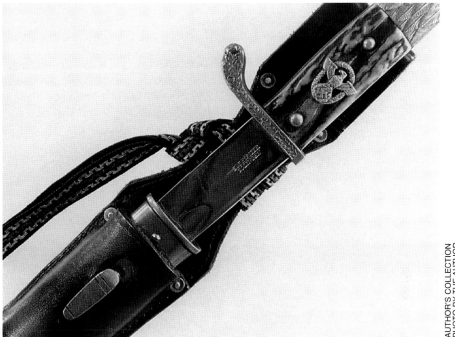

Long-slotted police bayonet by E.&F. Hörster. The Hörster firm's trademarks appear on both the obverse and the reverse blade ricasso. The bayonet is pictured complete with a black leather frog stamped with the date, "1939" and a police NCO bayonet knot.

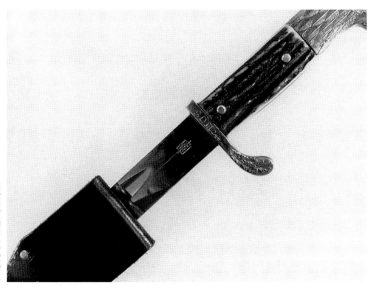

The long-slotted police bayonet by E.&F. Hörster is pictured—reverse view. The reverse crossguard is deeply stamped, "S.D. 111 244" (Municipal police property, Administrative District Arnsberg, Duty Station III, Weapon #244). A red felt plug is present in the slotted lug.

The rare SS security police bayonet. This long dress bayonet was reputedly worn by members of the SS Police Security Unit and the maker of the specimen shown was Alexander Coppel, Solingen. The bayonet scabbard is blued anodized seamless steel. Note the very detailed and intricate oak leaf engraving on the hilt fittings. The specimen shown is complete with black leather frog and silver portepee with black stripes. Detailed information on this extremely rare bayonet can be found on pages 262-264 of *Volume IV* of *Collecting the Edged Weapons of the Third Reich.*

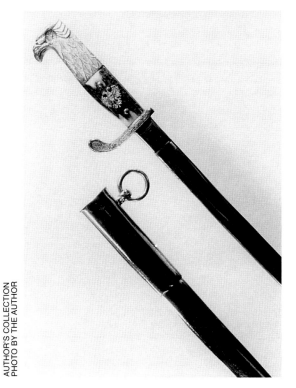

City of Lubeck Third Reich Police dress bayonet. This *extremely* rare Nazi-era police bayonet features a City of Lubeck double-headed Reich eagle pinned to the obverse stag grip plate. The city of Lubeck, Germany, was an independent city during the 1930s, similar to Hamburg. Thus, separate and distinctive sidearms were issued. Note the nickel-plated standard police-style eagle head pommel and oak leaf embellished crossguard. The scabbard is unique in that it is carried by a suspension ring rather than the more common scabbard lug.

◀

Detail of the obverse hilt of the City of Lubeck Third Reich Police dress bayonet. A silver washed City of Lubeck double-headed Reich eagle is pinned to the obverse stag grip plate. Note the exquisite detail of the embellished pommel and crossguard. The single scabbard suspension ring is also visible.

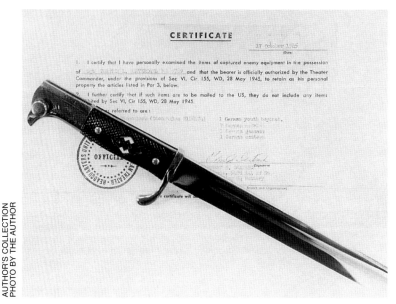

Rare Hitler Youth bayonet by Carl Eickhorn. Although many edged weapon collectors have doubted the authenticity of this model dress bayonet, the one pictured was veteran-acquired and is complete with the official U.S. Army WWII "bring-back" certificate dated 17 October 1945 authorizing the U.S. serviceman to retain "1 German Youth Bayonet" as his personal property.

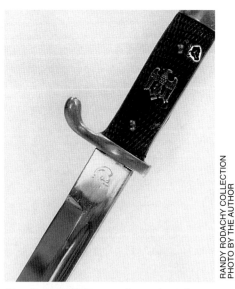

Possible RAD prototype bayonet by SMF—full-length, obverse view. Edged weapon collector Denny Matheney of Ohio states that this unusual sidearm was purchased directly from a World War II veteran along with several other German relics. The overall length is 13-1/4 inches. The well-known SMF "king's profile" trademark is visible directly under the clamshell.

Standard WWII German Army dress bayonet with a closed-wing Army eagle on the obverse grip and an unusual fire helmet trademark on the obverse blade ricasso.

Example of an early *Postschutz* (postal) dress bayonet by WKC. The *Postschutz* insignia is *perfectly* inset into the obverse checkered grip plate; i.e., note the absence of any gaps surrounding the grip insignia. Since this bayonet was purchased, as is, by the author in 1996 from a private source in Germany for less than twenty dollars, its authenticity would be difficult to question. The original postal insignia alone would be worth several times the price paid for the complete bayonet.

◄

THIRD REICH DRESS WEAPON ACCOUTERMENTS

Army officer dagger hangers were sold through military speciality shops in cardboard cartons as pictured. The English translation of the verbiage on the carton label is, "Army Officer's dagger hangers, D.R.G.M. with movable bar slides. Fits every position of wear of the dagger." Original hanger issue cartons are *extremely* rare.

Extreme close-up of the "Krauss, Böblingen" stock paper original issue tag which is wire attached to the upper hanger clip. The issue tag is stamped with the manufacturer's inventory number, "G875/3" and original price, 2.75 RM's. It is worth noting that the price of these hangers at 2.75 RM's was quite high compared to the price of a complete SA dress dagger at the time which was 6.5 RM's.

►

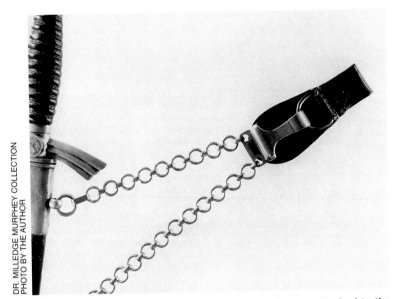

Small blue leather 1st model *Luftwaffe* teardrop hanger attached to the dagger chain hanger. These small accouterments were made for the *Luftwaffe* daggers in both brown and blue leather.

Unissued *Muster* (sample) of the fabric dress hangers designed for the Water Protection Police dagger. The metal banding clip shows that these sample hangers originated at the A. Bender accouterments firm located in Weissenburg, Germany. The fabric sewn to the obverse straps is gold with two thin black stripes. ▶

Close-up view of the original metal banding clip and cardboard identification tag on the sample Water Protection Police dagger hangers. The "AB" on the banding clip is the logo of the Albrecht Bender firm in Weissenburg. The "Nr. 78" represents the Bender identification number for this model dress hangers.

◀

Unissued set of Hitler Youth Leader hangers complete with an unissued HJ Leader belt loop and *RZM* metal control tag.

▶

◀

Close-up view of the bottom hanger clips and slides on the sample Water Protection Police dagger hangers. Note that one of the reverse fabric straps has been clipped by the accouterment firm. This was a common practice in order to insure that sample merchandise was not, inadvertently, sold or distributed.

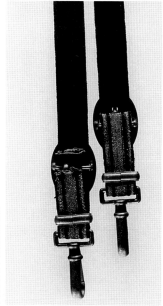

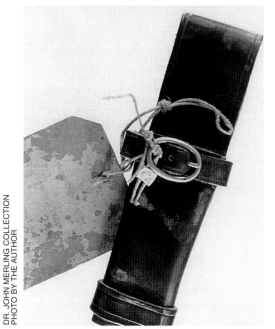

Pictured is a previously unpublished NSKK leader's prototype vertical hanger. The original cardboard identification tag reads, *"Original-muster"* (original sample), *"Dolchgehange Leder"* (leather dagger hanger). Additional typed identifications include "Art. Nr. 17439," *"NSKK Korpsführer"* and *"München,* 1939.*"* The cardboard tag is sealed to the hanger with a metal clip.

Extremely close-up view of the unissued Hitler Youth Leader hangers with belt loop and original *RZM* metal control tag—reverse view. Note that the control disc is stamped "4 39" (April 1939) and "013008." The upper hanging clip is stamped "U.E. 10" followed by the small encircled *RZM* stamping. The original factory lacquer is evident on all of the hanger hardware.

Interesting edged weapon factory box of sample 2nd model *Luftwaffe* dagger grips. The green cardboard box pictured was purchased by the author, as is, in Germany. The seller was a retired Solingen factory employee. A translation of the handwritten notation on the top of the carton reads, "Grip samples, Air Force Officer's Dagger, 2 January 1937." A second handwritten note on the side of the carton translates, "Not for sale. To be retained by the factory." The carton contains sample *Luftwaffe Trolon* grips in white, orange, cream, and several "marbleized" examples, as well as a couple of Army dress grips. Obviously, the factory was experimenting in 1937 (the same year of adoption for the 2nd Model *Luftwaffe* dagger) to determine the best color for the *Luftwaffe* dagger grip. ▶

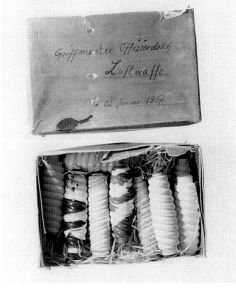

AUTHOR'S COLLECTION
PHOTO BY THE AUTHOR

An unusual 23 cm *Luftwaffe* dagger portepee, complete with the original string-tie and cardstock price tag still attached.

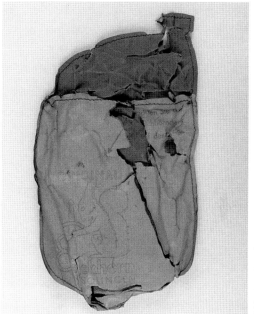

JASON P. BURMEISTER COLLECTION
PHOTO BY KEN DUMMINGER

Laminated paper Carl Eickhorn sword hilt cover. The above paper hilt cover was a direct vet acquisition and came with an unissued Eickhorn Field Marshal series *"Roon"* pattern sword. Collectors are more familiar with the Eickhorn felt sword hilt covers. A theory on the use of this paper hilt cover is that swords leaving the factory were shipped wrapped in paper, and the felt covers were furnished for home storage use.

AUTHOR'S COLLECTION
PHOTO BY THE AUTHOR

***Luftwaffe* sword hanger—obverse view. This style of *Luftwaffe* sword hanger has the protective blue leather cover and pebbled aluminum hardware. The upper leather part serves as a belt loop. The pebbled aluminum hanging clip is covered in the photograph by the protective cover.** ◀

Luftwaffe sword hanger—reverse view. The manufacturer's name and "Berlin 1939" are stamped on the reverse leather backing. Also the name of the original owner, "Lt. Rosch," can be seen written on the hanger reverse in ink.

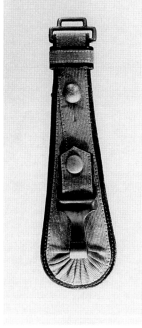

Pictured is a rare silver brocade teardrop sword hanger—obverse view.

▶

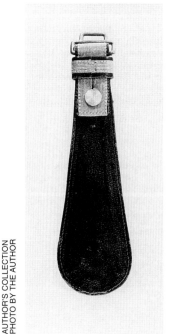

The rare silver brocade teardrop sword hanger is pictured—reverse view. The reverse of this hanger is constructed of a dark green leather backing. Although one school of thought is that these green-backed brocade teardrops are for the German Army swords and the black leather-backed ones are for SS swords, the author is of the opinion that all of the brocade teardrop hangers were for SS and Police swords. If the Army sword theory were correct, there, obviously, would be many more of these hangers available, as there are hundreds, if not thousands, of German Army swords in collections today.

◀

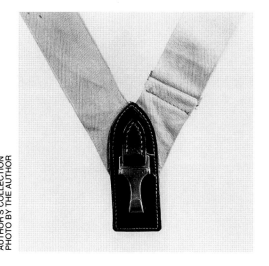

Pictured is a rare *green* leather over-the-shoulder device designed for use with the standard hunting and forestry dress daggers.

◄

Extremely rare SS Officer brocade sword hanger. Black leather hanger with a silver bullion front is shown complete with a black leather belt loop complete with a metal regain chain. Lower clip is stamped on the reverse with an anchor which is correct for this type of sword hanger. The overall length of the hanger pictured is 14 inches. ►

THIRD REICH EDGED WEAPON DISPLAYS

An outstanding idea for a militaria/gun show exhibit is the recreated German military shop window belonging to Texas collector Skipper Greenwade. This unique exhibit features numerous authentic unissued edged weapons, salesman sword samples, and factory point-of-purchase advertising.

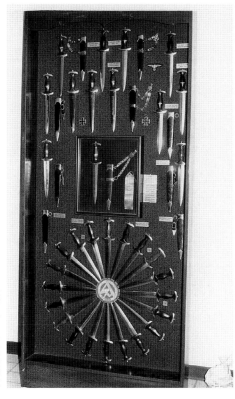

A portion of the Third Reich edged weapon collection belonging to P.W. Lefort of Thibodaux, Louisiana.

◀

Custom-made wooden sword case in the collection of advanced collector Robert Waitts of New Jersey. A provision has been included for the display of accompanying sword knots. The sword scabbards are neatly stored out-of-sight via a vertical side door on the back of the display case.

▶

The personalized 2nd model Damascus Navy dagger presented to Knight Cross winner *Kapitan zur See* Reinicke is professionally displayed alongside a cased ship model of the German heavy cruiser *Prinz Eugen*. The scale ship model is over three feet in length, of the finest quality workmanship, and is complete with two electric motors inside the hull that actually operate the ship. On 7 May, 1945, while anchored at Copenhagen, Denmark, the *Prinz Eugen* surrendered to the British. Ultimately, the vessel was taken by the U.S. Navy to Bikini Lagoon,where she was used as a target ship.

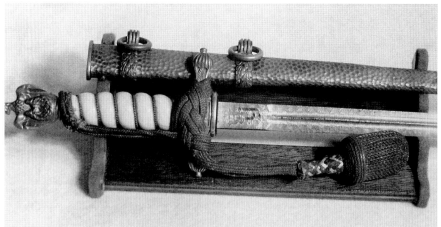

The personalized 2nd model Damascus Navy dagger presented to Hans-Jürgen Reinicke, the commanding officer of the *Prinz Eugen* heavy cruiser during the last two years of WWII. The obverse blade ricasso of the high quality "rosebud" pattern Damascus steel blade bears the monogram of *Kapitan zur See* Reinicke, "HR", in raised letters. The attractive wooden display stand for the dagger was handcrafted by collector Ed Leland of Massachusetts.

Pictured is the impressive miniature dagger/sword/bayonet collection belonging to advanced German edged weapon collector Andrew Gates of England.

GERMAN THIRD REICH EDGED WEAPON VALUATIONS

In an endeavor to assist the collector with the most practical and useful data available, **Volumes I-VII** of **Collecting the Edged Weapons of the Third Reich** provided the reader with an innovation of detailed pricing information for each standard model Third Reich sidearm and accompanying hanger in three different grades, i.e., Very Good, Excellent, and Mint. To reiterate **Volume I**, the Third Reich edged weapon market is so dynamic in most categories that values can easily change during any given period of time. Needless to say, the increased activity in the marketplace since the publication of **Volume VII** in 1994 has necessitated adjustments to the current valuations section. As a matter of fact, the Current Market Values section is so volatile that this section is purposely the last section of text to be compiled, in order to avoid having to constantly update the values during the preparation stages of the book, e.g., the values of authentic German edged weapons often escalate at such an astronomical rate that if this section is completed several months in advance, it, invariably, has to be completely updated prior to the book going to press. This was precisely the case for **Volume VI** of this series. The Current Market Values section was finished, typed, proofed, and forwarded to the printer prior to finalizing the last 50-75 pages of the book. When the remaining pages were submitted to the printer some three months later, it was obvious to the author that the valuations of dress daggers required a <u>complete</u> update.

The updated, revised section which follows is, again, based on values averaged from data supplied by numerous sources, e.g., current U.S. and foreign dealer sales lists; prices realized in militaria auctions in this country and abroad; asking prices at recent gun, knife, and militaria shows; values quoted by a number of advanced collectors; and, recent sale prices. Every attempt has been made to use actual sale prices versus a series of advertised asking prices in order to capture a barometer of the true value at a given time. All values as listed are based on the overall U.S. market. Albeit mathematically sound, the values reflected below are shown as a guide only and are not intended to serve as a price list for any dealer. Many weeks have been spent in the research, checking, and cross-checking of current sales, making this reference of current values the most authoritative and complete published to date. However, it should be noted that the prices of militaria not only vary from time to time, but also from country to country, although reference books belong to the international marketplace. Thus, a scale of values based on the current U.S. prices would be of little value to collectors elsewhere or, even, to the collectors in the U.S. within a couple of years after publication. In fact, the majority of militaria items are worth just as much, or just as little, as another collector is prepared to pay.

*(Author's Note: As with the preceding **Volume VII**, readers of this series will find listed below several additional models of edged weapons which were inadvertently overlooked in the first seven volumes. Also, approximate model types have been expanded, e.g., the SS Chained (1936) category has been expanded to include both the early nickel model and the later model*

with plated fittings; and the Forestry Cutlass category has been expanded to include the deluxe senior and subordinate models, as well as the standard production Forestry models. Additionally, this **Volume VIII** listing is also expanded to include, for the first time, current valuations in three different grades for the following: Gold Government Official (RMBO) dagger, Gold Railway Water Protection Police dagger, Fire Police dagger (as pictured on page 279 of **Volume VI**), Fire Official dress axe (in gold), 3/4-size Fire Official dress axe, and the Navy Diver's knife. In the Dress Sword category, the reader will find for the first time market values in three conditions for the Police/SS Degen (with SS pommel nut), the Police/SS NCO Degen (with SS pommel nut), and the Early Silver SS Lion Head Saber. Last, but not least, an entirely new section has been added to the Current Market Values section of **Volume VIII** providing current market values in three conditions for sword accouterments (knots and hangers).

CURRENT RETAIL MARKET VALUES
Dress Daggers

MODEL TYPE (Excluding Accouterments)	VG.	EXC.	MINT
Army Officer (Early Silver)	$345.	$425.	$600.
Army Officer (Late)	300.	375.	400.
Army Officer w/Engraved Blade	1,950.	2,700.	3,500.
Army General Officer	775.	1,050.	1,400.
1st Model (1934) *Luftwaffe* w/Silver Fittings	575.	750.	1,100.
1st Model *Luftwaffe* w/Aluminum Fittings	425.	550.	800.
2nd Model (1937) *Luftwaffe*	365.	475.	700.
2nd Model (1937) *Luftwaffe* w/Black Grip	600.	900.	1,100.
2nd Model (1937) *Luftwaffe* w/Engraved Blade	2,000.	2,900.	3,800.
1st Model Naval	1,000.	1,300.	2,000.
2nd Model Naval	650.	895.	1,200.
SA, Service Dagger (1933), Early Maker	400.	550.	750.
SA, Service Dagger (*RZM* Marked)	345.	400.	525.
SA, Marine Service Dagger w/Gilted Fittings	1,125.	1,400.	1,700.
SA, Marine Service Dagger w/Nickel-Silver Fittings and Black Scabbard	950.	1,275.	1,500.
SA, Chained (High Leader with Chain Hanger)	20,000.	27,000.	40,000.
SA, 1935 High Leader, No Chain	18,000.	24,000.	35,000.
SA, Honor w/Plain Nickel Blade	8,500.	10,000.	14,000.
SA, *Röhm*, Ground, Partial Inscription	700.	975.	1,200.
SA, *Röhm* Inscription, Unground	2,400.	3,200.	4,750.
SA, *Feldherrnhalle*	30,000.	38,000.	45,000.
SS, Service (1933) Early Maker	1,400.	1,800.	2,400.
SS, *RZM* Marked (1933) Service Dagger	1,000.	1,400.	1,850.
SS, Chained (1936) (Early Nickel)	2,650.	3,950.	5,500.
SS, Chained (Plated)	2,500.	3,700.	5,000.
SS, Himmler Inscription	5,500.	7,500.	11,000.
SS, *Röhm* Inscription, Partial Ground	2,400.	3,750.	5,000.
SS, *Röhm* Inscription, Unground	7,200.	14,000.	18,000.
SS, Honor w/Indented Scabbard Fittings	35,000.	50,000.	70,000.
SS, Honor, w/Raised Oak Leaf Scabbard Fittings	50,000.	65,000.	90,000.
SS, Honor w/Plain Blade	22,000.	35,000.	50,000.

NSKK Service (1933), Early Maker	500.	625.	800.
NSKK *RZM* Marked (1933) Service	450.	575.	750.
NSKK Chained (1936)	2,200.	3,500.	4,700.
NSKK Naval Chained (1936)	2,850.	4,200.	6,000.
NSKK High Leader w/Chain Hanger	19,500.	26,000.	38,500.
NPEA Student	1,500.	2,200.	2,700.
NPEA Staff Leader	2,100.	2,600.	3,500.
NPEA Leader	4,200.	5,000.	7,000.
RAD Enlisted Hewer	600.	700.	950.
RAD Full Stag, Enlisted	1,100.	1,450.	1,600.
RAD Officer	1,200.	1,650.	2,400.
Red Cross Enlisted Hewer	475.	550.	700.
Red Cross Leader	900.	1,300.	1,600.
1st Model DLV *(Luftsport-Verband)*	4,000.	4,900.	6,500.
DLV *Fliegerdolch*	700.	900.	1,200.
NSFK, Model 1934	750.	950.	1,250.
NSFK, Model 1936	750.	950.	1,250.
Hitler Youth Knife (with Motto)	275.	350.	550.
Hitler Youth Knife (without Motto)	250.	325.	500.
HJ Marine Youth Knife (Blue Emblem)	1,400.	1,800.	2,150.
NS Student League Knife	750.	975.	1,200.
DJ *Fahrtenmesser* With Emblem	400.	550.	750.
DJ *Fahrtenmesser* Without Emblem	325.	425.	550.
Hitler Youth Leader	2,200.	3,000.	4,200.
Hitler Youth Marine Leader	3,000.	4,000.	5,000.
1st Model (1936) *RLB* Enlisted	1,100.	1,650.	2,000.
1st Model (1936) *RLB* Officer	3,000.	4,000.	5,250.
2nd Model (1938) *RLB* Enlisted	1,050.	1,500.	1,950.
2nd Model (1938) *RLB* Officer	1,400.	1,700.	2,400.
1st Model (1935) Railway	1,200.	1,600.	1,900.
1938 Railway Leader (Early Silver)	2,650.	3,200.	4,500.
1938 Railway Leader (w/brushed steel scabbard)	2,400.	3,000.	4,000.
Railway Water Protection Police (Gold)	6,500.	8,000.	10,000.
Railway Water Protection Police (Silver)	5,000.	7,500.	8,550.
Land Customs	1,500.	1,800.	2,200.
Water Customs	3,500.	5,000.	6,800.
Postal Leader	3,250.	4,000.	5,000.
TENO Enlisted Hewer	1,800.	2,200.	2,650.
TENO Leader	3,000.	3,800.	5,000.
Government Official	3,200.	4,000.	5,200.
Gold Government Official (RMBO)	8,500.	9,500.	12,500.
Diplomatic	6,500.	8,500.	10,000.
Fire Police Dagger *(Feuer Losch Dolch)*	4,500.	5,800.	8,000.
Fire Official	1,200.	1,400.	1,650.
Fire Official Dress Axe (Silver)	1,600.	1,950.	2,200.
3/4-Size Fire Official Axe	2,000.	3,000.	3,450.

	VG.	EXC.	MINT
Gold Fire Official Axe	2,000.	2,400.	2,650.
Water Protection Police Leader w/o Insignia	2,200.	2,800.	4,000.
Water Protection Police Leader w/Insignia	4,000.	5,200.	7,500.
Hunting Association	1,400.	1,750.	2,200.
Deluxe Hunting Association	2,000.	3,250.	3,850.
Subordinate Forestry Cutlass w/Stag Grip	1,150.	1,400.	1,650.
Deluxe Subordinate Forestry w/Stag Grip	1,700.	2,000.	2,400.
Deluxe Subordinate Forestry w/Eagle & Swastika on Ferrule	2,100.	2,500.	2,900.
Senior Forestry Cutlass w/Celluloid Grip	1,200.	1,450.	1,700.
Deluxe Senior Forestry w/Celluloid Grip	1,750.	2,100.	2,500.
Deluxe Senior Forestry w/Eagle & Swastika on Ferrule	2,200.	2,600.	3,000.
Rifle Association	1,400.	1,650.	2,250.
Navy Diver knife	1,400.	1,750.	2,200.

DRESS DAGGER ACCOUTERMENTS
Hangers

HANGER TYPE	VG.	EXC.	MINT
Army	$100.	$140.	$195.
Luftwaffe	110.	150.	200.
SA	40.	60.	85.
SS	60.	85.	110.
SS (Vertical) 1933 Service Dagger	200.	275.	350.
SS (Teardrop) 1936 Dagger	300.	350.	450.
Navy (Brass Fittings)	295.	400.	475.
Navy Administrative (Aluminum Fittings)	350.	450.	525.
RAD Officer	450.	550.	600.
RAD EM (Large Leather Type)	275.	300.	400.
Red Cross	345.	475.	550.
Red Cross Enlisted Frog	50.	80.	100.
NPEA Frog	145.	195.	250.
Social Welfare	400.	500.	600.
RLB Officer	425.	475.	650.
TENO Leader (Leather) Service (Black)	1,100.	1,300.	1,700.
TENO Leader (Leather) Service (Brown)	1,350.	1,600.	1,950.
TENO Leader (Fabric) Dress	1,000.	1,200.	1,450.
TENO Enlisted	450.	500.	550.
Railway (Model 1935)	1,500.	1,800.	2,000.
Railway *(Bahnschutz)* Leader	750.	900.	1,100.
Land Customs	425.	475.	550.
Water Customs	1,100.	1,400.	1,750.
Water Protection Police	1,500.	1,750.	2,000.
Hitler Youth Leader	1,500.	2,000.	2,500.
Diplomatic/Government Official (Gold Fittings)	1,200.	1,500.	1,800.
Diplomatic/Government Off. (Silver Fittings)	1,100.	1,350.	1,450.

Diplomatic/Government Off. (Leather Straps)	1,900.	2,250.	2,650.
Eastern Territories Diplomatic/Government Official (Gold Fabric w/Gold Fittings)	**	**	**
Feldherrnhalle (Gold Fabric w/Gold Fittings)	**	**	**
Feldherrnhalle (Silver Fabric w/Silver Fittings)	**	**	**
Feldherrnhalle EM Frog	400.	650.	750.
Fireman Leader	575.	750.	950.

**Extremely Rare—No data available.

Portepees

PORTEPEE TYPE	VG.	EXC.	MINT
Army	$ 30.	$ 45.	$ 60.
Luftwaffe	40.	55.	70.
Navy (Gold)	90.	110.	145.
Red Cross Officer	200.	245.	350.
Postal	400.	550.	600.
Land Customs	375.	400.	550.
Water Customs	450.	500.	600.
Government/Diplomatic	400.	550.	700.
Forestry, Subordinate	70.	85.	100.
Forestry, Senior	80.	95.	125.
Hunting	145.	220.	300.
Railway (1935)	**	**	**
Railway (1938)	400.	450.	500.
Rifle Association	60.	85.	100.

**Extremely Rare—No data available.

CURRENT RETAIL MARKET VALUES
Dress Swords

MODEL TYPE (Excluding Accouterments)	VG.	EXC.	MINT
Standard Army Officer	$295.	$395.	$500.
Standard Army Officer w/Engraved Blade	1,100.	1,300.	1,500.
Standard Army Officer w/Damascus Blade	2,700.	2,900.	4,000.
Standard Army Lion Head	350.	450.	600.
Standard Amy Lion Head w/Engraved Blade	1,200.	1,500.	1,700.
Army Pattern Saber (Nickel Finish)	160.	200.	225.
Army Pattern Saber (Brass Finish)	185.	210.	250.
Eickhorn Field Marshal Series:			
"Wrangel," #1693	325.	375.	450.
"Scharnhorst," #1706	375.	500.	600.
"Blücher," #1710	400.	600.	700.
"Freiherr von Stein," #1714	350.	550.	600.
"Roon," #1716	275.	300.	375.
"Zieten," #1734	475.	725.	875.

"Derfflinger," #1735	350.	550.	650.
"Prinz Eugen," #1765	800.	1,100.	1,500.
"Lützow," #1767	1,400.	1,850.	2,450.
Army Ordnance	275.	345.	400.
Army Höller 21 Lion Head	1,200.	1,400.	1,600.
Army Cavalry (Crossed Sabers)	300.	375.	425.
Army Artillery (Crossed Cannons)	450.	550.	675.
Army ("Armistice")	1,200.	1,400.	1,650.
Luftwaffe, Model 1934 (Early Silver)	650.	800.	1,100.
Luftwaffe, Model 1934 (Aluminum)	550.	700.	950.
Luftwaffe, w/Engraved Blade	4,000.	5,000.	6,500.
Luftwaffe Presentation "Stab-Sword"	10,000.	12,000.	15,000.
Luftwaffe General Officer, #1732	9,500.	11,500.	14,500.
Navy	1,000.	1,300.	1,650.
SS Officer	2,700.	4,000.	5,500.
SS NCO	1,800.	2,400.	3,000.
SS Officer Candidate (Senior Pattern)	1,200.	1,600.	2,000.
SS Officer Candidate (Subordinate Pattern)	1,175.	1,550.	1,950.
SS Honor, Damascus	35,000.	40,000.	55,000.
SS Officer (Silver Lion Head, Early)	2,000.	2,750.	3,900.
Police Officer	550.	750.	1,000.
Police/SS Officer (w/SS pommel cap)	1,800.	2,450.	3,000.
Police NCO	550.	750.	1,000.
Police/SS NCO (w/SS pommel cap)	1,700.	2,300.	2,750.
Land Customs	975.	1,450.	1,800.
Water Customs	3,000.	3,750.	4,200.
Fire Official (Leather Scabbard)	1,000.	1,250.	1,500.
Justice Official (Silver)	2,400.	3,000.	4,000.
Prison Official (Gilted)	1,600.	2,000.	2,500.
Mining Official	850.	1,050.	1,300.
Diplomatic Official	15,000.	18,000.	26,500.

CURRENT RETAIL MARKET VALUES
Service and Dress Bayonets

MODEL TYPE (Excluding Accouterments)	VG.	EXC.	MINT
Model 84/98 Mauser Service	$ 75.	$100.	$140.
Standard Army/Luftwaffe, Short Model, Dress	90.	125.	170.
Standard Army/Luftwaffe, Long Model, Dress	90.	120.	165.
Standard Army/Luftwaffe, (Stag Grips), Dress	175.	250.	350.
Army Single-Engraved, Short Model	350.	450.	550.
Army Single-Engraved, Long Model	325.	425.	525.
Army Double-Engraved, Short Model	510.	650.	750.
Army Double-Engraved, Long Model	470.	600.	700.
Army Pioneer (Engineer), Dress	350.	450.	525.
Army Pioneer (Engineer), Engraved	**	**	**
Luftwaffe Single-Engraved, Short Model	525.	600.	795.

Luftwaffe Single-Engraved, Long Model	510.	575.	750.
Luftwaffe Double-Engraved, Short Model	695.	795.	900.
Luftwaffe Double-Engraved, Long Model	650.	750.	875.
Red Cross Prototype	**	**	**
RLB Prototype (as seen on p. 156 of **Vol. III**)	**	**	**
Fireman, Short Model, Dress	110.	175.	275.
Fireman, Long Model, Dress	125.	200.	300.
Fireman, Sawtooth, Short Model	350.	400.	550.
Fireman, Sawtooth, Long Model	400.	450.	600.
SS M98/05 Security Police	1,800.	2,400.	3,000.
Police, Long Model, Unslotted, Service	340.	400.	500.
Police, Long Model, Slotted, Service	375.	450.	575.
Police, Short Model, Dress	650.	850.	1,100.
Police, Clamshell, Dress	1,100.	1,450.	1,750.
Hitler Youth Honor	1,500.	1,750.	2,000.
Hitler Youth	950.	1,350.	1,650.
Customs	500.	600.	750.
Customs, Clamshell	**	**	**
Luftwaffe Gravity Knife, Non-Take-Down	350.	500.	750.
Luftwaffe Gravity Knife (Take-Down)	400.	550.	775.

**Extremely Rare—No data available.

CURRENT RETAIL MARKET VALUES
Bayonet Frogs

MODEL TYPE	VG.	EXC.	MINT
Army (Black)	$35.	$45.	$60.
Luftwaffe (Brown)	45.	65.	75.
Police (Black)	50.	70.	95.
Police (Brown)	60.	80.	100.

Note: Many of the other bayonets utilized the same frog as used on the Army and *Luftwaffe* bayonets. The value would, however, increase if they were marked to specific organizations.

CURRENT RETAIL MARKET VALUES
Miniatures

MODEL TYPE (Excluding Accouterments)	VG.	EXC.	MINT
Army Officer Dagger (Alcoso)	$600.	$850.	$1,200.
Army Officer Dagger (Small Size)	250.	350.	500.
2nd Model *Luftwaffe* (Alcoso)	600.	800.	1,100.
2nd Model *Luftwaffe* (SMF)	450.	700.	850.
2nd Model *Luftwaffe* (Small Size)	275.	325.	450.
1st Model *Luftwaffe*/DLV Long Model	450.	650.	725.
Luftwaffe Sword (Alcoso)	700.	850.	1,150.
Luftwaffe Sword, Base-Mounted (Propeller)	900.	1,250.	1,500.

Examples (Alcoso)

	VG.	EXC.	MINT
Luftwaffe Sword (Other Makers)	500.	625.	795.
Imperial Navy Dagger (Varied Sizes)	325.	450.	550.
2nd Model Navy (Alcoso)	2,200.	2,800.	3,400.
2nd Model Navy (Varied Makers)	750.	950.	1,200.
RAD Officer Dagger (Alcoso)	1,800.	2,200.	2,400.
RAD Officer Dagger (Other Makers)	1,350.	1,700.	2,100.
Hunting/Forestry Dagger (Alcoso)	1,500.	1,900.	2,400.
Hunting Dagger (Other Makers)	625.	750.	850.
Bayonets (Dress)	200.	250.	300.

CURRENT RETAIL MARKET VALUES
Sword Accouterments

HANGER TYPE	VG.	EXC.	MINT
Brown Teardrop	$60.	$75.	$100.
Brown Over-the-Shoulder	70.	95.	110.
Black Over-the-Shoulder	100.	125.	150.
Silver-faced Teardrop (Green Leather Backed)	450.	600.	700.
Braided Naval Leather Straps	150.	225.	300.
Black Police Teardrop	125.	175.	200.
Black SS-Marked Teardrop	275.	325.	375.
Long Silver-Faced SS Officer (w/Black Leather Back)	700.	950.	1,100.
Silver-Faced Teardrop (w/Black Leather Back)	600.	800.	900.
Long Silver-Faced Fire Police (w/Red Leather Back)	195.	250.	300.
Luftwaffe Teardrop	125.	145.	185.

SWORD KNOTS	VG.	EXC.	MINT
Standard Army	$40.	$60.	$75.
Navy	100.	125.	175.
SS Officer (w/Control Tag)	350.	400.	500.
SS Officer (w/o Control Tag)	275.	375.	450.
SS NCO (w/Control Tag)	500.	650.	750.
SS NCO (w/o Control Tag)	450.	500.	650.
Police Officer	45.	60.	75.
Police NCO	40.	50.	70.
Mining Official	200.	300.	400.

Note: No other information available on other types of sword knots.

Uncommon Manufacturers' Trademarks

A. CURT HOPPE SOLINGEN

B. WILM. HALBACH SOLINGEN

C. AUG. KULLENG SOLINGEN-GR.

D. R H E — RICH. & E. HARTKOPF SOLINGEN

E. DANIEL PERES SOLINGEN

F. GUST. WEYERSBERG NACHF. W S SOLINGEN

G. ARTUR MELCHER ARMESO SOLINGEN MERSCHEID

H. LEUCO

I. GUSTAV WIRTH W SOLINGEN GRAFRATH

J. J.E. DITTERT & CO. NEUSTADT i SA

K. ERNST KEMPER SOLINGEN

L. SPALTENEDER MÜNCHEN

M. JULIUS BAHRL JR. SOLINGEN

N. RICH. DREES & SOHN R D & S SOLINGEN

O. KARL MALSCH GUST. SOHN STEINBACH KR. MAIN

P. PAUL-KOHL SOLINGEN

Uncommon Manufacturers' Trademarks (Cont.)

ASSO

Q

R

S

Kolumbuswerk Eduard Becker

T

J. DIRLAM & SÖHNE
SOLINGEN

U

LEOPOLD

V

KUNO RITTER
SOLINGEN

W

HEINR. KAUFMANN & SÖHNE
SOLINGEN

X

E. SCHRICK & SOHN
SOLINGEN

Y

R B S
RUDOLF BUCHEL
SOLINGEN-MERSCHEID

Z

FLAMME   L^{ou}P$_{er}$
SOLINGEN

I

CARL HEIDELBERG
SOLINGEN

II

EMIL VOOS
SOLINGEN

III

SOLINGEN

IV

GUSTAV FELIX
GLORIAWERK · SOLINGEN

V

VI

Extreme close-up of the David Malsch "DM" Steinbach trademark. The David Malsch firm in the former East Germany (DDR) was well known for *Luftwaffe* and *DLV* edged weapons, but, evidently, manufactured very few SA daggers, as this represents a rare SA maker. Note the "He" (Hessen) SA identification symbol stamped on the reverse crossguard.

SA Dagger with double *RZM* number and trademark by Anton Wingen, Jr. Note that the reverse blade ricasso bears the Wingen firm *RZM* number *M7/51*, the date "1940" and the Anton Wingen, Jr., "knight with sword" trademark.

Extreme close-up view of a 1939 SS dagger with a rare J.A. Henckels "double" trademark. Note that both the well-known Henckels "twins" trademark *and* the *RZM* number assigned to the Henckels firm, *RZM M7/15*, as well as the date "38" are deeply stamped on the reverse blade ricasso. The dagger is complete with a felt blade buffer pad.

An unattributed Solingen manufacturer's trademark featuring a stag and "Solingen." The author would welcome any input concerning the identification of this particular trademark.

SELECTED YEAR THIRD REICH EDGED WEAPONS/ACCOUTERMENTS PRICE COMPARISON TABLE

(Author's Note: This table reflects actual retail prices for selected Third Reich edged weapons and accouterments for various years. All items selected were described as being authentic and in excellent or better condition.)

ITEM	1958	1961	1964	1967	1971	1975	1980	1985	1992	1994	1996	2-Yr. % Increase
Army Officer Dagger	$ 15.	$ 25.	$ 35.	$ 35.	$ 50.	$110.	$135.	$225.	$300.	$345.	$425.	23.2%
1st Model *Luftwaffe* Dagger	22.	25.	35.	50.	75.	150.	195.	285.	425.	575.	750.	30.4%
2nd Model *Luftwaffe* Dagger	15.	25.	30.	35.	65.	115.	140.	250.	310.	375.	475.	26.6%
2nd Model Navy Dagger	25.	35.	40.	50.	80.	165.	225.	300.	450.	595.	895.	52.1%
SS, 1933 Service Dagger	35.	37.50	60.	65.	95.	250.	335.	650.	1100.	1395.	1800.	29.0%
SA Service Dagger	10.	22.50	27.50	35.	50.	115.	135.	225.	365.	425.	550.	29.0%
2nd Model *RLB* Officer Dagger	45.	70.	95.	130.	220.	450.	550.	850.	1200.	1425.	1700.	19.2%
Red Cross Officer Dagger	40.	50.	65.	100.	150.	275.	350.	475.	785.	1000.	1300.	30.0%
Diplomatic Dagger	75.	150.	200.	275.	375.	925.	1500.	2200.	6500.	7300.	8500.	16.4%
Postal Dagger	90.	150.	175.	225.	650.	875.	1050.	1750.	2750.	2850.	4000.	40.3%
Army Officer Dagger Hangers	1.50	2.50	5.	8.	12.	18.	35.	55.	85.	110.	140.	27.2%
Dagger Portepees	.35	1.25	3.	4.	8.	10.	15.	25.	35.	35.	45.	28.5%
Eickhorn *Kundendienst* Catalog	10.	13.50	13.50	25.	35.	75.	135.	195.	325.	350.	400.	14.2%

UPDATE ON FACTORY SOURCE DOCUMENTS

As explained in the Introduction and on page 313 of **Volume VI**, as well as on page 238 of **Volume VII** of this reference series, I had the unique opportunity to acquire in 1989 the majority of the original records of the large WKC edged weapons manufacturing firm in Solingen, Germany, and to add this monument of reference materials to a large selection of the Carl Eickhorn firm's original records acquired many years ago from James P. Atwood (Jim Atwood's memorable forays into the blade city of Solingen are well documented in **Chapter 2** of **Volume II** of this series). Additionally, the author has managed to augment the WKC and Eickhorn records with pertinent 1933-45 correspondence and factory documentation from the Alexander Coppel (Alcoso), E. & F. Hörster, Ernst Pack, Puma, and Max Weyersberg firms. The vast amount of information contained in these files for the edged weapon collecting is, in a word, staggering! Each individual document can be analysis and add to the collecting community's overall knowledge on the intricacies of this complex and fascinating industry. As dagger collector Fred Fallgren of Stony Creek, Connecticut, so amply stated in a recent letter to the author, ". . . By the way, I really enjoyed your new book **Volume VII**—especially 'factory source documents', etc. A lot of arguments went out the window on that section!" A case in point, I can now prove that the large WKC firm in Solingen did, in fact, produce their own Government Official and/or Diplomatic daggers, although the "dagger experts" for years have been proclaiming that only two firms, Alcoso and Eickhorn, manufactured these two model Third Reich dress daggers.

A concentrated effort remains ongoing at Johnson Reference Books (JRB) to catalog and have translated reams of the WKC and Eickhorn source correspondence and paperwork pertinent to this interesting and ever-expanding hobby. As with the previous two volumes, several additional original source documents have been selected and are reproduced in this reference, along with the accompanying English language translations.

The first document translated and reproduced below is a 1940 order and bill of delivery from the J. L. Kruse firm in Kassel (a major WKC distributor) to WKC. It is interesting to note that one of the largest Solingen edged weapon manufacturing firms offered the service of repairing a single edged weapon. The Kruse company had obviously mailed a single 1st model *Luftwaffe* dagger (WKC Model Nr. 1009) from Herman Vockrodt (retailer) to WKC for repair.

Kassel, den 10. Februar 19 40.

Firma WKC. Waffenfabrik
    Solingen - Wald.
========================

     Beifolgend ein Auftrag u. ein Lieferschein von
Firma Herm. Vockrodt Kassel.

     Geben Sie bitte der Firma Nachricht ob der ein=
gesandte Fliegerdolch 1oo9 repar.u. zurück gesand ist.

         Heil Hitler

J. L. Kruse
Kassel, Wilhelmstr, 13
Fernruf 32521,

J. L. Kruse, Kassel Wilhelmstrasse 13

Kassel 10 February 1940

Firma WKC Waffenfabrik, G.m.b.H.

Solingen-Wald

Enclosed find an order and bill of delivery from the firm Herman Vockrodt of Kassel.

Please notify the firm, if the mailed-in flight dagger (Luftwaffe) Model 1009 was repaired and sent back.

Heil Hitler!

/s/

The second 1940 document is important to edged weapon collectors/ researchers as it provides insight into the types and colors of issue felt dagger and sword storage bags. Perhaps this single WKC price notice provides the serious collector/researcher with the first documented look at the correct color felt bag for the corresponding edged weapon. For example, Third Reich sabers were issued with brown, red, blue, <u>and</u> grey felt issue storage bags. Note that all of the felt bags originating at WKC were equipped with zipper tops, although drawstrings were used by some other accouterment and manufacturing firms. It is also interesting to note that dagger bags for Army and *Luftwaffe* daggers only came in grey or brown felt.

WKC-Waffenfabrik

G. m. b. H.
Blanke Waffen für Heer und Marine aller Länder

Sammelnummer 24915/16
.nsprech-Anschluss: Nr. 25559

Telegr.-Adr.: Helm Solingenwald
Postscheck - Konto Essen 22664

Solingen-Wald, den   17. April 1940

Preise für Futterale nur mit Reißverschluß.
===

Säbel- Filzfutterale (braun, rot, blau, grau)   2,40

Flieger Offz.-Schwert Filzfutterale (blau)   2,50

Heeres- und Fliegerdolchfutterale (grau, braun)   1,25

WKC-Edged-Weaponry Concern Solingen-Wald, April 17, 1940
*G.m.b.H.
Edged-weaponry for Army and Navy of all countries

<u>Prices for storage bags only with zippers.</u>

Saber-felt storage-bags (brown, red, blue, gray)   2,40
Air Force (Luftwaffe) Officer's-sword felt storage bags (blue)   2,50
Army-and Luftwaffe dagger storage bags (gray, brown)   1,25

* Limited Liability Company

Following is another original pricing structure letter from WKC for their complete line of Naval Officer's daggers. Several items of interest to the collector/researcher include: verification that 2nd model Naval dagger crossguards were made both with and without the release button on the reverse side; the additional cost of a genuine ivory grip was over one-half the cost of the complete dagger with a celluloid grip; the Imperial crown pommel was still being offered as late as <u>1940</u>; and there was an extra charge from the factory for a hammered scabbard. Additionally, the WKC firm which manufactured the majority of 2nd model Navy daggers offered some <u>thirteen</u> different embellished scabbards.

WKC-WAFFENFABRIK G. M. B. H.
SOLINGEN-WALD   Solingen-Wald   TAG **21. Mai 1940**   BLATT   **-1-**

EMPFÄNGER:

<u>Preise der verschiedenen Ausführungen</u>

<u>für Marine-Offz.-Dolche</u>

Vergoldeter, ciselierter, deutscher Marine Offz.-Dolch, mit Flammenknopf, weißem Holz-Cell.-Griff, Parierstange auf Wunsch , auf der hinteren Seite mit Druckknopf, polierte Zweibahnenklinge, regulär ciselierte Scheide					Rmk.	15,70
Dto. mit Elfenbeingriff kostet mehr					Rmk.	8,40
Dto. mit damaszierter Klinge kostet mehr					Rmk.	-,55
Dto. mit durchbrochener Kaiserkrone kostet mehr					Rmk.	1,05
Dto. mit gehämmerter Scheide kostet mehr					Rmk.	1,05
Dto. mit feinhandciselierte Scheide No. 57 kostet mehr .					Rmk.	4,75
Dto.	"	"	"	No. 39 " "	Rmk.	2,--
Dto.	"	"	"	No. 58 " "	Rmk.	6,60
Dto.	"	"	"	No. 59 " "	Rmk.	3,60
Dto.	"	"	"	No. 60 " "	Rmk.	6,60
Dto.	"	"	"	No. 61 " "	Rmk.	7,--
Dto.	"	"	"	No. 62 " "	Rmk.	4,75
Dto.	"	"	"	No. 63 " "	Rmk.	6,60
Dto.	"	"	"	No. 64 " "	Rmk.	6,60
Dto.	"	"	"	No. 65 " "	Rmk.	4,75
Dto.	"	"	"	No. 66 " "	Rmk.	7,--
Dto.	"	"	"	No. 67 " "	Rmk.	4,--
Dto.	"	"	"	No. 68 " "	Rmk.	7,--
Vergold. Marien Offz.-Dolch Scheide mit Blitzen " "					Rmk.	8,70

loser vergold. Dolch - 9.30
Mundblech - -,60
Scheide versnieren - 1.70

WKC-Edged-Weaponry Solingen-Wald, May 21, 1940

Receiver:

Prices of different types
for Naval Officer's daggers

Gold-gilded, chisled(?), German Officer's Naval dagger with flame-type pommel, white wood-celluloid-grip, crossguard on request on the reverse sides with button-release, polished two-runner blade, regular hand-fashioned scabbard	Reichsmark 15,70
Same with ivory grip additional cost	" 8,40
" " damask blade " "	" -,55
" " cut-out Imperial crown additional cost	" 1,05
" " hammered scabbard	" 1,05
" " elegant hand-fashioned scabbard No. 57 additional cost	" 4,75
" " " No. 39 " "	" 2, --
" " " No. 58 " "	" 6,60
" " " No. 59 " "	" 3,60
" " " No. 60 " "	" 6,60
" " " No. 61 " "	" 7, --
" " " No. 62 " "	" 4,75
" " " No. 63 " "	" 6,60
" " " No. 64 " "	" 6,60
" " " No. 65 " "	" 4,75
" " " No. 66 " "	" 7, --
" " " No. 67 " "	" 4, --
" " " No. 68 " "	" 7, --
Gold-Gilded Naval Officer's dagger scabbard with lightning bolts	" 8,70

gold-gilded dagger -	9,30
upper scabbard fittings -	-60
scabbard embellished	1,70

Something as simple as a single *Rechnung* (bill) can provide the collector with some usable information. Reproduced below is a bill from the Adams and Martin Horn and Celluloid Factory in Haan to WKC for 100 Army Officer dagger grips. This one original bill verifies the information contained in Rex Reddick's fine chapter on German edged weapon production (Grips) appearing in **Volume VI** on pages 50-66 and, also, identifies one of the outside grip makers for WKC.

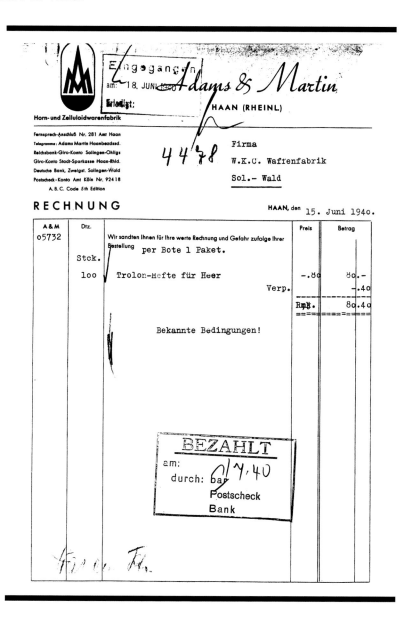

The following bill dated 26 June 1940 from the large Alexander Coppel Cutlery and Edged Weapons firm (Alcoso) to WKC is for <u>completed</u> silver Diplomatic daggers and <u>completed</u> Army dagger and *Luftwaffe* sword letter openers (miniatures). Note that the Army Officer's dagger miniature is referred to as a *"Reichswehr Offizier Dolch-Briefoffner"* (*Reichswehr* Officer Dagger-Letter opener). Why *Reichswehr* and not Third Reich? See the advertising postcard from the WKC firm, also reproduced below.

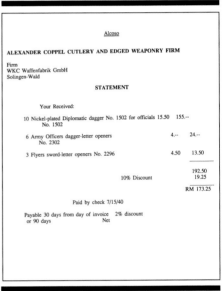

Alcoso

ALEXANDER COPPEL CUTLERY AND EDGED WEAPONRY FIRM

Firm
WKC Waffenfabrik GmbH
Solingen-Wald

STATEMENT

Your Received:

10 Nickel-plated Diplomatic dagger No. 1502 for officials No. 1502	15.50	155.--	
6 Army Officers dagger-letter openers No. 2302	4.--	24.--	
3 Flyers sword-letter openers No. 2296	4.50	13.50	
		192.50	
10% Discount		19.25	
		RM 173.25	

Paid by check 7/15/40

Payable 30 days from day of invoice   2% discount
or 90 days   Net

Reproduced below is a translation of a 1940 letter from the J. L. Kruse Company in Kassel written to WKC to accompany two orders and to inquire about a long-overdue sword shipment. It is interesting to note the postscript to the letter, "P. S. Incidentally, we are being visited every night by the English" (obviously, referring to the British RAF air raids on Kassel). The original of this letter is on file at Johnson Reference Books (JRB).

J. L. Kruse, Kassel Wilhelmstrasse 13

Factory for Edged Weaponry and Military Articles

Kassel, 22 July 1940
Firm WKC Waffenfabrik G.m.b.H.
Solingen-Wald

Enclosed two orders, please ship as soon as possible. The firm Herm. Vockrodt is very short of the short bayonets Nr. 92, perhaps it would be possible for you to send these first of all.

Firm Wilh. Welhausen, Kassel requests shipment of swords ordered a long time ago, it would be desirable, if you would ship these immediately.

In general business has become quite slow, the inquiry has abated.

Heil Hitler (mit deutschem Gruss)

/s/

J. L. Kruse

Incidentally, we are being visited by the English every night.

The same J. L. Kruse Company wrote back to WKC the following month registering several serious delivery complaints against WKC and compared the firm's service to that of the competition, specifically, the Ernst Pack and Carl Eickhorn factories, also located in Solingen. The original of this letter is on file at Johnson Reference Books (JRB).

J. L. Kruse, Kassel Wilhelmstrasse 13

Factory for Edged Weaponry and Military Articles

Kassel, 28 August 1940
Firm WKC Waffenfabrik G.m.b.H.
Solingen-Wald

Entered
29 August 1940

Enclosed two orders, please take care that the daggers are shipped as soon as possible.

Karl Diertich Nordhausen has been buying for some time from the Pack Firm, he said if he ordered today, the items would be there in three days, with you one must wait and still wait, that he couldn't do but if you are in the position to ship him 5 officers Flieger daggers 1042 within 8 days, then you can send them to him.

Wilh. Becker Nordhausen swore like a trooper, does not want anything to do with the Firm WKC any longer, already the manner of your letters was offensive, on the otherhand the Eickhorn Firm was a noble firm, also the Firm W. Becker has run it's course, I do not know what you have written, do not wish to engage in other disputes, because it was useless.

I was at the Leipziger-Fair, have then come back, various edged weaponry concerns had exhibited on the way back I visited Nordhausen I have prevailed upon Zapf Kassel to send you the order for Hitler Youth knives.

Kamberg Nordhausen has purchased Hitler Youth knives at another place because you have not shipped.

Heil Hitler

J. L. Kruse

The following *Rechnung* (statement) from the Alcoso firm dated 2 October 1940 provides yet another example of the large-scale interchange of parts that occurred among the Solingen edged weapon factories. In this statement Alcoso is billing WKC for 100 Police Officer sword pommel nuts.

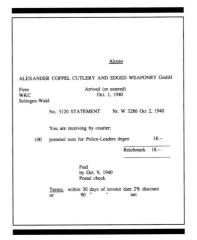

Following is a translation of a postcard from a small family business in Stuttgart to the WKC factory pointing out that some of the arms company salesmen were promising customers more than they could deliver. The original of this correspondence is on file at Johnson Reference Books (JRB).

The Emil Burling Company in Solingen-Hohscheid specialized in leather goods to include leather scabbards of all types. The 31 December 1940 bill below from Emil Burling demonstrates that the WKC firm both subcontracted the labor on covering grips and scabbards and performed the same function in-house. Note the last entry—Emil Burling on 27 December 1940 provided WKC with sufficient stock leather to cover 300 1st model *Luftwaffe* daggers.

Family E. Breunihger A.G. Stuttgart - East, Market Street

The above firm acknowledges your order from 26th No. 40. Enclosed find a new order No. 1098. You can be happy, that our firm has been promptly taken care of, because a local competitor tried its best to get me out of business. The competitor promised the firm to deliver 100 Wehrmacht daggers within 14 days. Of course, they didn't deliver and only came up with 10 pieces within 2 months. So, my firm cut out the competitor again. I sent a Christmas present to the two decision-making gentlemen.

I am asking you, to please make at least a partial delivery of our order #1058.

with German greetings,

/s/

B. Disposition

Reproduced below is a partial English translation of an early (July 1932) E. & F. Hörster letter which was used as an insert for the company's updated 1932 price list. This letter serves to verify that Solingen manufacturers would also repair and recondition edged weapons. Also, note the mention of Forestry Cutlass and Police bayonet conversions.

English Translation of a July 1932 E. & F. Horster Letter Insert for their 1932 Catalog.

Solingen, date of the poststamp.

P.P. We are permitting ourselves to submit to you our newest price list for officers and NCO sabers as well as deluxe-sidearms. For more than 80 years we have been manufacturing these articles for all the states of the world. Therefore, we are in the position to be able to guarantee you in every way prompt and reasonable service. Our edged weaponry is manufactured from first-class material. The manufacturing process is absolutely incontestable, gilting and nickel-plating processes are in every way solid and durable. Our edged weaponry finds complete satisfaction with all of our customers, <u>what the many voluntary letters of recommendation sent confirm to us.</u>
The damasking and engraving on the blades is applied by us in the most simple to the most delicate artificial execution and we solicit from time to time our special suggestions.-- <u>Reconditioning of used edged weaponry as well as repairs of all types will be executed promptly and under the least expensive estimate.</u> Conversions of Forester's cutlasses in accordance with the newest regulations in the least expensive and the best execution offers for the <u>Police-Service-cutlass model 1928 for Municipal Police as well as a Police deluxe cutlass</u> in various executions, as well as edged weaponry of the different states.
Terms of payment: 30 days from the date of account less charges 2% discount, immediate payment 5%, with C.O.D. 4%
We look forward to your important offers, which will be carried out with care, and we remain,

Respectfully,
E. & F. Horster

Next is a translation of a 1937 letter located in the company files of the Krebs firm in Solingen, which verifies that at least one firm other than Carl Eickhorn produced SS daggers with Damascus blades.

Federal Leader
of the German Empire War
Association
(Kuffhauserbund) e.v.

Berlin W30 the 29th
of April 1937
Geisberg Street 2

(e.v. = registered association)

Mr.

Max Krebs
Solingen
Beethoven Street 83

My Dear Krebs!

I thank you most cordially for the most beautiful SS-dagger with the most beautiful damask blade, which you gave to me!

Enclosed I'm sending you my picture in the hope, that it would bring you joy and remind you of me in years to come.

I have gladly taken notice of the fact that you yourself have been glad about the bestowal of the association pin. I would hope that the serious illness of your wife in the meantime is over and you are able to be free of apprehension in this respect.

With comradely greetings and
Heil Hitler

Yours always loyal, sincere

/s/

SS-Lieutenant-General, Colonel retired

(Rheinhart)?

The Carl Eickhorn invoice shown below is a 1945 bill from the firm to the Allied Military Government in Monchengladbach for *Luftwaffe* (two models) and SA daggers inscribed with "Field Day Germany 1945." Of significance is the date of the invoice (22 June 1945) which was only a few weeks after Germany surrendered. Note that the majority of the daggers (150 of 240 pieces) were delivered "*ohne Inschrift*" (<u>without</u> inscription). Obviously, the 150 daggers without inscription were either leftover *RZM M7/66* stock pieces or were assembled by Eickhorn shortly after the cessation of hostilities for the American troops.

EICKHORN Bestecke

CARL EICKHORN - SOLINGEN

BESTECKFABRIK

An die
Militär-Regierung

<u>M.-Gladbach</u>

2186

FERNSPRECHER: SAMMEL-NR. ~~25046~~
TELEGRAMM-ADRESSE: EICKHORNWERK
CODES: ABC 5. AUSG., WESTERN UNION, RUD. MOSSE
REICHSBANK-GIRO-KONTO NR. 373/834 SOLINGEN
POSTSCHECKKONTO: AMT KÖLN NR. 4372

RECHNUNG — NUMMER: Ob. 2093 — IHRE BESTELLUNG VOM — KOMM.-NUMMER — SOLINGEN 22.6.1945

			RM	Pf
	~~Wir danken Ihnen für Ihre Rechnung und Gerät~~			
20	Stck. Flieger-Offizierdolche unsere No. 1736 mit Inschrift "Field day Germany 1945"	15.80	316	--
40	" wie vor ohne Inschrift	13.50	540	--
40	" Flieger-Borddolche unsere No. 1696 mit Inschrift "field day Germany 1945"	19.80	792	--
80	" wie vor ohne Inschrift	17.--	1.360.	--
30	" SA-Dolche unsere Nr. 1750 mit Inschrift "field day Germany 1945"	11.20	336	--
30	" wie vor ohne Inschrift	8.50	255	--
	Verpackung		2	40
		RM.	3.601	40

Wir behalten uns das Eigentumsrecht für vorstehende Waren bis zur restlosen Bezahlung vor. Verpackung, außer Holzkisten, wird zum Selbstkostenpreis berechnet u. nicht zurückgenommen. Erfüllungsort für alle Verpflichtungen beider Teile ist Solingen. Bei Wechseln auf Nebenplätze übernehmen wir keine Verbindlichkeiten wegen rechtzeitiger Vorzeigung oder Protest. Reklamationen spätestens 8 Tage nach Empfang der Ware. Rücksendung von Leergut nach Solingen-Hbf.

Note: Original copy of this document was furnished by LTC (Ret.) James P. Atwood.

Reproduced below is a letter and corresponding English translation of a two-page letter from the Ernst Pack firm to their dealers. The only available date is "Aug./Sept." with no year being included. The "new catalog" mentioned on page 2 of the letter is, most likely, the E. Pack catalog reproduced in **Volume II** of this series.

SOLINGEN $\mathfrak{Pack}$-$\mathfrak{Nachrichten}$ SOLINGEN

IHRE ABTL.:		SCHRIFTL.:	F/K
GESCHÄFTSFÜHRUNG VERKAUFSLEITUNG WERBELEITUNG		Bericht Nr.: Seite 1 Monat:	Wa 6 Aug/Sept.

Z w e i   S i l b e n ...

... haben sich den Waffenhandel erobert -   " S i e g - f r i e d ".
Wenige Wochen haben genügt, um einen Begriff aus dieser Marke zu machen.

Eine gute Waffe heißt Siegfried
und ist von P a c k .

Das weiß nicht nur der Waffenhändler, darüber spricht bereits der Soldat ..
... und das ist viel, sehr viel bei der Vielzahl der Fabrikate. Was das seit
30 Jahren bestehende Bild nicht vermochte, haben diese zwei Silben in erstaun-
lich kurzer Zeit geschafft. Daß es nicht nur die Marke sein kann, ist selbst-
verständlich. Es muß auch etwas dahinter stecken:

Wer die "Siegfried"-Waffe führt,
hat mehr vom Geschäft.

Das ist der tiefere Sinn, der eigentliche Grund der erstaunlichen Erfolge.-

Die Lieferzeit ... ,

... das Sorgenkind der letzten Monate, wird uns allen keinen Ärger mehr brin-
gen. In verschiedenen Fällen mußte auf diese oder jene Waffe gewartet werden.
Niemandem war dieser Zustand unangenehmer als uns selbst. Was Sie aber heute be-
stellen, erhalten Sie prompt, meist sofort ab Lager.
Trotzdem dieser zeitweise recht leidige Zustand nun behoben ist, möchten wir Ihnen die Gründe nicht vorenthalten.
Seit Monaten waren wir für den Waffenexport außerordentlich beschäftigt. Die Ex-
portpflicht, die notwendige Bevorzugung der Exportaufträge, ist uns allen be-
kannt. In dieser Lage konnten wir es nicht immer jedem rechtmachen.
Sehen Sie deshalb auch unseren hohen Beschäftigungsgrad, unsere großen Erfolge,
als eine Empfehlung an .... und merken Sie vor:

"jetzt wieder p r o m p t e L i e f e r u n g".

... und nochmals die Lieferzeit ...

... aber anders herum. Wie, das sagt der beiliegende Brief. Er ist wichtig!
Deshalb lesen Sie ihn bitte recht aufmerksam.

-2-

WERBEMITTEL ALLER ART
AUS EISEN, STAHL,
EDLEREN METALLEN UND
ANDEREN HARTSTOFFEN
EXPORT

E. PACK & SÖHNE M.B.H., SOLINGEN, FABRIK UND LEITUNG RITTERSTR. 61-69

STAHLWAREN
HAARSCHNEIDE-
MASCHINEN
WAFFEN . EXPORT

Dieser Bericht ist ein Teilstück des uneigennützigen und kostenlosen Kundendienstes der Fa. Ernst Pack & Söhne. Alle Mitteilungen sind eingehend geprüft.

The English translation below of the letter from Ernst Pack & *Söhne* illustrates that the Solingen factories sent traveling salesmen (even out of the country) to their large accounts.

Pack New Copy

Two syllables....have conquered the weapons business "Sieg-victory-fried peace"

It only took a few business weeks to make an impact of this trade mark. A good weapon is called Siegfried, and is produced by Pack.

Not only the weapon's dealer knows about it, even the soldier is already talking about it...and that means a lot, a lot, because of the immense number of frabrications. What the situation during the last 30 years could not deliver (achieve), these amazing syllables were able to do in a short time span. Of course, it is without a doubt not only the brand name of this achievement, there has to be another motive behind it. Whoever carries the "Siegfried" weapon, has a better move on business. That is the deeper meaning, the true reason of amazing success.

The Delivery Time. Our "anxiety child" during the last month, will not be of any concern any longer. Although there are a few cases where customers had to wait for this or that weapon. Nobody could have been more embarrassed about this situation than us! But, whatever you order today, you will receive promptly, most of the time from storage. But never the less, although all the delays of the past have been taken care of, we wanted to inform you of the reasons.

For months, we were extra ordinarily busy with weapons export. The export duties, the necessary preferred shipment of export orders, is probably well known to all of us. Because of those conditions, it was impossible for us to take care of all requests. I hope, you will consider our high business grade (profile) and big success as a recommendation, and please take note: "now we will again deliver promptly." And once more about delivery time...how, the eclosed letter will tell you, it is important! So, please read it carefully!

The New Police Swords...are available (in storage supply department). You may order for delivery by return mail. We are sure you are familiar with our having production permit concerning those models? Advertising brochure is available for you.

How was that again...With the sword reclamation (rejection). Sword hilts from different material other than Tombak, are unsuitable. Every weapons' factory has had great difficulty with other material testing. The four year plan changed all of that and allowed the use of Tombak again. Today every Siegfried sword carries the Tombak hilt and will not have any reason for objection.

The New Catalog has been published and should be in the hands of our customers. The beauiful workmanship is admired everywhere and has been a valuable selling point. If we by any chance did not send a catalog to you (our friend) we ask you to notify us, and we will do so at once.

The Fall Messe starts August 27th. As always, we will be represented in the underground Messhallemarkt, Koje 78-78a. Should you come to Leipzig, it is very much our hope to see you at our stand.

The special attraction (weight) this year will focus on officers weapons. We are seeing it over and over again, that our swords and daggers are judged outstanding. During the last year, and also this year, we were able to win a large new customer circle for our Siegfried weapons and the assurance that we are certain, that the future will hold big successes. Our new catalog will show it in detail.

Eastmark prices have been dropping. Our many friends in the East-Mark are now buying with the reasonable prices of the alt (old) Reich. This makes it an opportune moment to present your order. In the interest of an always prompt delivery, we ask our east mark friends to promptly take care of orders for fast conclusions.

Those are the Pack news for August-September. You will hear from us again during the 1st month of the year.

Ernst Pack & Sons

A 1930s letter from the Max Weyersberg firm makes it clear that edged weapons from the Weyersberg firm and deliveries are made exclusively to wholesale businesses and <u>not</u> to individuals and/or formations.

WAFFENFABRIK MAX WEYERSBERG
Solingen, Green Street
Special Concern for Hunting and Sport Knives

Solingen, date of postal stamp

To all customer, business associates and interested!

<u>With regard to offers for the Reichswehr, Police and</u>
<u>Annex Formations.</u>

From customers I hear now and then that the notion is being represented that <u>my</u> firm is submitting offers directly to the above buyers. This is to be refuted, since offers are <u>not</u> being handled by me to these customers.

My offers and deliveries are made exclusively to the individual-and major wholesale businesses.

Furthermore I must call attention once again to the exact address of our firm since, in spite of constant reminders on my documents, letters, etc., returns often give occasion to confusion by uncertain firm trademarks. In order to avoid mistakes I offer the most exact address once again, as follows:

<u>Waffenfabrik Max Weyersberg</u>
Solingen, Grunstrasse

Heil Hitler
Waffenfabrik Max Weyersberg

Note the unusual "Aryan" comment found in an April 1934 Paul Weyersberg letter to a customer in Dortmund. The P.S. of this letter verifies that the 1st model *Luftwaffe* dress dagger was introduced in 1934.

PAUL WEYERSBERG & CO.,
EDGED-WEAPONRY CONCERN
SOLINGEN
April 25, 1934

Mr. Markoff: <u>Dortmund</u>

We confirm your prompt inquiry and include our current sales list, which illustrates

our sidearms and sabers.

From the list prices we will still guarantee you a reduction of 12%.

In order to document the quality of our products, we inform you that we are a 93-

year-old pure Aryan edged-weaponry concern, and supplier of the state government, Army and

Naval departments as well as the ministries.

With confirmation of contract for sabers, we ask for height (of persons) and for belts

the waist sizes.

We would be very happy if we might expect an order, and we guarantee beforehand

our best and most prompt service.

With a German greeting

/s/

P.S. Are you interested in our new Air Force daggers? If so, we ask for your prompt reply and we will make you an offer.

D.O.

The rear cover of the WMW sales catalog outlines exactly which model edged weapons Max Weyersberg manufactured. Note the inclusion of a *Zoll Dolche* (Customs dagger), not normally associated with this particular manufacturer.

Das Zeichen **WMW** für Qualität

WAFFEN

Eingetragene Schutzmarke

Ich liefere Ihnen:

1. Heer
Säbel für Offiziere und Mannschaften, Heeres-Offizier-Dolche, Seitengewehre, Koppelzeug, Portepees usw.

2. Luftwaffe
Fliegerschwerter, Flieger-Offizier-Dolche und Fliegerdolche, Seitengewehre, Koppelzeug, Portepees usw.

3. Polizei
Degen für Führer und Unterführer, Seitengewehre, Koppelzeug, Portepees usw.

4. Bahn- und Postschutz
Säbel, Seitengewehre, Koppelzeug, Portepees usw.

5. Zoll-, Justiz- und Strafanstaltsbeamte
Säbel, Dolche, Seitengewehre, Koppelzeug, Portepees usw.

6. Feuerlöschpolizei, Feuerwehr
Säbel für Branddirektoren, Wehrführer
Faschinenmesser für Offiziere und Mannschaften, Koppelzeug, Portepees usw.

7. Forst
Hirschfänger in vorschriftsmäßiger Ausführung, Koppelzeug, Portepees usw.

8. Deutsche Jägerschaft
Hirschfänger für D. J., Koppelzeug, Portepees usw.

9. Deutsches Jungvolk und Hitlerjugend
Vorschriftsmäßige Fahrtenmesser

10. SA, NSKK, Reichsarbeitsdienst
Vorschriftsmäßige Dolche und Führer-Haumesser

11. Miniatur-Waffen als Brieföffner

12. Reparaturen jeder Art, aufpolieren, vergolden, versilbern, elektrisch oxydieren, vernickeln, verchromen, emaillieren, brünieren, Ersatz- und Zubehörteile, Sonderanfertigungen nach Wunsch, Damaszierungen, Ätzungen, Inschriften, Monogramms usw.

Angebote und Lieferungen werden von mir nicht direkt an Heeresangehörige vorgenommen. Meine Lieferungen erfolgen nur an Wiederverkäufer.

Zwecks Vermeidung von Verwechslungen
mit einer ähnlich lautenden Firma bitte genauestens adressieren, besonders den Vornamen beachten!

Lastly, the following invoice from the famous H. J. Wilm firm in Berlin, while not edged weapon related, does vividly illustrate that deluxe items were not cheap during the 1933-1945 timeframe. Note that the price for a cased General Field Marshal's baton was 6,000 *Reichsmarks*. We have seen earlier that an HJ knife during the same time could be purchased for a mere three *Reichsmarks* and an SA or NSKK dress dagger for only six *Reichsmarks*. Hopefully, in the future, a 1930s factory invoice for an Honor dagger or sword will surface for comparative purposes.

SUMMARY

Again, the factory source documents reproduced in this reference and the preceding two volumes of this ongoing series only touch the surface of the records saved from the Solingen edged weapon manufacturing firms and on-hand at Johnson Reference Books (JRB). The author will continue to translate and publish additional information from these invaluable documents in future references.

Excellent studio portrait of a *Luftwaffe Feldwebel* grasping his 1st Model *Luftwaffe* dress dagger with nickel silver fittings. The cloth patch on his left sleeve is a specialist badge for anti-aircraft personnel.

Chapter 5

THIRD REICH EDGED WEAPONS IN WEAR

"A good uniform must work its way with the women, sooner or later."
—*Pickwick Papers* (1837)

The researcher of military history normally taps three potential sources of information—previously published references on the subject; official military documents, orders, and photographs; and private sources. A well-researched piece of work will draw information from all three of these primary sources.

The purpose of this particular chapter is to concentrate on only one of the aforementioned sources—photographs, and in doing so, provide the collector/researcher with an addition to his reference library to augment his existing references. Undoubtedly, one primary source of research information is period photographs. Here the collector/researcher of World War II memorabilia is blessed by both the quality and the quantity of available materials in the nature of available photographs. The state-of-the-art of photography was well enough advanced in the 1930s-40s to provide a sharp, well-defined product, as attested to by the period photographs appearing in the seven previous reference works of this **Collecting the Edged Weapons of the Third Reich** series.

Additionally, the quality of the photography is exceeded only by the quantity. There exists no period of history which is better documented than the era of Hitler's Third Reich. The general trend of German thoroughness prevailed in documenting and recording every detail of the life and times of the Third Reich. Not only do tons of official orders and documents remain in existence today, but, also, an infinite number of period photographs are available. As a case in point, the Hermann Göring personal photograph collection which is presently housed at the U.S. Library of Congress in Washington, D.C. consists of over forty mammoth albums, each filled with hundreds of photographs!

The quality photographs appearing in this pictorial study are the result of a screening of, literally, tens of thousands of period photographs at numerous learned institutions in this country and abroad, including the U.S. Library of Congress, National Archives, the U.S. Marine Corps Museum and Historical Center, United States Military Academy Museum and Library, the Imperial War Museum in London, the German *Deutsches Klingenmuseum,* the *Stadtarchiv-Solingen,* and the *Wehrgeschichliches* Museum. In addition to countless minor photo collections, the entire Hitler, Göring, von Ribbentrop, and Heinrich Hoffman (Hitler's personal photographer) collections were painstakingly reviewed one photograph at a time in a dedicated search for selected pictures of Third Reich edged weapons in wear. Additionally, thousands of 1933-1945 period postcards and pictures were studied in Europe over the past several years, and the appropriate ones purchased for use in this reference by the author. Additionally, many of the photographs appearing in this chapter were graciously provided by fellow dealers, collectors and researchers in this country and abroad. For example, collector/researcher Dirk Stefanski from Germany provided many valuable source photographs and documents from his extensive research library. Last, but not least, well-known dealer Johannes Floch of Vienna, Austria gave the author free rein of his extensive WWII photo archives (over 55,000 original newspaper press release photographs).

The resulting portfolio, while pictorial in content, can be considered one of the most significant reference additions in this entire field of endeavor. Here, the reader is afforded the firsthand opportunity to study the individual sidearms in their authentic settings. A wealth of information concerning the associated uniform and trappings, correct method of wear, use of accompanying accouterments, etc., is available in each individual picture. In sum, each photograph which follows provides an intricate study in itself by showing a little more clearly the relationship of the edged weapon to the spectacular pageantry that surrounded it.

Some "in wear" period photographs continue to elude the author. For example, after having researched literally **tens of thousands** of period photographs in this country and abroad, clear photographs of the 1st Model Rail and the *TENO* Officer dress dagger in wear have not been located, to date.

During the early volumes of this ongoing reference series, the list of "not to be found" photographs of World War II German dress daggers in wear was much longer and included the *TENO EM Heuer* and the *Bahnschutz* dagger. During the interim period, several period photographs of both of these sidearms have surfaced and been reproduced in previous volumes. There is little doubt that clear pictures of these last two models will surface and be brought to the attention of the author sooner or later.

When treasure hunter/researcher Ben Swearingen of Lewisville, Texas, discovered the one-of-a-kind Sepp Dietrich SS Honor sword in the hands of a World War II U.S. Army veteran in Florida who brought the sword to the U.S. (see **Volume V,** pages 114-126, and **Chapter 4** of **World War II German War Booty, Volume II,** pages 14-18 for complete details on the discovery), an all-out search began for period photographs showing Dietrich wearing his massive sidearm. A few American dealers and collectors were naive enough to even question the authenticity of this superb work-of-art, citing the absence of any period photographs showing Dietrich wearing his prized possession. Thanks to the likes of serious researcher/historian Andrew Mollo of England and Derek Chapman of Canada, not one, but several pictures of this sword in wear have come to the attention of the author. Other pictures continue to surface (see the photo below and page 110 of this volume). Once again, the "too quick to criticize" skeptics were proven drastically wrong, courtesy of the art of photography. The point is that, given enough time and effort, period pictures of the remaining two models of dress daggers in wear will eventually come to the fore, and will, hopefully, grace the pages of this reference series in the future.

Pictured above is one of several period photographs which clearly shows *LAH* Commander Sepp Dietrich wearing his one-of-a-kind SS honor sword while inspecting his SS troops.

A German *Leutnant*, a combat veteran of WWI service, poses wearing his Army officer dagger. The upper hanger clip is clearly visible just beneath the left lower pocket flap.
◀

This period portrait of an Army private provides an excellent view of a plain hilt enlisted man's sword complete with sword portepee. Clearly visible on the sword scabbard are scratches where the lower clip of the sword hanger has rubbed away the black enamel.
▶

An Army *Feldwebel* poses with an Army dove head sword complete with bullion portepee. On the lower left sleeve are the pre-1936 Army marksmanship and sharpshooter awards.

◄

An Army *Feldwebel* assigned to Infantry Regiment Nr. 488 poses with what appears to be an Alcoso model Nr. 119 lion head pattern sword complete with an officer pattern bullion portepee. Under close examination, the eagle with outstretched wings is clearly visible.

►

An Army *Feldwebel* holding a lion head sword complete with officer pattern portepee with bullion acorn poses with his bride. Rarely are photographs encountered showing the reverse hilt and langet of the edged weapon.

◀

An Army *Oberfeldwebel* poses with his lion head sword complete with portepee. Based on the configuration of the knuckle-bow and langet, the sword is possibly an Eickhorn model 1734, *Zieten Offiziersabel*. The double rows of braid on the cuff of the great-coat indicate the duty as a *Hauptfeld-webel* (company First Sergeant). ▶

In this studio portrait an Army *Hauptfeldwebel* is shown holding his Army dove head sword complete with officer pattern portepee with bullion acorn. The two rings of aluminum braid on the lower sleeves designate the position of *Hauptfeldwebel* (company First Sergeant).

An Army *Leutnant* poses in this formal portrait wearing what appears to be a Carl Eickhorn model 1765 *Prinz Eugen* officer saber complete with bullion portepee. Visible at the right of the scabbard is the rare bullion sword hanger.

A reserve *Oberleutnant,* a Veteran of WWI service, poses with his lion head pattern officer's sword. Note the Maltese cross in the center of the visor cap cockade which indicates his reserve status.

◀

In this wedding portrait, the groom, an Army *Obergefreiter,* poses with a jawless lion head officer sword with an NCO sword knot. The insignia on his visor hat is the first pattern with the short wing eagle. The tunic appears to be a variation dress/service pattern with piped front with six bright metal buttons, dress color patches and officer-style, turn-back cuffs.

▶

This period photograph shows an S84/98 Mauser service bayonet being worn with the parade dress uniform. The bakelite grips are clearly visible in the photograph.

◄

An Army private in an old style service tunic without the dark green collar and shoulder straps is shown wearing a dress bayonet with stag grips. Upon close examination, the strap of the portepee can be seen wrapped around the bayonet frog.

►

In this period portrait, a *Luftwaffe Obergefreiter* poses with a first model *Luftwaffe* dagger. On the left breast of his flight blouse, the *Obergefreiter* wears a radio operator/air gunner badge. The photograph, in the form of a postcard, is signed "Your Son Willi."

◄

In this wedding photograph, the groom, a *Luftwaffe Obergefreiter* is pictured with his bride and his aluminum 1st model *Luftwaffe* dagger. The bullion braid on his shoulder strap indicates he was a non-commissioned officer candidate on the date of his wedding. His awards and decorations include the Bomber Operational Flying clasp, 1939 Iron Cross 2nd Class and the Observer's badge.

►

This period photograph provides an excellent study of the first model *Luftwaffe* dagger worn by an *Unteroffizier*. Based on the toning on the metal parts, the dagger appears to be a silver model with 9 upper and 14 lower links in the chain hanger. The Trade badge on the lower left sleeve indicates flight personnel not authorized to wear a Flight Qualification badge.

In this formal portrait, a *Luftwaffe Unteroffizier* poses wearing a first model *Luftwaffe* dagger in silver. The photograph clearly shows the chain hanger attached to the leather belt loop and waist belt.

◀

In this period studio portrait, a *Luftwaffe Feldwebel* is pictured wearing his 1st model *Luftwaffe* dagger complete with 23cm bullion portepee. Note that the portepee is tied in the correct "tie" as specified in *Luftwaffe* Directive #77 dated 1 March 1935. ▶

This photograph dated 18 September 1939 provides an excellent study of the first model *Luftwaffe* dagger complete with 23 cm portepee in correct "tie." The *Feldwebel* wears both the *Luftwaffe* marksmanship lanyard and the German Sports Award on his uniform tunic.

A *Luftwaffe Oberfeldwebel*, a decorated veteran of WWI service, poses wearing his first model *Luftwaffe* dagger complete with portepee. Close examination of the photograph reveals the portepee is tied in one of the styles often seen on first model *Luftwaffe* daggers.

◀

In this December 1937 photograph, a *Luftwaffe Leutnant*, with WWI service, poses with his 1st model *Luftwaffe* Dagger with 23cm portepee. Under close examination, the hilt and scabbard fittings appear to be constructed of aluminum indicating a later production model.

▶

PHOTO COURTESY OF ADAM J. PORTUGAL, GERMANY

In this undated portrait, a *Luftwaffe Feldwebel* poses wearing his 1937 model *Luftwaffe* dagger with 23cm portepee. A portion of one hanger strap with deluxe lower fitting is visible below the lower edge of the tunic. The Specialist badge on the lower left sleeve designates anti-aircraft artillery.

◀

A *Luftwaffe Feldwebel* poses for his wedding portrait holding his *Fliegerschwert*. Visible in the photograph is the gilt swastika on the pommel and the double wire wrap on the leather grip. Note that the groom is wearing both the Commemorative medal of 1 October 1938 and the Defense Wall ("West Wall") medal when regulations specified that members of the Armed Forces were not authorized to receive both awards.

▶

LTC (RET.) THOMAS M. JOHNSON PHOTO COLLECTION

A *Luftwaffe Oberfeldwebel* wearing a silver model *Fliegerschwert* poses with his bride. The sword is suspended from beneath the flap of the lower left tunic pocket. The specialist badge on his left forearm is for flight technical personnel.

This period portrait of *General der Flieger* Kurt Student, founder of the German Airborne Forces, provides an excellent view of the 2nd model *Flieger Generaldegen* worn with a standard 23cm bullion portepee. General Student wears both the Imperial and Third Reich pilot's badges on his left breast. For his leadership as Commanding General of the 7th Air (Parachute) Division during the invasion of Holland, General Student was awarded the Knights Cross on 12 May 1940. He ended his career in April 1945 as a *Generaloberst* when he was captured by the British.

◀

In this studio portrait General Hermann von der Lieth-Thomsen poses wearing a 1st model *Luftwaffe* General's sword. This photograph provides an excellent view of the rarely seen special portepee worn with these swords. Note the two dark (blue) lines on the portepee fabric strap.

▶

LTC (RET.) THOMAS M. JOHNSON PHOTO COLLECTION
PHOTO BY FOTO SANDAU

Hermann Göring as a *Generalfeld-marschall* is shown wearing the special tunic (*Kleiner Rock*) for *Luftwaffe* Generals complete with the 2nd pattern *Luftwaffe* General officer sword. Attached to the hilt of the sword is the special porte-pee designed for this model sword; gilt strap with blue lines and gilt slide, stem, and acorn. The reverse of the photograph is dated 27 April 1939.

◄

In this period studio portrait, Hermann Göring as a General *Feldmarschall* is shown wearing the second pattern wedding sword. For a detailed account of this one-of-a-kind sword, see pages 103-105 of **Volume IV** of **Collecting the Edged Weapons of the Third Reich** by LTC (Ret.) Thomas M. Johnson. Of interest to medal collectors is the fact that Göring is wearing the three decorations on his lower left breast incorrectly. Normally, these decorations were worn in the reverse order to that shown here.

►

LTC (RET.) THOMAS M. JOHNSON PHOTO COLLECTION
PHOTO BY PHOTO-HOFFMANN, MÜNCHEN

HERMANN GÖRING
General der Flieger

Hermann Göring as a *General der Flieger* poses in one of his nonregulation uniforms wearing the duplicate wedding sword. Of particular interest in the photograph is the sword pommel which shows a representation of the *Pour le Merite* (Blue Max). As depicted on the dust jacket cover of **Volume IV** of **Collecting the Edged Weapons of the Third Reich** and described on pages 103-105, the duplicate wedding sword bears a stylized sunwheel design swastika while the reverse pommel is adorned with the complete Göring coat of arms. The original wedding sword, by contrast, has an enameled *Pour le Merite* on the obverse pommel while the reverse pommel depicts only the crest of the Göring coat of arms (mailed arm and fist), and not the entire coat of arms. Could this mean that the duplicate sword had more than one pommel, that the pommel of the original wedding sword could be transferred to the duplicate sword, or is there possibly a third pattern wedding sword in existence?

In this wedding photograph, a DLV *Fliegerkomandant* wears the rare 55cm flyer's dagger suspended by the chain hanger from beneath the tunic. The officer, a veteran of WWI service, wears his medal bar as well as the Iron Cross 1st Class and wound badge.

In this undated photograph, the DLV officer in the foreground is wearing a rare 55cm DLV flyer's dagger with unique scabbard fittings. Note that the fittings have convex edges as opposed to the normal concave edges. Also visible in the photograph is an SA dagger and two 1933 SS daggers.

A DLV *Fliegerkapitan* is shown wearing the rare 55cm DLV flyer's dagger. Close inspection of the photograph reveals the flat pommel with inset gilted swastika and long tip on the lower scabbard fitting which is unique to this rare dagger.

A *Luftwaffe Unteroffizier* poses with a *Luftwaffe* survival machete complete with canvas web frog. The three dark spots on the blade were probably caused by contact with the internal scabbard retaining bands. See page 103 of **Collecting the Edged Weapons of the Third Reich, Volume III** for additional information on this unique edged weapon.

◀

A *Kriegsmarine Oberfeldwebel* is shown wearing his 2nd model Navy dagger with lightning bolt scabbard and portepee in the regulation "reef knot" tie. The dagger is suspended from the hanger straps that were sewn under the pocket flap on the left side of the greatcoat. The greatcoat is being worn with all buttons buttoned as prescribed by regulations for noncommissioned officers on duty.

▶

The detail on this studio portrait of a naval officer candidate is such that the engraving on the lightning bolt pattern scabbard is clearly visible. The dagger is suspended from the under-the-tunic waist belt. The decorations include the Iron Cross ribbon in the second buttonhole and the Destroyer badge on the lower left breast.

A Naval medical officer *Leutnant* poses wearing his second model Navy dagger complete with portepee. Closer inspection of the photograph reveals that the dagger is suspended from only *one* hanger strap.

◀

This period photograph provides an excellent view of the 2nd Model Naval dagger worn with the naval officer's great coat. The dagger is suspended from two sew-in fabric hangers which can be slipped inside the pocket when not in use. Close inspection of the photograph reveals the dagger has the lightning bolt scabbard and is complete with a portepee in the "reef knot" tie.

▶

PHOTO COURTESY OF DIRK STEFANSKI, GERMANY

A group of naval officers is greeted by *Grossadmiral* Raeder. All of the officers wear the white dress uniform with 2nd model Navy daggers complete with 42cm portepee.

Oberster SA-Führer (OSAF) Franz von Pfeffer is shown in conversation with Deputy *Führer* Rudolf Hess during one of the annual Nurnberg party rallies. Von Pfeffer is wearing what appears to be a standard SA service dagger, although upon close examination, the dagger appears to be longer and narrower than the standard pattern.

▶

NATIONAL ARCHIVES COLLECTION
PHOTO COURTESY OF JILL HALCOMB SMITH

A Marine *SA-Obertruppführer* poses in his 1934 pattern dark blue service uniform complete with the rare Marine SA dagger. Note the gold anchor insignia on the right collar patch, the shoulder strap with dark blue and white alternating cords and the adjutant's aiguillette suspended from the right shoulder.

Previously unpublished photograph of SA *Obergruppenführer* and adjutant to the *Führer,* Wilhelm Bruckner, with Deputy *Führer,* Rudolf Hess. Bruckner is wearing an SA honor dagger with unique interlocking loop-type link (similar to an ID bracelet) chain hanger. See page 37 of *The Daggers and Edged Weapons of Hitler's Germany* by LTC James P. Atwood for photograph of similar dagger.

This 1939 photograph shows the Count of Baillet-Latour honoring the team leaders from Hungary, Italy, and Finland at the National Sports Arena events. Of note is National Sport leader von Tschammer-Osten on the left who is wearing the extremely rare *SA Feldherrnhalle* dress dagger and suspension straps.

During a visit to Italy, SA Chief of Staff Viktor Lutze poses with *Il Duce* and *Reichssportführer* Tschammer und Osten. Lutze and the SA officer behind Lutze both wear ultra-rare *Feldherrnhalle* high leaders daggers. Close examination of the photograph reveals that Lutze's dagger is in gilt while the other dagger appears to be the silver model. Also, there appears to be a difference in the color of the hangers.

In this studio portrait SA *Stabschef* Viktor Lutze is wearing his specially designed 1935 SA honor dagger. Close examination of the photograph reveals the raised oak leaves on the crossguard, the unadorned links in the double-chain hanger, the unadorned scabbard fittings and the overall larger proportions of the dagger (see page 47 of ***Daggers, Bayonets & Fighting Knives of Hitler's Germany*** by John R. Angolia for additional information on this dagger). In addition to his military awards for WWI service, Lutze wears the *NSDAP* golden party badge and the badge of the SA Rally at Brunswick in 1931 which was hosted by Lutze as *Führer* of *SA-Gruppe Nord*.

In this press release photograph dated 5 August 1939, Hitler greets a Hitler Youth leader at the May Day Youth Rally at the Berlin Olympic Stadium. The HJ leader wears his leader dagger suspended from beneath his tunic. For classic automobile collectors, the photograph also provides a detailed view of Hitler's Mercedes Benz 770 open limousine. The *Führer* standard is clearly visible just above the right front fender.

◀

This studio portrait provides a clear view of the DLV flyer's knife, integral hanger, and beltloop being worn by a DLV technical specialist.

▶

In this period studio portrait, a German Red Cross *Oberwachtführer* poses wearing his Red Cross leader's dagger suspended from the fabric hangers. The detail of the photograph is such that the slots in the pommel cap of the dagger and the pebbled finish of the scabbard are clearly visible. The two bullion stripes on the lower left sleeve indicate ten years of Red Cross service.

◀

The Hermann Göring presentation Forestry dagger featured in chapter 4 is shown "in wear." Also, visible in this photograph is a standard senior Forestry cutlass, complete with portepee.

Two members of the German Rifle Association pose for a formal portrait with the individual on the right wearing his rare Rifle Association dagger. This is only the second photograph printed which shows this model dagger being worn. In addition to the large numbers of shooting medals the men are wearing, the individual on the left is wearing his WWI military awards.

In this wedding portrait the groom, a police *Leutnant* (Lieutenant) wears his 1936 pattern *Polizei Führer Degen* with officer portepee. Clearly visible in the photograph is the silver police grip emblem and large bullion acorn on the portepee. Although undated, the photograph is signed, "Josef U. Pauli."

In this 1938 photograph, *Oberstleutnant* von Axhelm, Commander of the Regiment Her-mann Göring, presents the traditional emblem ("Cross of the South") to the Commandant of the *Schutzpolizei* of Berlin, *Generalmajor* von Kamptz. The emblem had been previously used by the Regiment Göring. General Kamptz wears a 1936 pattern *Polizei Führer Degen* suspended from a teardrop hanger. The original caption of the photograph notes the mounted troop of the Berlin *Schutzpolizei* would carry on the traditions of the East African police troop. Veterans of the former German East African territories are in the background.

An *SS-Obersturmführer* and Knight's Cross winner poses with an Imperial Bavarian cavalry officer sword with SS officer portepee in a very unique "tie." Under close examination, the SS runes on the portepee stem are clearly visible.

▶

This 30 September 1935 photograph shows English Prime Minister Neville Chamberlain and von Ribbentrop inspecting an SS unit. Note the SS sword and accompanying SS sword knot.

An *SS-Untersturmführer* assigned to the staff of *SS-Junkerschule Braunschweig* poses with his 1936 pattern SS officer Degen complete with bullion sword knot. The SS runes are clearly visible on the stem of the sword knot. On his left chest, the officer is wearing the Hitler Youth pin, the German National Sport badge and the SA Sport badge.

Der Führer and *Il Duce* are shown at a ceremony during the May 1938 German state visit to Italy. Hitler is wearing a special version of the Fascist party leader's dagger presented to him by Mussolini. This is one of the few photographs of Hitler wearing an edged weapon. There are no known photographs of Hitler wearing a German edged weapon. In the center background, German Foreign Minister Von Ribbentrop wears a Diplomatic dagger with his 1st pattern Diplomatic uniform designed especially for the Italian visit.

This previously unpublished press photograph dated 10 May 1938 depicts Adolf Hitler at Michelangelo Square in Florence, Italy wearing the Italian dress dagger presented to him by Mussolini. The Italian dagger pictured appears to be the standard M.V.S.N. leader's dagger model 1932. To the best of the author's knowledge, this is the only dress dagger that Hitler was personally pictured wearing, i.e., no photograph to date has surfaced of Adolf Hitler wearing a German edged sidearm.

U.S. Army Staff Sgt. Robert Thibodaux, 269th Combat Engineer Unit, of Thibodaux, Louisiana is pictured during May, 1945, holding two presentation swords from Hermann Göring's "Aladdin's Cave" near Berchtesgaden. The massive gold sword in his left hand was a gift to Göring from Mussolini. The officer pictured on the right of the photograph is SSG Thibodaux's platoon leader, Lt. Eckberg. SSG Thibodaux is the U.S. Army Sergeant who shipped home the famous Hermann Göring wedding sword and later sold it to James P. Atwood.

SSG (Ret.) Robert Thibodaux of Louisiana stands in front of his U.S. Army Bronze Star Award Document and photographs of the Hermann Göring Wedding Sword which he personally "liberated" from Göring's "Aladdin's Cave" near Berchtesgaden during May, 1945. The author visited and interviewed Sgt. Thibodaux at his home in Louisiana during January 1996.

321

This U.S. Army combat photograph of a heavily armed German soldier provides an excellent study of a World War II boot knife "In wear." Although pictured in previous contemporary reference books, it is certainly worth reprinting here as it clearly shows how a boot knife could also be attached to another part of the combat uniform by means of the metal clip.

Chapter 6

THE THIRD REICH BOOT KNIFE

By Robert Heiduk

"To face an adversary in armed combat is one of the most exciting experiences in life."

—Aldo Nadi

*(Author's Note: Robert Heiduk is a native of Santa Barbara, California, and a veteran of the U.S. Air Force. He began collecting German militaria while in high school in the mid-1950s and began specializing in German dress daggers and fighting knives in the early 1970s. Bob authored the chapter on Imperial Trench Knives appearing in **Collecting the Edged Weapons of Imperial Germany, Volume I,** and is the author of this chapter on the subject of the Third Reich Boot Knife appearing in **Volume VII** and continuing in this reference. Bob Heiduk also made major contributions to **Volume V** of this ongoing series and has conducted a professional seminar on the subject of German Boot Knives at a recent Militaria Antiques Xtravaganza (MAX) Show in Pittsburgh.)*

FAKES AND REPRODUCTIONS

In any hobby where there is money to be made, there are the un-scrupulous who are waiting and willing to sell fakes and reproductions to the unaware. Unfortunately, this statement holds true with boot knives as well as all other areas of edged weapon collecting.

Collectors/researchers must read as much as they can in contemporary reference books and become as familiar as possible with their particular area of collecting by talking with other collectors and examining the genuine arti-cle firsthand against a reproduction or fake, if possible. Shown below are two out-and-out fakes.

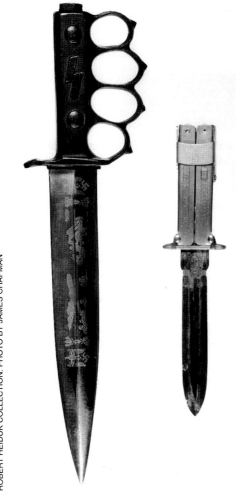

Fakes. The "knuckle knife" shown is supposed to be a Hitler Youth "private purchase" piece. Except for the scabbard, the entire knife is a fake. It first appeared on the market in the early 1960's. The source from which it came is unknown to the author. The knife on the right is the much publicized "*SS panograph knife*" which never existed during the Third Reich period. For complete details on this spurious piece, refer to earlier volumes of this reference series (Vol. I, p. 279; Vol. II, p. 306; Vol. III, p. 191).

The first is the much publicized "*SS panograph knife*" that never existed during the Third Reich era. It was actually manufactured in Great Britain during the 1960s. It has a 4 1/2-inch double-edged blade with the 1933-1934 Eickhorn trademark stamped on it. One side of the brass handle is marked "*M7/66/34,*" has "*RZM*" in a circle and the SS runes. The other half has the SS runes and is marked, "*Streifendienst.*" The aluminum clip has the early SS eagle over the swastika. The knife has been aged, but is definitely not of good quality. Although this particular knife has been widely publicized as a fake, it is still seen at shows and in antique shops, sometimes with a very high pricetag.

The second knife is supposed to be a Hitler Youth "private purchase" "knuckle knife." The 8 1/2-inch, SA style double-edged blade has no maker mark or motto, but does have a very light photo-etched Army scene. The blackened aluminum knuckles and nonfunctional rivets have a pebbled texture. A Hitler Youth single rune is on either side of the hilt. The threaded tang is held to the hilt by a pommel nut with a swastika on the top. The scabbard seems to be an authentic SA scabbard with the lower scabbard fitting hardware removed. This knife was made in the 1960s. What quantity may currently be in circulation is unknown to the author.

The illustration below shows a World War I trench knife that was utilized in World War II, manufactured by the Gottlieb-Hammesfahr firm.

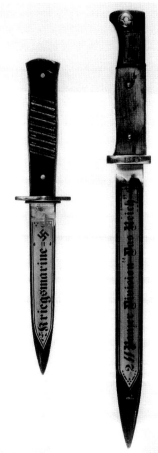

Two original items that have been "enhanced" with the addition of blade etchings to increase the sales and value of a normally low-cost, common knife and bayonet. The knife was manufactured by *Gottlieb-Hammesfahr, Solingen-Foche.* Both sides have been etched. The obverse side is etched, *"Kriegsmarine"* plus a swastika. The reverse side is etched *"Bismarck 1939."* The bayonet has been highly polished and etched, *"2 Panzer Division-Das Reich"* on the obverse side and *"Meine Ehre heisst Treue"* (My Honor is Loyalty) on the reverse side. There are runic symbols etched on the pommel. The quality of the etchings is certainly good enough to fool the novice collector.

This particular knife is enhanced with some outstanding acid etchings on both sides of the blade. One side is etched, *"Bismarck 1939,"* and the other side has, *"Kriegsmarine"* plus a swastika. The style and quality of the etchings are reminiscent of the supposedly SS bayonets which were etched in Great Britain during the 1960s to increase the sales and value of normally low-cost, slow-moving items.

ORDNANCE ACCEPTANCE MARKINGS

The *Reichszeugmeisterei (RZM)* (Nazi Party Department of Ordnance) was officially established in 1934 to control the manufacturing, quality, quantity, and price of Nazi Party-related goods. The *RZM* is mentioned in this chapter only to clarify its authority and areas of responsibility. Cutlers applied for permission to manufacture *RZM*-controlled edged weapons, and upon approval, were assigned a control number which identified their individual firms. An example of this is on a Hitler Youth knife manufactured by the Carl Eickhorn firm, on which the marking, *"M7/66"* appears. The *"M"* stands for an item made from metal; the *"7"* means a duty dagger or hunting knife manufacturer; the *"66"* is the unique numeric code assigned to the Carl Eickhorn firm. Blades are found with both the *RZM* marking as well as the cutler's name and trademark. *RZM* inspectors conducted periodic inspections of firms assigned control numbers to verify adherence to required specifications.

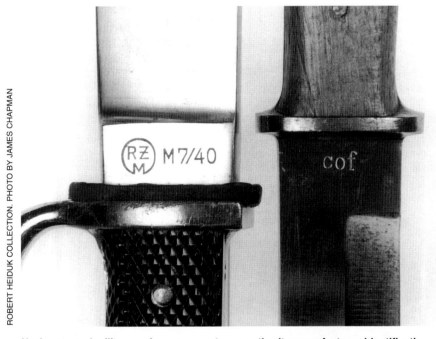

Nazi party and military ordnance acceptance authority manufacturer identification code markings. The "M7/40" is the *RZM* control number assigned to *Hartkopf & Co., Solingen*. The "cof" is the military ordnance acceptance authority three-letter group manufacturer identification code assigned to *Carl Eickhorn Waffenfabrik, Solingen* after 1940 to the end of World War II.

The military ordnance acceptance authority's inspection mark utilized after 1937 on military combat sidearms shown on the top edge of a boot knife blade and on the pommel of a bayonet. This style marking is commonly referred to as the *"Waffen-Amt"* mark.

The military ordnance acceptance stamp of a stylized eagle with folded wings over the number "5" as it appears on the spike of a *Luftwaffe* gravity knife.

The *Heereswaffenamt (HWaA)* (Military Ordnance Acceptance Authority) was responsible for quality assurance on military and combat items, including knives. The *Wehrmachtswaffenamt (WaA)* (Army Ordnance Acceptance Authority) was the predecessor of the *HWaA,* while the *Luftwaffewaffenamt* (Air Force Ordnance Acceptance Authority) was a subordinate of the *HWaA.*

The *Waffen-Amt* stamp on a boot knife signified acceptance, but not necessarily that the manufacturer was in absolute compliance with the specification. That is why, in some cases, knives manufactured by the same cutler can be compared and differences noted.

Combat items were required in the field quickly and in larger quantities as the war progressed. Fabrication and quality control were not completed as carefully, nor were the best materials available for use towards the end of World War II.

The marking utilized by the *HWaA* Regional Bureaus was a stylized eagle with its wings spread over a number, or a number preceded by *WaA.* The eagle used prior to 1937 had its wings folded. After 1937, the eagle's wings were plainly extended or were extended over a swastika in a circle.

HWaA assigned an "S" plus <u>three number</u> group manufacturer identification code number during the period 1936 to 1940 (for example, *"S/175"* was assigned to the Carl Eickhorn *Waffenfabrik*). From 1940 until the end of the war a <u>three-letter</u> group manufacturer identification code was assigned (for example, *"cof"* was assigned to the Carl Eickhorn *Waffenfabrik*). The author has not encountered the "S" plus three-number designation on any "boot" knives; however, the three-letter codes are occasionally found.

The *HWaA* Assigned One-, Two-, and Three-Letter Manufacturer Identification Codes and *RZM* Codes for Known Third Reich Era Edged Weapon Makers:

i   *Elite Diamantwerke A.-G. Siegmar-Schönau b/Chemnitz. (Bayonet maker)*

ab   *Mundlos Aktien Gesellschaft, Nähmaschinenfabrik, Magdeburg-N. (Bayonet maker)*

ce   *Sauer & Sohn, J.P., Gewehrfabrik, Suhl, Thuringen. (S-147)*

uc   *Unknown bayonet maker.*

agv   *Berg & Co., Solingen-Ohligs. (Bayonet maker)*

aso   *Fichtel & Sachs, Schweinfurt, Bayern.*

asw   E. & F. Hörster, Stahl und Metallwarenfabrik, Solingen. RZM M7/36

bgj   Bremshey & Co., Solingen-Ohligs. RZM M2/181

bym   Genossenschafts Maschinenhaus der Buchsenmacher, Ferlach/
      Karnten, Austria. (Bayonet maker)

byn   Lasch & Co., Albin, G.m.b.H., Dresden N 30. (Bayonet maker)

cap   Völker, Adolf, Zangenfabrik, Schmalkalden; Hessen-Nassau.

chg   Osterreichische Drahtgitter-Siebwaren und Metallmobelfabrik, Linz,
      Austria. (Bayonet maker)

clc   Richard Herder, Drahtgitter-Siebwaren und Metallmobelfabrik
      Gesenkschmiede, Solingen. RZM M7/18

cof   Carl Eickhorn, Waffenfabrik, Solingen. (S-175) RZM M7/66

cqd   Pränafa-Werke G.m.b.H., Solingen-Gräfrath.

cqh   Clemen und Jung, Solingen.

cqu   Eck & Söhne, Josef, Maschinenfabrik, Düsseldorf. (Bayonet maker)

crs   Paul Weyersberg & Co. Waffenfabrik, Solingen. RZM M7/43

csd   Dürkoppwerke, A.G., Werk III, Bielefeld. (Bayonet maker)

csr   Gebrüder Heller, G.m.b.H., Marienthal bei Schweina. RZM M7/50

cud   Wilhelm Pfeiffer & Co., Metall-Besteck-Fabrik, Solingen.

cul   Ernst Pack & Söhne, Stahlwarenfabrik, Solingen.

cve   Schönbaumsfeld's Sohn, DMK, Metallwarenfabrik, Korneuburg. (Bay-
      onet maker)

cvl   WKC, Waffenfabrik, G.m.b.H., Solingen-Wald. (S-185) RZM M7/42

cvp   Gottlieb Hammesfahr, Stahlwarenfabrik, Solingen-Foche. RZM M7/67

ddl   Remscheider Hobelmesser-Fabrik, Josua Corts Sohn, Remscheid.

dlu   Ewald Lüneschloss, Militar-Effekten-Fabrik, Solingen. (Accouter-
      ments)

dnv   Fahr A.G., Stockach. (Bayonet maker)

dot   Waffenwerke Brunn, A.-G., Werk Brunn. (Bayonet maker)

dqg   Noelle, Gebrüder, G.m.b.H., Bestecke, Ludenscheid 1/Westfalen.

edg   J.A. Henckels, Zwillingswerk, Schneidwarenfabrik und Stahlwerk, Solingen. RZM M7/10

fdx   Heller, Gebrüder, Bohrerfabrik, Schmalkalden/Thuringen-Wald. RZM M7/50

ffc   Friedrich Herder, Abr. Sohn, Stahlwarenfabrik, Solingen. RZM M7/49

ffv   Wilhelm Benze, Stahlfabrik, Eimbeckhausen, Provinz Hanover. (S 84/98 Bayonet and scabbard maker)

fnj   Alcoso-Stahlwarenfabrik und Waffenfabrik, G.m.b.H. (formerly Alexander Coppel & Cie), Solingen.

fxo   C.G. Haenel Waffen und Fahrrad-fabrik, Suhl, Thuringen.

fze   F.W. Höller Waffenfabrik, Solingen. RZM M7/33

gcj   Melzer & Feller, Fabrik feiner Werkzeuge und Maschinen, Zella-Mehlis, Thuringen.

ghh   Kober & Co., Wilhelm, Haarschneide-Maschinenfabrik, Suhl, Thuringen.

gyq   Anton Wingen, Jr., Solingen. RZM M7/51

gyr   Hugo Linder, Deltawerk, Solingen.

har   Müller, Friedrich Augustus, Stahlwaren-Fabrik, Solingen-Gräfrath. RZM M7/4.

hat   Gebrüder Gräfrath, Fabrik feiner Stahlwaren, Solingen-Widdert. RZM M7/30

hfu   C. Friedrich Ern, Metallwarenfabrik, Solingen-Wald.

hpp   Helbig F.u.A., Steinbach Krs. Meiningen. M7/73

jkh   Busse, Carl, Fabrik für Ausrustungen aus Stoff und Leder, Mainz. (Accouterments—bayonet frogs) *jue* Dick, Paul F., Stahlwaren und Werkzeugfabrik, Esselingen a/N.

juv Eduard Wüsthof, Dreizackwerk, Solingen. RZM M7/19

jwh Staatliche Waffenfabrik, Chatellerault, France. (Bayonet maker—under German supervision)

jwn Fischer jun., Rudolf, Knopf-u. Metallwarenfabrik, Nixdorf/Sudenten-gau. (Bayonet maker)

lca Kamphausen und Plumacher, Stahlwarenfabrik, G.m.b.H., Solingen-Ohligs.

ltk Robert Klaas, Messerfabrik, Solingen-Ohligs. RZM M7/37 (Alternate M7/1051)

mjf Justus Brenger & Co., Justinuswerk, Solingen-Wald. RZM M7/16

mkm Lüttgens & Engels, Tempergiesserei, Solingen-Gräfrath. RZM M2/177

sgx Unknown bayonet maker.

pyy Unknown bayonet maker.

The above represents only a partial listing of letter codes assigned to edged weapon manufacturers during the Third Reich period. Although researchers have put forth much effort checking volumes of documents, the list remains incomplete. Many companies and their records were destroyed during the war. Others ceased to exist in the war's aftermath or were just as happy to "forget" their participation in the manufacturing of weapons during that period.

PATENT MARKINGS

A few edged weapons are encountered for which the manufacturer had applied for a patent because of an innovative design or some unusual manufacturing technique. If a patent was granted, a cutler would have protection for his investment, as well as the design or technique. Another firm could not utilize a particular design or manufacturing technique without prior approval from the originating firm. Also, after approval of a patent, the item was stamped with a patent marking to indicate its level of protection. The protections given by law to various items are listed below:

D.R.P.u.A.P.—Deutsches Reich Patent und Ausländische Patente (German Empire and Foreign Patents). This mark has not been seen on an edged weapon, to date, by the author.

Two examples of patent markings. *"Ges. Gesch." (Gesetzlich Geschutz)* means "protected by law." *"D.R.G.M." (Deutsches Reich Gebrauchsmüster)* means "German Registered Design."

D.R.P.—Deutsches Reich Patent (German Empire Patent). This mark was stamped on items to indicate the granting of a German letter patent only. This marking is not to be confused with the *"DRP" (Deutsches Reichs Post)* marking of the *Postschutz* (Postal Protection Service).

D.R.G.M—Deutsches Reich Gebrauchs Müster (German Registered Design). This mark was used to indicate a design patented during the German Empire and/or Third Reich. It is a common patent marking found on many Third Reich items.

Ges. Gesch.—Gesetzlich Geschützt (Protected by Law). This mark implied the design or technique had been registered with the *Deutsches Patentamt* (German Patent Authority) and had been granted some protection from being copied. This commonly-found marking was used to signify the registering of a design or technique for which there was not enough difference to justify a true patent.

MANUFACTURERS' NAMES AND TRADEMARKS

Many of the boot knives encountered by the collector will have a particular manufacturer's name and trademark stamped on them. However, a large quantity of knives manufactured during the Third Reich era will be found totally unmarked. One of the reasons so many of the knives are found unmarked, particularly during the World War II period, is that as the war progressed, larger quantities of knives were required. Therefore, manufacturers, out of necessity, did not fabricate the complete knife themselves, but obtained some parts from other sources and then assembled the knives. In some cases, middlemen obtained all the parts from various sources and then had them assembled by yet another company.

Pictured above are the names and trademarks of four large manufacturers of combat boot knives during the Third Reich.

Some of the privately purchased knives are found with either a whole-saler's or retailer's name stamped or etched on them.

SCABBARDS

The scabbards most commonly used for boot knives during the Third Reich era are the all-metal variety with steel spring clips on the back. They are almost always painted black.

Some of the World War I and transitional fighting knives used the common World War I style scabbard made with a metal body, leather belt loop and hilt strap. The metal body is usually painted black and the leather fittings are either brown or black.

ROBERT HEIDUK COLLECTION. PHOTO BY JAMES CHAPMAN

Various all-metal scabbards utilized with boot knives during the Third Reich period.

Examples 1, 3 and 4 above are leather scabbards with metal tips. Example 1 has no extra throat protection. Number 3 has a metal throat, and number 4 has an additional leather throat. Scabbards 2 and 5 are the World War I style with painted metal bodies and leather belt loops and hilt straps. Example 2 is painted dark green and number 5 is painted the standard black.

Privately purchased commercial knives are found in either brown or black all-leather scabbards, all-metal scabbards, or the metal-bodied scabbards with leather fittings.

ALL-METAL FIGHTING KNIFE UPDATE

Since the publication of my chapter on Third Reich boot knives in **Volume VII,** some information has surfaced which should shed some light on the mystery surrounding the origin of the all-metal, double-edged fighting knife described and pictured on pages 344 and 345 of that volume.

The knife in question has been pictured and described in various publications as being of German origin or at least captured, tested and used by the German military. The knife itself is completely unmarked, however. The

German origin theory came about due to a *Waffen Amt* marking of an eagle and swastika over the alpha/numeric code *HZajt21* which was stamped on the upper reverse side of the leather scabbard. The author has interviewed an individual in North Carolina who stated that years ago he was in possession of the knife and the *Waffen Amt* stamp in question and actually stamped the scabbard himself sometime prior to selling the knife at an Atlanta, Georgia show!

The reality of this all-metal knife is as follows. Three of the four knives of this type known to the author were made during the period May through July 1944 by an Iowa native, Hersel McMurry, while he was attending a war production vocational training shop program in Springfield, Missouri. The fourth knife (the one with the *Waffen-Amt* stamp on the back of the scabbard) could have been made by someone else at the school.

It is unknown where or by whom the brown leather scabbards were actually made. However, it is quite feasible they were also made at the vocational school. The snaps on the straps of the two scabbards examined by the author have stamped American markings.

Hersel gave one of the knives to his older brother, Howard McMurry, who was in the United States Army and on his way to Europe in October 1944. Howard was initially assigned to the 9th Army, Company B, 258th Engineers (C) Battalion and later to Company F, 357th Engineers (G.S.) Regiment. It appears Howard used the knife as a utility tool, as he wore out the first one digging up mines, opening cans, etc. and asked Hersel to send him a second one. Howard returned with the second knife to the United States and was discharged in April 1946. At some point after Howard's discharge, his wife returned the knife to Hersel. It remained with Hersel until it was discovered in his basement in 1981.

The fate of the first knife is unknown, but it was, most likely, disposed of by Howard when he received the second one. The second knife is in the possession of military collector, Lyn Gamelson. A third knife is in the possession of the author. The current location of the fourth knife with the marked scabbard is unknown.

COMMEMORATIVE KNIFE

It was mentioned by the author in **Volume VII** that knives are occasionally found from the Third Reich period engraved or etched with special dates and events. Pictured is a small knife with a blade etching commemorating War Christmas 1940 and presented to some member of the 17094E Field Security Police. This unit was attached to the 61st Infantry Regiment which was headquartered in Munich, Germany.

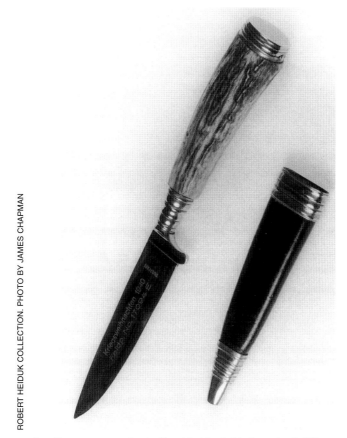

Small commemorative knife with 4-inch blade etched, "War Christmas 1940, Field Security Police Number 17094E."

SUMMARY

The German fighting knife has become an item of great interest to many militaria collectors. Unfortunately, unscrupulous individuals are producing fakes and reproductions and selling them to the unaware and unprepared.

Collectors must become thoroughly familiar with their area of collecting by reading reference books, having discussions with other collectors, examining as many as possible of the genuine items, and examining the fakes and reproductions when possible. A "sixth sense" or feel develops through experience. The old adage, "if it seems too good to be true, it probably is" definitely holds truth in the knife-collecting world.

Ordnance acceptance markings, patent markings, manufacturers' names, trademarks and codes are of interest to the collector/researcher in grasping more information related to a particular edged weapon.

Entertaining the American troops during World War II seems to have been fun for none other than Hollywood film star Mickey Rooney. Standing before a microphone in the field, Rooney wears a German trench knife which appears to be identical to the one pictured on page 315 (center) of *Collecting the Edged Weapons of Imperial Germany*.

U.S. ARMY PHOTOGRAPH

APPENDIX 1

LUFTWAFFE GENERAL DIETRICH VON CRIEGERN'S
2ND MODEL *LUFTWAFFE* DAGGER

—By Doug Gow, New Zealand

*(Author's Note: Fellow collector Doug Gow of New Zealand has been an invaluable contributor to the last several volumes of this ongoing reference series. Doug is not only an avid German edged weapon collector, but has become an accomplished researcher and photographer. The reader of this volume will find some quality color and black & white photographs shot through his camera lens. Additionally, he credits the earlier volumes of **Collecting the Edged Weapons of the Third Reich** in teaching him how to properly research the historical background of an individual sidearm. Several years ago Doug purchased the personal 2nd Model Luftwaffe dress dagger of Luftwaffe General Dietrich von Criegern. Utilizing <u>solely</u> a translation of von Criegern's service record, Doug Gow has provided us with a study of von Criegern's life and military service career. This appendix shows that a brief, accurate account of a World War II Wehrmacht Officer's life can be established from a <u>single</u> source document. Doug Gow is presently contacting relatives of General von Criegern in hopes of expanding his research file on the General.)*

Dietrich von Criegern was born in Dresden, Germany on 2 December 1886, the son of Friedrich Georg and Ida Maria von Criegern. His father was a *Generalleutnant* in the Imperial Army. In his younger years Dietrich was educated by private tutors at his home until entering the Bochow Institute in Dresden. In furthering his education he joined the Royal Corps of Cadets, also in Dresden, which he left with certified approval for college entrance examinations.

Following his father's military career, he entered the 18th Regiment of Hussars as an Officer candidate on 26 February 1907, and he received his Officer commission as a *Leutnant* on 24 January 1908. After taking leave of absence for a year he was transferred in February 1910 to the Officer Reserve.

In April 1914 he joined the Trained Reserves *Landwehr 1*, but shortly after World War I broke out, he was declared unfit for service in both garrison and field duty. However, due to the mobilization, he rejoined the Reserves in the 2nd Regiment of the Guard Regiment which, in early 1914, was united with the Frontline Regiment. Later that year (on 24 December 1914) he was awarded the Iron Cross 2nd Class. Von Criegern's promotion to *Oberleutnant* of the Reserve occurred on 27 January 1915, which resulted in his taking command of the 4th Company. With this unit he saw action on the Rawka River in East Prussia. By the middle of June he was placed in charge of a machine gun company, Reserve Infantry Division 232, and during this time he was involved with fighting on the borders of Poland and Galicia, the Battle of Hrubieszow, and the Battle of Cholm. A further transfer in August saw him briefly in a Reserve Officer's Cavalry Regiment.

By late October 1915 von Criegern's career led him to the position of acting Regimental Adjutant of the 232nd Reserve Infantry Regiment. He soon became their Regimental Adjutant, a position he was to hold until 20 October 1916. Over this period he took part in the Serbian Campaign, position warfare in the front at Dunaburg, and fighting on the Upper Styr and Stochod. With this action came the award of his Iron Cross First Class, which was received on 27 January 1916. Further promotion followed when he became Captain of the Guard Regiment in March 1917, and shortly thereafter, Brigade Adjutant.

In November 1917 von Criegern was ordered to take the position of 2nd General Staff Officer to the 46th Reserve Division with the responsibility of training, and, for a short period, he remained in training and course roles. By March he had seen some limited action in the battle of pursuit through White Ruthenia, but within a month his orders had him recalled into the regular Army. While fighting in the Lorraine he was wounded, and on 6 May 1918 he received the Black Wound Badge. After recovering from his wounds he was dispatched to the post of Artillery Commander of the 239th Infantry Division and, for a short time, was assigned to a battery. Following further courses in the General Staff and involvement in fighting late in the war at the Maas and Moselle, he was transferred to the General Staff on 28 October 1918.

After the war, in January 1919, he was appointed Leader of the Guard Command of Fortress Koenigstein and, shortly thereafter, became General Staff Officer for the Governor of Thorn. His recall came in June 1920 for the position of Acting Major to the *Reichswehr* Ministry in Berlin, but after just a year in this position he retired from the *Reichswehr* on 15 June 1921. Almost a decade later, in Berlin on 4 January 1930, Dietrich von Criegern married Helene Hansmann of Dresden, the daughter of a cutting mill owner.

Following a substantial time period away from the military, in September/October 1934, von Criegern took part in Cavalry exercises in Salzbrunn and Annaberg. From 2 January 1936, *Luftwaffe* Command kept him on probation for entrance into the Airforce; then he was promoted to Major before serving with the 1st Flak Regiment 10 in Dresden in June and July. After a short term of service with the 2nd Flak Regiment 13, Merseburg, he was transferred during July 1937 to Airforce Group Command, Berlin. September and October 1938 saw him involved in action in Czechoslovakia and the Liberation of the *Sudetenland*. In February 1939 he joined the Staff of Air Fleet Headquarters 1. With March and April came the occupation of Bohemia and Moravia, and he received further promotion to *Oberstleutnant* (Lieutenant Colonel) on 1 October 1939. In May 1940 he was transferred to Air Fleet 5 Headquarters, and he took on the position of Deputy Chief of General Staff, Supplies and Administration.

By the end of 1940 von Criegern had risen to the rank of *Oberst*

(Colonel), and mid-1941 saw him return to the Staff of Air Fleet 1 Headquarters, followed later in the year with the award of his War Merit Cross 1st Class with Swords. His great abilities of organizing, improvising, and being able to master difficult situations culminated on 3 November 1942 with the award of the German Cross in Silver. On 1 April 1943, von Criegern was promoted to *Generalmajor* (Major General), and in August of that year he was appointed to the Administration Reichs Airforce Ministry. The highest point of his career came on 1 July 1944 when he attained the rank of *Generalleutnant* (Lieutenant General) and the position of General Quartermaster of the *Luftwaffe*.

After a long and distinguished career with the German Armed Forces, Dietrich von Criegern died at Hechendorf/Pilsensee (near Munich) on 6 November 1952 at age 65.

The General Dietrich von Criegern personalized 2nd model *Luftwaffe* dagger is pictured alongside a period photograph of the General and a portion of his service record. General Criegern ended his career as the General Quartermaster of the *Luftwaffe*.

APPENDIX 2

THE *LUFTWAFFE* DRESS DAGGER THAT WENT
ON A COMBAT MISSION

—By Hinrik Steinsson, Reykjavik, Iceland

(Author's Note: Hinrik Steinsson is a young (24 years old) collector whose home is Reykjavik, Iceland. Although he has only been collecting WWII militaria for a little over three years, he is considered the top Icelandic expert on German daggers and medals. Hinrik is one of the founders of a recently established organization which is dedicated to preserving items related to the WWII period in Iceland. He is quick to point out that not many Americans know that more than 60,000 U.S. troops were stationed in Iceland during WWII. Hinrik reports that he is giving up his medal collection and will concentrate solely on German dagger collecting.)

I am writing these few lines to tell you an interesting story concerning a WWII German 1st Model *Luftwaffe* dagger which ended up on my island of Iceland. On 24 April 1943, at 1405 hrs. a German Junkers Ju-88 reconnaissance plane was shot down in flames six miles west of Lake Kleifarvatn in Iceland. The plane was shot down by American Lieutenants James M. McNulty and Harry R. Stengle of the 50th Fighter Squadron flying Lockheed Lightning P-38s. Three of the four crew members of the German plane were killed in the crash. The wireless operator, Sergeant Anton Mynarek, parachuted to safety and was taken prisoner. Mynarek was the first POW to be captured alive by the Allied Forces stationed on Iceland during WWII. A 1st

American GI kneeling beside a section of the Junkers fuselage from which Sergeant Mynarek parachuted to safety. The 1st model *Luftwaffe* dress dagger featured in this appendix was found in the wreckage. Note that the Junkers fuselage bore a painting of the outline of Iceland and the word "Island" (the German word for Iceland). Apparently, this German airplane was a regular "guest" over Iceland during WWII.

Luftwaffe Sgt. Anton Mynarek is pictured after his capture at the U.S. Army Intelligence Headquarters at Camp Pershing, Iceland. Note the medals on his tunic: Reconnaissance Flight Clasp, Iron Cross First Class, and a Wireless Operator Flight Badge. Sgt. Mynarek was the first German recovered alive after being shot down by American pilots in Iceland. ▶

OFFICIAL U.S. ARMY PHOTO. PHOTO COURTESY OF HINRIK STEINSSON, ICELAND

Model *Luftwaffe* dagger was recovered from the Junkers plane wreckage. This indicates that one of the crew members took his dress dagger with him while on a combat mission!

This dagger became the property of an Icelandic Police officer living in a nearby town from where the plane crashed. It is quite possible that the dagger was found by a U.S. soldier and then passed onto the policeman as a gift. The dagger is a transitional type with nickel scabbard fittings and aluminum chain. The blade has a Tiger maker's mark, and the crossguard and pommel are missing all of the silver plating with the lower part of the pommel broken off. The overall appearance would, indeed, suggest that this dagger had been in an aircraft crash. The old policeman gave the dagger to a young Police officer in 1980, and the dagger is still in his possession. The older Police officer passed away on Iceland in 1982.

PHOTO COURTESY OF HINRIK STEINSSON, ICELAND

Pictured above is the 1st model *Luftwaffe* dagger by *Tiger Stahlwaren* which is the subject of this Appendix—the *Luftwaffe* dagger which went on a combat mission.

Anton Mynarek, the survivor from the plane, was, when last known, still alive, living in retirement in Germany. Icelandic Aviation enthusiasts were able to locate him a few years ago, but the old man refused to talk to them about an incident that brought back such a sad memory of his long-lost friends who were killed in the crash.

Mynarek is possibly the only man left alive who can tell the complete story of this mysterious WWII German dress dagger. While just an ordinary 1st Model *Luftwaffe* dress dagger, the history surrounding this particular artifact makes it somewhat unique.

APPENDIX 3

NAVY *OBERINSPEKTOR (OBERLEUTNANT)* HEINRICH EHRLICH'S 2ND MODEL NAVY DAGGER

—By SGM (Ret.) Ken Rouse, Germany

(Author's note: SGM (Ret.) Kenneth Rouse is a native of upstate New York and recently retired with over twenty-seven years service with the U.S. Army. His lifelong interest in German militaria surfaced when he began seriously collecting Third Reich edged weapons about ten years ago. Ken was able to combine his collecting with his interest in European history when he was assigned to Germany eight years ago.)

Since the possibility of researching the original owner of an edged weapon, be it a dagger or sword, is one of the areas of the hobby that I have always enjoyed a great deal, it was with pleasant anticipation that I purchased a 2nd Model Naval dagger from one of Tom Johnson's edged weapons catalogs. I knew that it had come to Tom complete with an original mailing carton and additionally had a near mint set of silver administrative hangers as well as sleeve patch indicative of the administrative service *(Hoherer Dienst)*. A complete description of the ensemble as it appeared in the Johnson Reference Books (JRB) Spring 1995 List #70 was as follows:

Item #8. <u>RARE Grouping—2nd Model Naval Dagger w/Hammered Scabbard w/Administrative Hangers in Original Box as Mailed Home by German WWII Naval Officer During the War.</u> Carl Eickhorn (small, double oval) trademark. This RARE grouping was purchased in Germany and features the original cardboard shipping box with label and wartime Third Reich postage stamps. Box is in very nice condition showing age. Inside the box is the original 2nd Model Naval dagger with hammered scabbard, which shows 100% of its original factory gilding. White grip is perfect, has all of the gilding to the pommel and crossguard, has its twisted wire wrap intact, and has its original portepee attached. Portepee is beautifully toned and has never been off the dagger. Double-engraved blade grades excellent++ and has the stamped Eickhorn double oval proofmark. Administrative hangers are the white aluminum type utilized during WWII and are in near mint condition showing basically no wear. Has its original waist belt with gray woven cloth and brown leather. Also in the box is an Administrative button, as well as his original rank patch, which was for the High Grade Career Naval Technical Officer *(Hoherer Dienst)*. Patch features the Naval eagle with swastika in its talons in bullion on a black background. An outstanding and RARE grouping, which is totally untouched and in near mint condition.

Thus, I was fortunate enough to have three points of reference to start from, i.e., the officer's name as well as his home address at the time, and the fact that he was in the technical services.

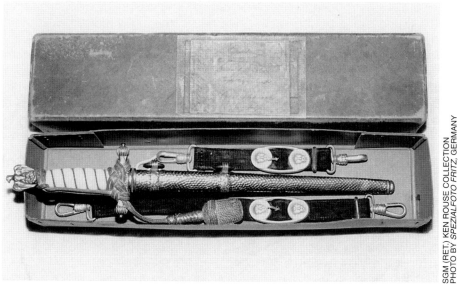

2nd model Navy dagger with administrative hangers in the original mailing carton as mailed home by German WWII Naval Officer *Oberleutnant* Heinrich Ehrlich.

The first challenge I faced was with the mailing label itself. It was, of course, some fifty years old and had been written with fountain pen in a combination of old Gothic-style German with a touch of Sutterlin script thrown in. For those of you who have never seen it, Sutterlin script is a now all-but-extinct form of writing that bears comparison only with an EKG printout of someone with heart fibulations. Be that as it may, I was fortunate that the label was decipherable as being addressed to the family of a naval officer named Ehrlich who had lived in a small town in the *Rheinland-Pfalz* area of Germany. I was doubly fortunate in that the town lies only some forty-odd miles from my own residence outside of Heidelberg which allowed me to do a lot of my own detective work.

When I happened to be in the immediate area of the town in question, the first thing I did was to hop into the first telephone booth I found, look up the village, and then write down the names and addresses of everyone with the same last name of Ehrlich. Then I wrote a general letter that served to introduce myself to them and explain a little bit about the hobby and why I was writing to them. Since the period of the Third Reich can still be a sensitive topic of discussion, I made sure that I told them that my interest was strictly historical. I also apologized, in advance, for intruding on their privacy. I then took the letter to a German friend of mine who was kind enough to translate it into German and laser-print it for me. Since I found five Ehrlichs still living in the town, I printed out four more copies, sent them all out in the mail and then sat back and did the hardest thing of all—I waited for any responses that I might get. The first couple I got back thanked me for writing an interesting letter but said that, unfortunately, they could not help me. I had all but given up when another letter arrived that was, regrettably, also from the wrong family, but the writer, blessedly, came to my aid by giving me a tip—the name and address of another Ehrlich family in town who was not listed in the phone book. He also stated that he remembered during the war having seen the man's father (now, unfortunately, deceased) home on leave from the *Kriegsmarine* wearing his dagger and that he had been in the *"Technisches Dienst"*! Needless to say, I was electrified by this good news and immediately sent off another letter to whom I felt <u>had</u> to be the son of the original owner of my dagger.

Some time passed without a reply, and I was almost despairing of hearing anything when I happened to mention my plight to another German friend who had helped me with the writing on the mailing label when I first got started on this research project. A dynamic individual in her own right, she immediately got on the phone and dialed directory assistance for me. No luck. Her next call was to the *Rathaus*, or town hall, where we struck paydirt. In short, within ten minutes, I had not only made contact with *Oberleutnant* Ehrlich's son, but had made an appointment to meet with him at his electrical shop and chat with him about his father and the dagger!

When the day came, I spent a part of the afternoon in pleasant conversation with *Herr* Ehrlich, whom I found to be a most gracious and friendly person. (Again, I could not have done it without another German friend, Werner, going with me to help with the translating.) I was able to tell him a little bit about the hobby and made some educated guesses with him about how his father's dagger may have come to be listed in the JRB sales catalog, as the last time he had seen it himself was a year or two before when he had sold it to a man who went around buying up things to sell at flea markets. It was at this time I found out to my great disappointment that *Herr* Ehrlich had disposed of his father's entire uniform at the same time. How the dagger and uniform had come to be saved from simply evaporating into the chaos at the end of WWII made an intriguing story in itself. It seems that when the war ended, *Oberinspektor* Ehrlich found himself in the Eisenach area of the province of *Thuringia*. Before he made his way back to the *Pfalz*, where he wound up in a prisoner-of-war (POW) camp outside Bad Kreuznach, he left his uniform and dagger in the safekeeping of a family there. When it was realized that the Russians were going to occupy what later became East Germany (the DDR) and all the barbed wire started going up, the family boxed the ensemble and mailed the grouping back to *Herr* Ehrlich at his home where they arrived in mint condition! The uniform and dagger then rested securely in the family home, stored away with the pride of all veterans for the next half-century until they found their way into the collecting community.

Formal portrait of Navy *Oberinspektor* Heinrich Ehrlich and his wife. This "in wear" period photograph shows the 2nd model Navy dagger featured in this Appendix.

◄

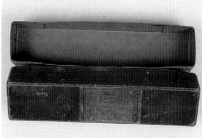

Original 1940s mailing carton used to mail Heinrich Ehrlich's 2nd model Navy dagger by Carl Eickhorn to his home address.

▶

Mailing label and Third Reich postage stamps on the original 1940s mailing carton used to mail Heinrich Ehrlich's 2nd model Navy dagger by Carl Eickhorn.

◄

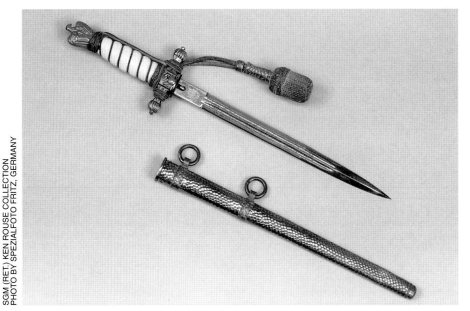

Navy *Oberinspektor* Heinrich Ehrlich's 2nd model Navy dagger by Carl Eickhorn—full-length, reverse view. Of interest is the fact that the reverse ricasso is stamped with the early 1933-1934 Eickhorn double oval trademark and *Oberinspektor* Ehrlich did not enter the German Navy until 1939, which once again proves that it is impossible to accurately date the various trademarks used by the Eickhorn firm.

The author of this Appendix, SGM (Ret.) Kenneth H. Rouse and *Herrn* Theo Ehrlich are pictured examining the 2nd model Navy dagger worn by *Herr* Ehrlich's father. In the foreground is a small photograph showing the identical World War II dagger "in wear."

After the end of the war, *Herr* Ehrlich was held for a time in the POW camp at *Bretzenheim* by Bad Kreuznach. Upon his release, he returned to his family and home where he spent the rest of his life working as an *"Elektro Meister"* (master electrician) until his retirement.

Of course, there is more that can be learned about the original owner of my dagger, hopefully, by initiating research requests through the various German archives (which I plan to do in the near future).

Preliminary Sketch of the Military Service of
Oberinspektor Heinrich Ehrlich

Born: 5 July 1899 in *Friensheim/Pfalz*, Germany

World War I: Served as a Private in the German Army

Decorations: Iron Cross 2nd Class

World War II: Served as an *Oberinspektor (Oberleutnant)* in the *Technische Dienst* in the German *Kriegsmarine*, stationed at the *Versuchts Amt* (Research Department) in Wilhelmshaven working on electrical systems for U-boats. At the war's end was in the Eisenach area of *Thuringia*.

Decorations: War Service Cross 2nd Class with Swords

VOLUME VIII MAJOR CONTRIBUTORS

*(Author's note: In order to recognize the valuable contributions provided for this reference and to better acquaint the collecting/research community with who's who, a photograph of each major contributor was requested. With the collective expertise and talents of the individuals below, the success of a reference book on the subject of German edged weaponry is practically assured. From the multitude of names listed in the Acknowledgements section, it seems unfair to select a few for individual thanks; yet it would be unthinkable not to acknowledge the major contributions made to **Volume VIII** by the following persons:)*

Mrs. Thomas M. (Tink) Johnson
—Assisted in research efforts for Volumes II-VIII.
—Provided proofreading assistance.
—Provided liaison with the U.S. Library of Congress and National Archives.

Barry Brown, U.K.
—Eminently qualified researcher/historian.
—Provided photographic and written input for previous volumes.
—Wrote the update on the Sepp Dietrich sword.

Bram Wasmus, The Netherlands
—Co-author of **Collecting the Edged Weapons of the Third Reich Cross-Index.**
—Ardent collector/researcher of German and Italian edged weapons.
—Provided photographic and written input for previous volumes.

350

Albert "Skipper" Greenwade
  —Author of **Me Fecit Solingen.**
  —Editor of "The MAX Gazette."
  —Wrote the Preface.
  —Provided photographic input for previous volumes.

Gailen L. David
  —Well-known collector and dealer of German edged weapons.
  —Major contributor to several contemporary edged weapon reference books.
  —Provided input for **Volume VIII** "Current Market Values" section.

Doug Gow, New Zealand
  —Well-known collector and researcher of Third Reich dress daggers since the early 1980s.
  —Provided photographic and written input for previous volumes.
  —Wrote Appendix 1.

Robert Heiduk
—Avid collector and researcher of Imperial and Third Reich boot knives.
—Made major contributions to **Volume VII** and **Collecting the Edged Weapons of Imperial Germany.**
—Authored Chapter 6.

Brian Molloy, U.K.
—Outstanding military artist.
—Provided quality artwork for Volumes II-VIII, **Collecting the Edged Weapons of the Third Reich,** and for **World War II German War Booty,** Volumes I and II.
—Official artist for MAX Promotions, Inc.

Gunter Bastian, Germany
—Lifetime resident of Solingen.
—Extremely knowledgeable of Solingen edged weapon industry.
—Provided major assistance to the author for Chapter 1.

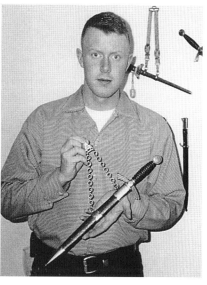

Ben Swearingen
—Eminently qualified researcher/historian.
—Author of **The Mystery of Hermann Göring's Suicide.**
—Wrote Chapter 3.

Hinrik Steinsson, Iceland
—Top Icelandic expert on German daggers and medals.
—One of the founders of an Icelandic organization dedicated to preserving WWII items associated with Iceland.
—Wrote Appendix 2.

Siegfried Rosenkaimer, Germany
—<u>Seventh-generation</u> Solingen edged weapon maker.
—Grandson of Paul Seilheimer.
—Provided major assistance to the author for Chapter 1.

SGM (Ret.) Kenneth Rouse, US Army
—Enthusiastic collector and researcher of Third Reich edged weapons and German militaria.
—Provided material for other references on collecting Third Reich edged weapons.
—Wrote Appendix 3.

Mark Ready
- —Ardent collector of German and Russian militaria.
- —German language teacher.
- —Provided countless translations for Volume VIII and previous volumes.

LTC (Ret.) Michael E. Little, US Army
- —Advanced collector and researcher of German edged weapons.
- —Made major contributions to all eight volumes.
- —General Manager of Johnson Reference Books (JRB).
- —Wrote numerous Volume VIII "in wear" photo captions and the dust jacket biographical sketch of the author.

Donna M. Kines
   —Typed the entire Volume VIII manuscript.
   —Provided proofreading assistance.
   —Longtime personal secretary to the author.
   —Office Manager of Johnson Reference Books (JRB).

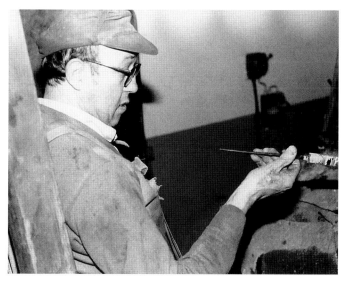

Willi Ulrich, Germany
   —Solingen sword maker.
   —Extremely knowledgeable of Solingen edged weapon
     industry.
   —Provided assistance to the author for Chapter 1.

VOLUME VIII PHOTOGRAPHERS

The Author

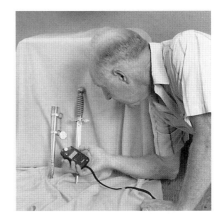

Charles H. Jenkins, III

James Chapman

Andy Southard, Jr.

Jack Arnold

THE STAFF OF JOHNSON REFERENCE BOOKS (JRB)
PREVIOUSLY NOT PICTURED

Office Complex in Fredericksburg

Bonnie T. Andrews

Sandra P. Bruce

BIBLIOGRAPHY

"A Reference on Daggers and Dress Bayonets," R and L Enterprises, Cleveland, Ohio, R and L Enterprises, 1959.

Atwood, Major James P., "The Daggers and Edged Weapons of Hitler's Germany," Berlin, Germany, *Omnium-Druck* and *Verlag*, 1965.

Atwood, Major James P., "World War II Treasure Hunt for Hitler's Daggers of Glory," SAGA (Vol. 34, No. 2) May, 1967, p. 8.

Bender, Roger J., "The *Luftwaffe*," Mountain View, California, R. James Bender Publishing Co., 1972.

Berger, Robert J., "World of Dress Daggers 1900-1945, Vol. I," Chino Valley, Arizona, Blacksmith Corporation, 1994.

Berry, David, "An Introduction to the Daggers of the Third Reich," The American Blade (Vol. 1, No. 2), July-August 1973, p. 22.

Cooper, Matthew, "Uniforms of the *Luftwaffe* 1939-1945," London, England, Almark Publishing Co., Ltd., 1974.

"Daggers of the German Third Reich," ZM Military Research Co., New York, ZM Military Research Co., 1958.

Davis, Brian L., "German Army Uniforms and Insignia 1933-1945," New York, New York, The World Publishing Co., 1972.

Davis, C.R., "Handbook of *RZM* Codes, Volume I, Metal," Runic Press, Houston, Texas, 1975.

Flook, R.E., "A Photographic Primer of Military Knives," Southdown, Bath, Avon, England, published privately by the author, 1990.

Glemser, Kurt, "A Guide to Military Dress Daggers, Vol. I," New Hamburg, Canada, published privately by the author, 1991.

Glemser, Kurt, "A Guide to Military Dress Daggers, Vol. II," New Hamburg, Canada, published privately by the author, 1993.

Greenwade, Albert ("Skipper"), "*Me Fecit Solingen*," Houston, Texas, published privately by the author, 1987.

"Handbook on German Military Forces (TM-E-30-451)," Washington, D.C. United States Government Printing Office, 1945.

Hughes, Gordon, "A Primer of German Military Knives of the Two World Wars," Brighton, England, Benedict Press, 1976.

Hughes, Gordon U., "German Military Knives," Brighton, England, The Benedict Press, 1976.

Husken, Andre, "*Katalog der Blankwaffen Des Deutschen Reiches 1933-1945,*" Hamburg, Germany, Galerie d'Histoire, 1995.

Johnson, Thomas M., "Application of Edged Weapons to Modern Warfare," The American Blade (Vol. 1, No. 4), November-December 1973, p. 38.

Johnson, Thomas M., "Bayonets of Adolf Hitler's Thousand Year Reich," The Classic Collector (Vol. 2, No. 1) Spring, 1974, p. 44.

Johnson, Thomas M., "Collecting the Edged Weapons of the Third Reich, Volume I," Columbia, South Carolina, The R.L. Bryan Co., 1975.

Johnson, Thomas M., "Collecting the Edged Weapons of the Third Reich, Volume II," Columbia, South Carolina, The R.L. Bryan Co., 1976.

Johnson, Thomas M., "Collecting the Edged Weapons of the Third Reich, Volume III," Columbia, South Carolina, The R.L. Bryan Co., 1978.

Johnson, Thomas M., "Collecting the Edged Weapons of the Third Reich, Volume IV," Columbia, South Carolina, The R.L. Bryan Co., 1981.

Johnson, Thomas M., "Collecting the Edged Weapons of the Third Reich, Volume V," Columbia, South Carolina, The R.L. Bryan Co., 1985.

Johnson, Thomas M., "Collecting the Edged Weapons of the Third Reich, Volume VI," Columbia, South Carolina, The R.L. Bryan Co., 1992.

Johnson, Thomas M., "Collecting the Edged Weapons of the Third Reich, Volume VII," Columbia, South Carolina, The R.L. Bryan Co., 1994.

Johnson, Thomas M. and A. Bram Wasmus, "Collecting the Edged Weapons of the Third Reich Cross-Index," Columbia, South Carolina, The R.L. Bryan Co., 1989.

Johnson, Thomas M., "Third Reich Edged Weapon Accouterments," Columbia, South Carolina, The R.L. Bryan Co., 1978.

Johnson, Thomas M., "Wearing the Edged Weapons of the Third Reich, Vol. I," Columbia, South Carolina, The R.L. Bryan Co., 1977.

Johnson, Thomas M., "Wearing the Edged Weapons of the Third Reich, Vol. II," Columbia, South Carolina, The R.L. Bryan Co., 1992.

Johnson, Thomas M., "Collectors' Handbook of German WWII Daggers," Columbia, South Carolina, The R.L. Bryan Co., 1979.

Johnson, Thomas M. and John Ormsby, "Daggers of World War II Germany," Special Collector's Edition Magazine (Vol. 1, No. 1), Clay Communications Group, 1980.

Johnson, Thomas M., "Don't Get Stuck By a Nazi Dagger," Guns & Ammo (Vol. 21, No. 11), November 1977, p. 72.

Johnson, Thomas M., "The Era of Military Edged Weapons," The Classic Collector (Vol. 1, No. 1), Fall 1973, p. 34.

Klietmann, Dr. Kurt-Gerhard, "German Daggers and Dress Sidearms of World War II," Falls Church, Virginia, Field and Fireside, Inc., 1967.

Klietmann, Dr. Kurt-Gerhard, Selected Monographs.

Maeurer, Herman A., "Military Edged Weapons of the World 1800-1965," College Point, New York, H.A. Maeurer, 1967.

Mason, David, "Who's Who in World War II," Boston, Massachusetts, Little, Brown and Co., 1978.

McFarlane, R., "Bluebook of Identification of Reproduction Nazi Edged Weapons," Oxon, England, published privately by the author, 1969.

Mermet, Charles and Jean Marfault, "*Les Dagues du IIIe Reich*," Portail-de-Ville, France, Editions du Portail, 1981.

Militaria-Sammler-Shop-Volz, "Blanke Waffen und Ehrendolche des III Reiches," Herne, Germany.

Mollo, Andrew, "Daggers of the Third German Reich 1933-1945," London, England, Historic Research Unit, 1967.

Niederhofer, Ernst J., "The Cold Steel Weapons of the SA, the SS, and the NSKK of the *NSDAP*," Norderstedt, Germany, *Militair-Verlag* Klaus D. Patzwall, 1993.

Ormsby, John R., Jr., "Daggers of the Third Reich," Charlotte, North Carolina, published privately by the author, 1971.

Patzwall, Klaus D., "*Der Reichsluftschutzbund 1933-1945*," Norderstedt, Germany, *Militair-Verlag* Klaus D. Patzwall, 1989.

"Presentation and Rare Daggers of Hitler's Third Reich," Dowd Private Research Project (United States Military Academy), 1962.

Seitz, Heribert, *"Blankwaffen,"* 2 Vols., Brunswick, 1965-1967.

"Solinger Tageblatt," Solingen Local Newspaper, 1932-1945.

Stephens, F.J., "A Guide to Nazi Daggers, Swords, and Bayonets," Leigh, Lancs, England, published privately by the author, 1965.

Stephens, F.J., "The Collector's Pictorial Book of Bayonets," Harrisburg, Pennsylvania, Stackpole Books, 1971.

Stephens, F.J., "Daggers of the German Third Reich," Battle (Vol. 4, No. 3), March 1977, p. 108.

Stephens, F.J., "Edged Weapons of the Third Reich, 1933-1945," London, England, Almark Publishing Co., Ltd., 1972.

Stephens, F.J., "Edged Weapons: A Collector's Guide," Buckinghamshire, England, Spurbooks Ltd., 1976.

Stephens, F.J., "Fighting Knives, An Illustrated Guide to Fighting Knives and Military Survival Weapons of the World," Stoney Creek, Ontario, Canada, Fortress Publications, Inc., 1980.

Stephens, F.J., "Reproduction? Recognition!," Leigh, Lancs, England, published privately by the author, 1976.

Swearingen, Ben, "The Mystery of Hermann Göring's Suicide," New York, New York, Harcourt, Brace, and Jovanovich, 1985.

"Uniformen Markt," German Military Uniforms, etc., Various Issues, 1932-1945.

Venner, Dominique, *"Les Armes Blanches du IIIe Reich,"* Paris, France, Pensee Moderne, 1977.

Walker, Gary L., and Ronald J. Weinand, "German Clamshells and Other Bayonets—A Collector's Guide," Quincy, Illinois, published privately by the authors, 1985.

Walter, John, "The German Bayonet, A Comprehensive Illustrated History of the Regulation Patterns, 1871-1945," Stoney Creek, Ontario, Canada, Fortress Publications, Inc., 1976.

Walter, John, "The Sword and Bayonet Makers of Imperial Germany 1871-1918," Essex, England, The Lyon Press, 1973.

Weinand, Ronald J., "NPEA Daggers and Associated Knives, A Collector's Guide," Quincy, Illinois, published privately by the author, 1988.

Welser, Mike, *"Reichswehr and Wehrmacht Bayonets 1920-1945,"* Escondido, California, published privately by the author, 1985.

Wittmann, Thomas T., "Exploring the Dress Daggers of the German Army," Pennsylvania, Alcom Printing Group, Inc., 1995.

ORIGINAL THIRD REICH CATALOGS

Alcoso, Illustrated Sales Catalog, Solingen, Germany, cira 1938.

Alcoso, Illustrated Sales Catalog, Solingen, Germany, circa 1941.

Anton Wingen, Jr. Sales Catalog, Solingen, Germany, circa 1938.

"Blanke Waffen—A Study of Prototype Designs," Solingen, Germany, Chamber of Commerce, 1941.

Carl Julius Krebs, Illustrated Sales Catalog, Solingen, Germany, circa 1938.

"Das Schwert," Richard A. Herder Sales Catalog, Solingen, Germany, circa 1938.

"Die Klinge," Solingen Cutlery Trade Magazine, 1932-1942.

E. & F. Hörster, Illustrated Sales Catalog, Solingen, Germany, circa 1938.

Eickhorn, Illustrated Sales Catalog, Solingen, Germany, 1931.

Eickhorn *"Blanke Waffen,"* Illustrated Sales Catalog, Solingen, Germany, circa 1936.

Eickhorn *"Blanke Waidmannswaffen,"* Illustrated Hunting Sidearm Sales Catalog, Solingen, Germany, 1932.

Eickhorn *"Kundendienst,"* Illustrated Sales catalog, Solingen, Germany, circa 1938.

Eickhorn *"Leisten und Dienen,"* Illustrated Catalog, Solingen, Germany, 1940.

Emil Voos, Illustrated Sales Catalog, Solingen, Germany, circa 1938.

Ernst Pack & *Söhne "Waffen von Pack,"* Illustrated Sales Catalog, Solingen, Germany, circa 1938.

F.W. Assmann & *Söhne,* Illustrated Sales Catalog, Ludenscheid, Germany, circa 1938.

F.W. Höller, Illustrated Sales Catalog, Solingen, Germany, circa 1938.

F.W. Höller, Illustrated Sales Catalog, Solingen, Germany, circa 1941.

Gebrüder Gräfrath, Illustrated Sales Catalog, Solingen-Widdert, Germany, 1935.

Gebrüder Gräfrath, Illustrated Sales Catalog, Solingen-Widdert, Germany, circa 1938.

Paul Seilheimer, Illustrated Sales Catalog, Solingen, Germany, circa 1938.

Paul Weyersberg, Illustrated Sales Catalog, Solingen, Germany, circa 1938.

Puma, Illustrated Sales Catalog, Solingen, Germany, 1940.

Puma, Illustrated Sales Catalog, Solingen, Germany, 1941.

Richard Herder, Illustrated Sales Catalog, Solingen, Germany, circa 1938.

Robert Klaas *"Blanke Waffen,"* Illustrated Sales Catalog, Solingen, Germany, circa 1937.

WKC, Illustrated Sales Catalog, Solingen, Germany, circa 1935.

WKC, Illustrated Sales Catalog, Solingen, Germany, circa 1938.

WKC, Illustrated Sales Catalog, Solingen, Germany, circa 1939.

BOOK REVIEWS AND UNSOLICITED READER COMMENTS ON VOLUMES I-VII OF COLLECTING THE EDGED WEAPONS OF THE THIRD REICH

"This 372-page book is the 7th volume in an excellent and authoritative series on the Third Reich German Daggers and Swords. The author has done much research and traveling to provide the most current information on this fascinating aspect in the field of militaria collecting. Many one-of-a-kind and rare pieces are depicted in highly detailed black & white and color photos. The chapters include descriptions of the raw materials and manufacturing processes used to make their desirable and decorative edged weapons used by every organization of the Third Reich, as well as information on the firms that produced them. The author even takes us with him into the town of Steinbach, in the former East Germany, where several of these firms existed. . . . Tom Johnson promises us a continuation on this series of books, as more information comes into his office daily. He is an expert on the subject of German edged weapons, is President and Co-founder of the world famous annual MAX Show, and has done much to promote and legitimize the hobby of militaria collecting."

—Marc Cohen
Book Review

"Johnson Reference Books—The Hobby's Best Work. This seven volume series has become the 'bible' of edged weapon collecting. You can not enjoy this hobby without possessing all seven of these reference books. Each and every one is as exciting to a blade collector, as 'Gone with the Wind' is to the avid reader of fiction. . . . You need these books. Please order them, so you may enjoy this great hobby to its fullest."

—Thomas T. Wittmann
Book Review, "The Wittmann Offering—No. 28"

"*Collecting the Edged Weapons of the Third Reich* by LTC (Ret.) Thomas M. Johnson, all-purpose books about daggers, sabers, swords, bayonets, portepees of German Reich from 1933-1945, detailed descriptions and illustrations, no doubt the most outstanding books about the edged weaponry of the Third Reich, English language, **Volume I** through **Volume VII**."

—Book Review
"Berlin *Auktionshaus* Catalog"

"I must start by thanking you for your effort in helping other collectors in this field, by publishing all those great books. I just bought the whole series of *Collecting the Edged Weapons of the Third Reich, Volume I-VII*, and frankly they are without doubt the best of the best that has been written on this subject. After reading the first two volumes, my interest in collecting daggers/bayonets increased significantly, so I traded in a couple of rare medals in my collection for two daggers. Don't stop writing!"

—Hinrik Steinsson, Collector
Reykjavik, Iceland

"I am an avid collector of Third Reich militaria, especially of edged weapons and their accouterments. I have all Volumes of your reference books and have read them cover-to-cover many times over. Let me say I am thoroughly pleased with these books and very much impressed with your extensive knowledge and research of the subject. I enjoy reading and reviewing your books as much as I enjoy my collection of edged weapons themselves. I would greatly appreciate seeing your list of German edged weapons for sale."

—Gregg Canavan, Collector
Holliston, Massachusetts

"It was nice seeing you at the 'OVMS' Show this last weekend and I want to thank you again for purchasing the enclosed dagger. It pleases me when 'the master' in the dagger collection world is interested in one that I have pruned out of my collection. It is a pleasure to know you, especially after thoroughly having read all of your super seven reference books!"

—Henry Kortz, Collector
Brentwood, Tennessee

"My name is John Whalen. I have a small collection of edged weapons. I purchased a copy of your book, *Collecting the Edged Weapons of the Third Reich*. I have managed to buy **Volume II** and **Volume VI**. I have tried to locate more of your books but to no success. I live in a small, rural town with little or no references on this subject. I would like to purchase **Volumes I, III, IV,** and **V** of these great works. If you could let me know how much it would cost to have these items posted over, as one parcel, I must have the full set, as the information is invaluable! The two volumes I have already make other books I have on the subject childish. I would just like to thank you for sharing this knowledge."

—John Whalen, Collector
Dumfrieshire, Scotland

"I have just recently purchased your five volumes of *Collecting the Edged Weapons of the Third Reich*. I must say I could not put them down—absolutely fascinating, to say the least. I particularly liked the various articles on the edged weapons owned by Hermann Göring and also the photos showing various liberated war booty. This brings me to my next question. In **Volume V**, a book is mentioned, *World War II German War Booty*. Can I purchase this book from you? If so, can you kindly advise price, postage, etc. Before I sign off may I, like so many others, extend my congratulations on a job well done in putting together your five volumes of *Collecting the Edged Weapons of the Third Reich*. I can't tell you how much pleasure it gave me reading them. Although I don't collect these things (as my bag is Japanese swords, etc.), I have genuine interest in all edged weapons, especially presentation pieces."

—Brenton Williams, Collector
West Beach, South Australia

"... As much as I would like to visit what I believe should be called 'The Third Solingen', i.e., JRB, 312 Butler Road, Fredericksburg, Virginia, finances do not permit such a pilgrimage, but I would welcome the chance to show you the dagger grips and explain my thoughts more fully. ... Perhaps on your next visit to Great Britain we could arrange a mutually agreeable time and place to meet each other. In the meanwhile, I hope that the photographs are of some interest, albeit they are not perfect. ... Although rather lengthy, I hope my thoughts ... were of interest to you. Over the years you have given so much to the collector, I think it is about time we gave you something back in return. My best wishes to all at JRB."

—Bavin J. Lane, Collector
Gwent, Great Britain

"Where to start? I think firstly with a big THANK YOU! In the first instance for the continued dedication and effort you show to this fine hobby. Secondly for the ability of your books to bring together those around the world who possess both the weapons and knowledge, and then to communicate these in such a clear, informative, and accessible way. Finding your books was my first great hunt as a militaria collector. Having been persuaded by references on other aspects of Third Reich collecting ... the wisest step to take is that of understanding your subject as well as possible and, therefore, investing in the relevant reference books. Being a British soldier living in the north of Germany, this did not, at first, seem an easy prospect! However, I found a small book shop in the town of Soltau (on the edge of the Luneburg Heath in Lower Saxony) which had copies of **Volumes I** to **VI**—these were instantly snapped up, much to the pleasure of the shop owner. ... Once again, thank you very much for such an outstanding set of reference books. Long may you continue to attract the praise so richly deserved. I look forward to any reply which time may permit you send."

—Sgt. D.J. Armstrong, Collector
Bergen, Germany

"... You also see that I have ordered, for the second time, **Collecting the Edged Weapons of the Third Reich, Volume VII**. Of course, it is not for me, because I have your book already a couple of months and have read it already a couple of hundred times. It is for a friend of mine—I have shown him your books, and he was very interested! He asked me to order **Volume VII**—maybe a new client and collector for you."

—Kurt Van Laere, Collector
West Vlaanderen, Belgium

"Received my **Vol. VII** today and have been buried in it 'til now! Thanks for the signature, and thank LTC (Ret.) [Johnson] for me too— he's done it again. Put me down for **Vol. VIII**, will you?! The best. No one should bother writing about this hobby/obsession—they should just leave it to TMJ (Ret.)."

—Lemmy Kilmister, Collector
West Hollywood, California

"I can't tell you how much I've enjoyed **Volume VII**. It's nothing less than historically significant! As always, your coverage of the hobby is phenomenal! Personally, I think the chapter on personalized edged weapons was the highlight (perhaps a rather biased opinion). In terms of being an historical study, however, your chapter on your visits to East Germany is of profound importance. Since the fall of the Wall in 1990, I have read numerous accounts of life in the East. Most have been either too broad in scope with only minimal focus on personal lives, or too factual and lacking feeling altogether. When you presented me with my personalized copy of **Volume VII**, you indicated that you thought I would enjoy the chapter on 'The Other Solingen.' Well, Tom, I can hardly tell you how moved I was after reading that chapter! You presented it in a way that made me feel like I was there. Actually, I would have loved to have been there to hold the David Malsch 1st Model *Luftwaffe* [dagger], to talk with former employees of the factories, and to see 'the other Solingen.' Nevertheless, I believe the manner in which you described your experiences is the next best thing to being there myself. The whole book, and especially the chapter about 'The Other Solingen,' will be cherished by both collectors and historians. I congratulate you on your outstanding work!"

—Robert Johns, Collector
Alexandria, Virginia

"... Your **Collecting the Edged Weapons of the Third Reich** series is truly a work of art. A thoroughly masterful blend of storytelling, technical precise information, wonderful illustrations and drawings, and the definitive books on the subject. Looking forward to **Volume VIII** and beyond. I have collected edged weapons of the Third Reich since I was 16—I am now 54 and still learning, thanks to you!"

—Donald Braunstein, Collector
Phoenix, Arizona

Original Solingen 1930's photograph of factory workers hard at work producing Third Reich dress daggers.